100 Best
cross-country
SKI TRAILS in

WASHINGTON

D0356005

100 Best cross-country SKI TRAILS in

WASHINGTON

Third Edition

Vicky Spring & Tom Kirkendall

THE MOUNTAINEERS BOOKS

Published by
The Mountaineers Books
1001 SW Klickitat Way, Suite 201
Seattle, WA 98134

© 2002 by Vicky Spring and Tom Kirkendall

All rights reserved

Third edition, 2002. Revised and combined edition of: *Cross-Country Ski Tours, Washington's North Cascades*, 2nd edition, 1996; and *Cross-Country Ski Tours, Washington's South Cascades and Olympics*, 2nd edition, 1995.

No part of this book may be reproduced in any form, or by any electronic, mechanical, or other means, without permission in writing from the publisher.

Published simultaneously in Great Britain by Cordee, 3a DeMontfort Street, Leicester, England, LE1 7HD

Manufactured in Canada

Project Editor: Laura Slavik
Editor: Christine Clifton-Thornton
Layout Artist: Kristy L. Welch
Mapmaker: Tom Kirkendall
Photographers: Vicky Spring and Tom Kirkendall

Cover photograph: © Kirkendall/Spring
Frontispiece: *Skier at Reflection Lakes in Mount Rainier National Park, Tour 74*

Library of Congress Cataloging-in-Publication Data
Spring, Vicky, 1953–
  100 best cross-country ski trails in Washington/Vicky Spring and Tom Kirkendall.— 3rd ed.
     p. cm.
  Rev. and combined ed. of: Cross-country ski tours/Tom Kirkendall & Vicky Spring. 2nd ed. c1996; and Cross-country ski tours—Washington's south Cascades & Olympics/Tom Kirkendall & Vicky Spring. 2nd ed. c1995.
  "First edition."
  Includes bibliographical references (p.   ) and index.
  ISBN 0-89886-806-8 (pbk.)
  1. Cross-country skiing—Cascade Range—Guidebooks. 2. Cross-country ski trails—Cascade Range—Guidebooks. 3. Cascade Range—Guidebooks. 4. Cross-country skiing—Washington (State)—Olympic Mountains—Guidebooks. 5. Cross-country ski trails—Washington (State)—Olympic Mountains—Guidebooks. 6. Olympic Mountains (Wash.)—Guidebooks. I. Title: One hundred best cross-country ski trails in Washington. II. Kirkendall, Tom. III. Kirkendall, Tom. Cross-country ski tours. IV. Kirkendall, Tom. Cross-country ski tours—Washington's south Cascades & Olympics. V. Title.
  GV854.5.C27 S67 2002
    917.97—dc21
                                    2002005094

✿ Printed on recycled paper

CONTENTS

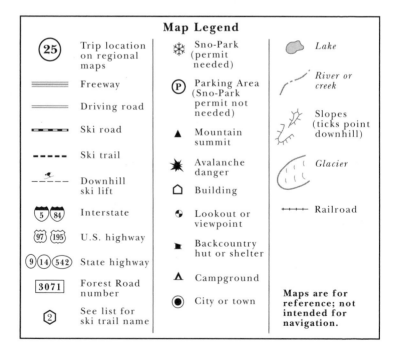

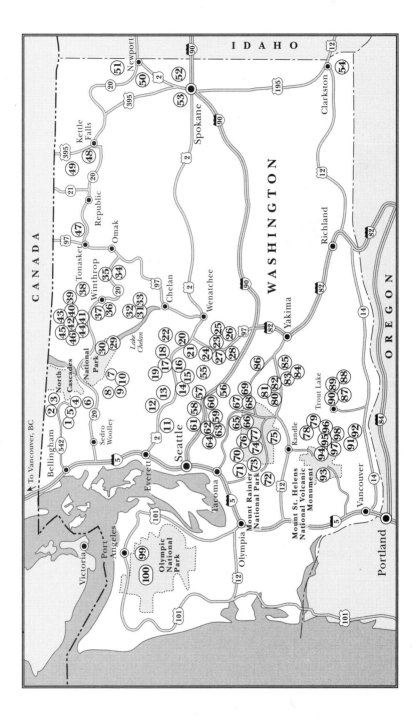

Skiers at Artist Point approaching Table Mountain, Tour 4

INTRODUCTION

The mountainous terrain throughout the entire state ensures that all of Washington's residents have access to excellent cross-country skiing, whether on groomed trails, on scenic logging roads, or on open slopes of glacier-covered volcanoes. The 100 trips outlined in this book are designed to serve only as an introduction to cross-country skiing opportunities in Washington. When choosing these trips, preference was given to those with low avalanche hazard, high scenic value, and ease and reliability of access. Consequently, most of the trips start from sno-parks or resorts.

To repeat the caution that any guidebook must offer (especially one that deals with such an undependable a substance as snow): Keep in mind that the authors have absolutely no control over the amount of snow that falls. Some years there is so much snow that the parking lots are never plowed, and other years the snow fails to arrive at all. The authors also admit to having no control over (1) the building of new roads or washing out of old ones, (2) the rules and regulations of government agencies, and (3) the falling of trees. In a word: Conditions are never the same twice, so be flexible in your plans.

HEADING OUT INTO WINTER

This book does not explain how to ski, just where. However, the following are some tips to help orient skiers toward wintertime fun. More information can be found in Suggested Reading in Appendix A.

Be Flexible

During research for this book, many Forest Service personnel and ski patrollers were interviewed and the one point they stressed repeatedly was: *Be flexible.* Have an alternate, safer trip plan if weather changes create a high-avalanche potential in your chosen area. If your second choice is also unsafe, consider an alternate activity.

Sno-Parks and Permits

Many of the tours in this book start at sno-parks. These are designated parking areas plowed throughout the winter for the convenience of recreational users. Permits are required to park in these areas, and the fees are used to keep the parking sites plowed, bathrooms open, and trails maintained. Cars parking without permits can count on a ticket and possible towing. Sno-park permits are sold by the day, week, or season. Before you head out, be sure to check the Access section of your chosen tour to determine if a permit is required.

Some sno-parks require a second, groomed area sticker to be added to the basic sno-park permit. Money from these stickers helps defray the costs of machine grooming. Sno-parks currently (in 2001) requiring a Special Groomed Area sticker are: Keechelus Lake, Price Creek Eastbound, Cabin Creek, Lake Easton State Park, Lake Wenatchee State Park, Kahler Glen, Chiwawa Road, and Mount Spokane State Park.

Sno-park permits and Special Groomed Area stickers are available at many outdoor equipment retail stores, or by mail from: Washington State Parks and Recreation Commission, 7150 Cleanwater Lane KY-11, P.O. Box 42650, Olympia, WA 98504-2650.

Other Access Fees

Northwest Forest Pass: These passes are sold by the Forest Service and most outdoor gear shops. They are designed to help the Forest Service defray the costs of maintaining trailheads and trails. At the time of this writing, Tour 21, Tour 32, and Tour 33 are the only tours in this book that require a Northwest Forest Pass for parking rather than a state-sponsored sno-park permit. Northwest Forest Passes can be purchased at the Leavenworth Ranger Station, located on the north side of Highway 2 at the east end of the town of Leavenworth. These passes can be purchased for a day or for an entire year, covering the summer hiking season as well as the winter skiing season.

Leavenworth Trail Pass: In Leavenworth, skiers are required to buy

Skiing among snow-plastered trees on the crest of Amabilis Mountain (Tour 58)

a trail pass before using the city-sponsored trails discussed in Tour 20. Trail passes are sold at the golf course, at the Leavenworth Ski Hill, and at the Icicle River trail access. Seasonal passes are available.

MVSTA Pass: Skiing the groomed trails in the Methow Valley requires a MVSTA (Methow Valley Sport Trails Association) Pass. A sno-park permit is not required for skiing in the Methow Valley unless you choose to park at the Goat Creek Sno-Park as suggested in Tours 43 and 44, or if you would like to ski out from the Loup Loup South Summit Sno-Park, Tour 34. Bear Mountain, at the Loup Loup Ski Area, Tour 35, requires a separate fee not covered by the MVSTA Pass.

Other Commercial Cross-Country Ski Areas: Stevens Pass Cross-Country (Tour 14), Bear Mountain at the Loup Loup Ski Area (Tour 35), and Snoqualmie Pass Nordic Center (Tour 64) are operated in conjunction with the adjoining downhill ski areas. Fees are charged for skiing the groomed trails at these locations. Annual passes may be purchased.

Huts and Cabins

What could be more fun than spending a long winter night in a warm and cozy cabin? If there is a storm screaming outside, it just makes it all the better. There are many cabins available for rent for a moderate fee. Of course, the hardy have endless choices for tent camping.

Starting at the northern border of the state, the first you'll encounter are the Rendezvous Huts. These six commercial huts are located on the hills overlooking the Methow Valley. Five of the huts are accessed by the immaculately groomed trails of the Methow Valley Trail system. The sixth hut can be reached by skiing the groomed snowmobile routes from the Goat Creek Sno-Park (Tour 44). Gear-hauling services are available (see Tour 40 for more information).

High in the Kettle Range is a Forest Service shelter. Reservations are made many months in advance for stays at this backcountry cabin. Skiing to the cabin is difficult. For more information, see Tour 48.

The Chiwaukum Mountains are the home of the Scottish Lakes High Camp, another commercial venture. The camp offers visitors tent cabins and cooking facilities. Gear- and people-hauling services are available. See Tour 16 for more information.

Mt. Tahoma Trails Association operates three huts, scenically located on hilltops overlooking the Nisqually River valley. Skiers who wish to use these huts pay only a refundable damage deposit and a minimal paperwork fee. The huts are open to everyone; however, advance reservations are required. See Tour 72 for more details.

The old Burley Mountain Lookout has been turned into a public hut by the innovative people at the Cispus Valley Ranger Station.

Ski-N-Yurt in the North Fork Tieton River valley (Tour 84)

Advance reservations are a must before you start the long, arduous trek to the lookout; see Tour 78.

In the North Fork Tieton River area, a yurt can be rented for overnight stays. This beautiful facility is a commercial venture. Check Tour 84 for details on how to make reservations.

Finally, the old Prairie Creek Guard Station is available for winter use. The cabin is a fun destination, with easy winter access from the Atkisson Sno-Park, near Fish Lake. Skiers can follow a groomed snowmobile route or a well-marked trail to the cabin. Tour 90 has the reservation details.

Winter Camping

Most Forest Service campgrounds are closed in winter. However, some State Parks remain open, with plowed access roads, one or two campsites, and the added joy of heated bathrooms. One campground is usually kept open near the Nisqually entrance to Mount Rainier National Park, and Olympic National Park keeps Heart o' the Hills open.

When winter camping takes you away from established campgrounds, set camp wherever you feel safe. Avoid pitching a tent under snow-laden trees; when least expected (day or night), "mushrooms" may fall from above and crush your tent.

Whether in the backcountry or on groomed tracks of a resort, carry out your garbage. (If you packed it in full, you can pack it out empty.) Burying leftovers under a few inches of snow only hides them until the spring melt. Also be careful with human waste. Use good judgment about where you deposit human waste. Look for areas that are away from roads, trails, and parking lots. Remember that you, or someone else, may walk there in the summer. Make sure that your chosen spot is at least 200 feet away from dips that could be streams when the snow melts in the spring. If possible, dig down into the soil. Carry out your toilet paper.

Water can be difficult to find in winter. Most small streams are either hidden beneath the snow or flowing in grand white canyons. If day-skiing, carry water. On overnight or longer trips, carry a long string for lowering a bucket to an open stream as well as a stove and enough fuel to melt snow. Water from creeks or melted from snow should be thoroughly boiled and filtered before drinking.

When spending the day or several days out skiing, take care where you park your car. A sudden winter storm can turn bare and dry logging roads into a winter wonderland, leaving your car stranded—maybe until the spring melt. Always travel with a shovel in the car and a watchful eye on the weather.

Stehekin

Located at the upper end of Lake Chelan, the only winter access to Stehekin is by boat or floatplane. Most visitors take advantage of the relatively inexpensive boat service. In the winter the *Lady Express* runs five times a week. You may board the boat in Chelan or save a little money and pick it up at Fields Landing. In Stehekin, accommodations range from hotel rooms and cabins at the North Cascades Lodge to bed and breakfast facilities. Of course, you may camp; the North Cascades National Park leaves the campground near the boat dock open all winter. If camping, bring a shovel to level a tent platform on the hard snow under the trees. Running water is available at the park office, located above the post office.

The primary skiing areas are located upvalley from the town of Stehekin. Transportation can be arranged through the hotel or at the store in Stehekin. Snowshoe and ski rentals are available. For information concerning boat passenger rates and schedules, contact the Lake Chelan Boat Company at (509) 682-4584. For lodging and transportation reservations, call (509) 682-4584.

Technique

Cross-country skiing looks simple enough, but proper technique is very important to ensure a good time. Even expert alpine skiers have problems the first day on cross-country gear. The narrowness of the skis, flexibility of the bindings, and softness of the shoes give an entirely different feeling. Books are helpful in learning technique, but one or two lessons may be needed. Many organizations offer a two-lesson plan, the first to get you started in the right direction and the second to correct any problems you may have.

Pets

Although in some jurisdictions the family pet is permitted to tag along on summer hikes, wintertime should be left to the two-legged family members. Skiing through knee-deep powder is a lot of fun, but not for the skiless family pet, floundering in a white morass. Pets also tend to destroy ski tracks by leaving behind deep paw prints and brown klister. Pets are not allowed in national parks or on any machine-groomed ski trails.

What to Take

Every skier who ventures more than a few feet away from the car should be prepared to spend the night out. Winter storms can come with great speed and force, creating whiteouts that leave the skier with nowhere to go. Each skier's pack must include the Ten Essentials, plus one:

1. **Extra clothing**—more than needed in the worst of weather. (See More Words Concerning Clothing, later in this section.)
2. **Extra food and water**—there should be some left over at the end of the trip.
3. **Sunglasses**—a few hours of bright sun on snow can cause a pounding headache or temporary blindness.
4. **Knife**—for first aid and emergency repairs.
5. **First-aid kit**—just in case.
6. **Firestarter**—chemical starter to get wet wood burning.
7. **Waterproof matches** (in a waterproof container with a striker that you have tested before you leave home)—to start a fire.
8. **Flashlight**—be sure to have extra batteries as well as an extra bulb.
9. **Map**—make sure it's the right one for the trip.
10. **Compass**—keep in mind the declination.

Plus one: Repair kit—including a spare ski tip, spare screws, duct tape, and a combination wrench/pliers/screwdriver.

Other items you may want to carry include a small shovel, sun block cream, and a large plastic tarp to use as a "picnic blanket" or for emergency shelter. All these items should fit comfortably into a day pack. Obviously, a fanny pack is not large enough. Fanny packs are strictly for track and resort skiing, where one might carry only a sandwich and a few waxes.

More Words Concerning Clothing

No dress code exists for the cross-country skier. Clothing can be anything from spandex to mismatched army surplus. Many of the garments sold for cross-country skiing are designed for resort skiing or racing, providing flexibility and style, but not much warmth.

In the wilderness, warmth is crucial. Covering your body from head to toe in synthetic long underwear and using two or more layers on the upper body to regulate heat ensure a pleasant journey rather than a bone-chilling ordeal. So go ahead and wear that designer outfit, but be sure to have a layer of long underwear on underneath and another layer with you that can be put on top.

With a maritime climate creating frequent and rapid weather changes, waterproof gear is essential for skiing in Washington. Rain pants and jackets made of coated nylon or breathable waterproof material work best for warmth, dryness, and flexibility.

Equipment

What length of ski to buy, with side-cut or without, with metal edges or without, hard or soft camber? What boots are best, flexible or stiff? These and many more questions could fill a book—and they do (see Suggested Reading, in Appendix A, for recommendations). Our one and only suggestion is to purchase a waxless ski as your first pair. Learning to ski can be complicated enough without the frustration of trying to wax for Washington's ever-changing snow conditions. When looking for that new pair of skis, avoid stores that just happen to have a few cross-country skis in stock. Stores that have special cross-country departments and employees who enjoy cross-country skiing will be able to give you the right information so you will have a better understanding of what you need and what you don't.

Cross-country boots come in numerous varieties. The type of skis you have will determine which boots are appropriate, and the type of boots you have will determine the type of bindings you need.

Dressed for fun in any weather

GUIDE TO THE GUIDEBOOK

This section provides a brief explanation of the terms used in the information blocks preceding each tour description. It also explains how to best use the information in this book and what some of the commonly employed terms mean in non-skier English.

Information Blocks

Located at the beginning of each tour, the "information block" includes vital information for that specific trip, ranging from the kinds of equipment allowed on the trail to what maps are needed. Following are brief explanations of the information you will find in each of the ten categories.

Open to . . .

To help you decide if this is the right trip for you, the *Open to* category notes the type of equipment that is appropriate for or allowed on the trip. There are four classifications: *skis only, skis and snowshoes, nonmotorized,* and *all uses.*

Skis only: This designation is used for groomed trails. Some snowshoe use may be allowed in the skating lane, or there may be special trails set aside for snowshoe use.

Telemarking the open slopes below Coleman Pinnacle, Tour 4

Skis and snowshoes: This designation is used for areas shared by skiers and snowshoers. Usually these areas are not machine groomed.

Nonmotorized: Cross-country skiers may be joined by snowshoers and even hikers on these routes. If it is a road, you may even see a dogsled.

All uses: This is restrained language that indicates snowmobiles are allowed on these trips. All nonmotorized users are allowed in these areas; however, caution is recommended when skiing with young children. When skiing on roads shared with snowmobiles, take care to stay to the right when you hear one coming and always be prepared to move quickly out of the way of the fast-moving machines.

Surface

This lists the kind of trail you will be skiing on. There are five types.

Groomed: These are skis-only or skis and snowshoe trails that have been smoothed out by a machine to provide the best possible skiing conditions. You will find several types of grooming; the simplest is snow compacted by a snowmobile on a regular basis. Many groomed trails are set with machine-made tracks for your skis. Groomed trails may also include a skating lane. No dogs are allowed on groomed trails.

Groomed for snowmobiles: These are logging roads where the snow has been smoothed and compacted for optimal, high-speed snowmobile riding. When the machines are absent they make excellent skating lanes and downhill runs.

Forest road: This category covers all ungroomed roads that are open to cross-country skiers. The first skiers to head up a forest road after a storm will have to break trail, which can be slow and exhausting work when the snow is heavy. Some forest roads are referred to as "cat roads" or "skid roads." Cat roads are primitive routes through the trees, just wide enough for a tractor to get through. Skid roads are a type of cat road found on the east side of the Cascades Mountains. These rough paths through the trees are used by tractors to haul logs from a selected cutting area (as opposed to a clearcut) to the main road.

Trails: Hiking trails are narrow, never groomed, and can be very challenging on cross-country skis. Trails are rarely recommended for beginners.

Ungroomed slopes: These are open hillsides covered with a layer or two of snow. With no trails or roads to follow, you are free to create your own route up and carve as many turns as you can on the way back down.

Skiers on the Beaver Pond trail at Sun Mountain in the Methow Valley, Tour 37

Rating

Each tour has been rated for difficulty based on the amount of skill required to enjoy the trip. For the sake of simplicity we have used five categories that tend to be broad and somewhat overlapping; consider them to be merely suggestions.

Easiest: No skill requirement. Anyone can have fun, even if it's the very first time on skis, and families will find these to be great places for very small children. These are also areas where sleds loaded with gear or children can be pulled with relative ease. These tours generally are in open meadows, along valley bottoms, on level logging roads, or on abandoned railroad grades.

More difficult: The minimum skills required are good balance, kick and glide, and simple stopping techniques such as pole dragging, snowplowing, or sitting down—and a good sense of humor. The tours at this level generally are on logging roads, marked Forest Service loops, or prepared tracks, and will cover some steep terrain.

Most difficult: Tours with this designation may be long, very steep, or both. Skiers who attempt these tours should have endurance and the ability to descend precipitous slopes in all types of snow conditions. Minimum required skills include the kick-turn, herringbone, and snowplow turn. Skiers who can telemark will enjoy these tours more than those who cannot. These tours are generally on narrow, steep logging roads and may have optional off-road side trips and descent routes.

Backcountry: The minimum skills required for these tours are full control of skis at all times, mastery of the telemark or any turn you wish to use, and the ability to stop quickly. Some backcountry tours require basic routefinding to navigate unmarked trails.

Mountaineer: In addition to backcountry skiing skills, mountaineer trips require competence in routefinding, knowledge of snow and avalanche conditions, glacier travel techniques, weather savviness, winter camping skills, winter survival skills, and mountaineering skills.

Trail marked for difficulty

Mileage

This entry has several types of listings. The most common listing is the *round trip*, which tells you the number of miles you will ski from your car to the turnaround point and back again. The *loop trip* indicates the number of miles skied to complete a loop, which starts and ends at the same place. In the Methow Valley section, a couple of trip mileages are indicated as *one way*. Skiers on these trips frequently start at one location and end at a second location. This generally requires the use of more than one vehicle or the aid of a designated driver.

Please remember that snow levels vary from year to year and even day to day. When skiing on logging roads, the starting point may vary. In these cases, the mileages are figured from the parking area suggested in the text. You will have to adjust to the total mileage to fit the actual situation.

Skiing Time

This is the time spent skiing to and from the destination and does not include lunch or rest stops. The times are calculated from the tour's base point. If the snow line is above this point, plan less time; if below, plan more. The times given for each trail assume good conditions and an "average" fitness level. If a track must be broken through heavy snow or the surface is extremely hard ice, add a generous amount of extra time.

Elevation Gain

This entry simply helps you determine the amount of climbing you must do between the parking lot and your destination. Ups and downs have been calculated into the total elevation gain.

High Point

This entry notes the highest point you will reach on your tour. You will find the high point an important piece of information when the snow level is either fluctuating wildly or when the winter has been unseasonably warm and you are trying to guess if you will find any snow at all.

Best

"Best" is an attempt to answer the unanswerable. When is the "best" time to do the tour? The times we provided are guesses based on an average year. However, as any long-time skier can tell you, there is no such thing as an "average" snow year in Washington. There are winters when skiing must be done at 5,000 feet or above; other years, skiing is good through June at 3,000 feet. Some years the skiing is superb on Seattle's golf courses and Spokane has no snow at all.

Avalanche Potential

Tours in this book have been selected for their safety and no known areas of extreme hazard have been included. The warnings given here are about areas to avoid at times when the snow is unstable. To know when these times are, skiers must make it their responsibility to inform themselves about current weather and snow conditions. The best source for up-to-date information on the weather and avalanche conditions in Washington is a weather radio with continuous reports from the NOAA (National Oceanic and Atmospheric Administration). For specific tours, call the ranger station in that district; on weekends there will be a recorded message.

Your best defense against avalanches is knowledge. Check Suggested Reading, in Appendix A, for books with detailed discussions of avalanche safety. Following are several things to particularly watch for when in avalanche country.

Avalanche danger is especially high during warming trends or after a heavy snowfall; at these times, avoid leeward slopes, the side of the ridge opposite the prevailing wind, where unstable snow and cornices may build up and travel is safe only on the very crest of the ridge.

Steep hillsides, particularly those facing north, receive their first dose of sun for many months in the spring. After being stable all winter, these slopes may be covered by climax avalanches.

Wind causes snow to build up on the leeward side of ridges, creating dangerous overhanging crests of snow called cornices. Use caution when approaching a ridge top—you may walk out atop a cornice with empty air beneath. A good rule is never to ski beyond the line of trees or snow-blown rocks that mark the true crest of a ridge. It is equally as dangerous to ski under a cornice as over it.

Forecasting agencies express the daily hazard in the following four classifications:

Low avalanche hazard: Mostly stable snow.

Moderate avalanche hazard: Areas of unstable snow on steep, open slopes or gullies.

High avalanche hazard: Snowpack is very unstable. Avalanches are highly probable on steep slopes and in gullies.

Extreme avalanche hazard: Travel in the mountains is unsafe. Better to head for the beach.

These classifications of hazard have to do with the weather's contribution to the avalanches. Each trail in this book has been rated as to the potential of the terrain for avalanches. *The two factors of hazard and potential must be put together by the skier to make an accurate judgment of the situation.*

If the avalanche potential for the trail is listed as none, the trail may be safely skied on days when the hazard is low, moderate, or high.

Areas with low avalanche potential normally may be skied on days when the hazard is low or moderate.

A moderate avalanche potential indicates the area is always to be skied with caution and then only when the hazard is low.

Avalanche forecasting is not an exact science. As when driving a car, one has to accept a certain amount of risk when skiing and use the forecast as a guide, not as a certainty. It is important always to seek up-to-date avalanche information before each trip, even for trips of low to moderate avalanche potential.

Maps

Blankets of snow add difficulties to routefinding. Signs may be covered, road junctions may be obscured, and trails can blend into the surrounding countryside. Never start out without a good map of the area to be skied.

The maps provided in this book are for general reference only. All routefinding outside a groomed ski area requires a topographic map that shows elevation and contours. To help you find the best map, we have recommended one or more topographic maps *(USGS, Green Trails, Custom Correct, or USFS)* for each tour description. The *USGS* maps, which cover every location in the country, are published by the United States Geological Survey and are unequaled for off-road and off-trail routefinding. Unfortunately, USGS maps are not kept up-to-date in terms of roads and trails. The *Green Trails* maps are published in Washington and updated with some regularity; however, these maps do not cover areas beyond the heartland of the Cascades and Olympics.

Custom Correct maps cover only the Olympic Mountains. Unlike Green Trails, these maps do not follow the USGS established grids. Instead, Custom Correct maps cover a usage area, creating a series of maps that overlap each other. To date, Custom Correct maps have the best record of keeping current with the road and trail changes in the Olympics.

Each *USFS* (United States Forest Service) *Ranger District* map covers an entire Ranger District, showing contours, roads, and trails. These are outstanding maps and are sold at a bargain price. They are generally the most up-to-date maps available. Unfortunately, the maps are huge and tear easily.

Both the USGS and Green Trails maps are available at outdoor equipment retailers and many Forest Service Ranger Stations. The USFS Ranger District maps are available only through the Forest Service and may be purchased in person or by mail-order from the Ranger District offices or from the Forest Service Headquarters office.

Another excellent resource is an up-to-date *Forest Service Recreation Map*, available for a small fee at ranger stations (on weekdays) or by writing the district offices.

In groomed ski areas, we recommend the free map you receive (or should ask for) when you buy your ticket. These maps are essential in finding your way through the maze of trails in places like Sun Mountain, Mount Spokane, and Snoqualmie Pass Nordic Area.

A NOTE ABOUT SAFETY

Safety is an important concern in all outdoor activities. No guidebook can alert you to every hazard or anticipate the limitations of every reader. Therefore, the descriptions of roads, trails, routes, and natural features in this book are not representations that a particular place or excursion will be safe for your party. When you follow any of the routes described in this book, you assume responsibility for your own safety. Under normal conditions, such excursions require the usual attention to traffic, road and trail conditions, weather, terrain, the capabilities of your party, and other factors. Because many of the lands in this book are subject to development and/or change of ownership, conditions may have changed since this book was written that make your use of some of these routes unwise. Always check for current conditions, obey posted private property signs, and avoid confrontations with property owners or managers. Keeping informed on current conditions and exercising common sense are the keys to a safe, enjoyable outing.

—*The Mountaineers Books*

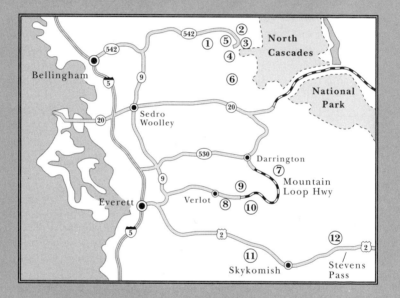

North Cascades: West Side Region

From Stevens Pass north to the Canadian border lies a wide swath of rugged mountains known as the North Cascades. These are impressive mountains, with glacier-clad summits and side slopes that plunge with stark abruptness to valley floors.

A typical winter in the North Cascades sees storm after storm dropping several feet of snow at a time on higher elevations. In the lower valleys, that translates to more than 120 inches of rain annually, making for extremely hazardous travel conditions during the winter months. Avalanches are common occurrences in the steep, mountainous terrain, forcing Highway 20 to close from November through April.

Cross-country skiing on the west side of the North Cascades is limited by the terrain. Many of the popular skiing areas are located at relatively low elevations, in densely forested valleys at the base of mountains. Weather is a factor, and west-side skiers are advised to watch the snow level: Some years there is not enough snow to ski at the lower elevations.

The main high-elevation accesses to mountains are the Mount Baker and Stevens Pass Ski Areas. The snow at both locations is notoriously good, as is the scenery. Avalanches are an ever-present hazard for anyone straying off the standard routes.

1 HELIOTROPE RIDGE

Open to: nonmotorized
Surface: trail
Rating: backcountry
Round trip: 13 miles; 26 miles to Coleman Glacier viewpoint
Skiing time: 1–2 days
Elevation gain: 3,700 feet
High point: 6,500 feet
Best: November and March–May
Avalanche potential: low
Map: *Green Trails* Mt. Baker #13

From a camp near the edge of the crevasse-slashed Coleman Glacier, carve ski tracks across miles of untracked slopes on Heliotrope Ridge. In the evening, watch one of nature's best shows, as a brief, brilliant winter sunset casts pinks and golds over the snowy ramparts of Mount Baker—or maybe crawl in the tent and peer out at a blizzard.

The route to the northwest side of Mount Baker culminates in 3 miles of trail, but starts with 10 miles of road, some or all of which may have to be skied. Because the road is extremely popular with snowmobilers, human-powered travelers are advised to do this trip in the fall or spring when the road is partially snow free. A special warning about late fall: If you are not careful, your car could be snowed in for the winter. When 6 inches of snow pile up at your camp in the mountains, it is time to leave—or already be gone.

Access: Drive Highway 542 to Glacier and register your trip at the

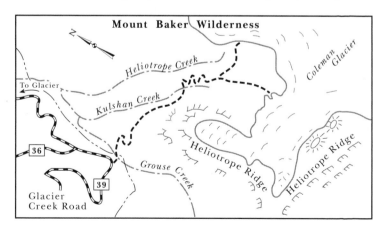

Skier on the upper slopes of Heliotrope Ridge

Forest Service Information Center, at the east end of town. Continue east 0.6 mile beyond the Information Center, then turn right (south) on Glacier Creek Road and follow it to the snow line or trailhead. At 5 miles the road bumps over Coal Creek and starts serious climbing. This generally marks the start of spring skiing, so park in one of the pullouts along the side of the road just before the corner (2,000 feet).

The Tour: Occasional views of Coleman Glacier and its headwall on the glacier-tracked face of Mount Baker enliven the initial miles up the steadily climbing road. Stay left at the large junction at 2½ miles on Road 39 for the final ¼ mile to the trailhead parking lot (3,700 feet).

To find the trail, descend into the heavy timber at the edge of the parking area. Cross a small creek then begin climbing. Skiers with skins will probably wish to use them. Many find it preferable to walk.

Two miles up the trail (4,700 feet), reach the old Kulshan Cabin site, torn down in 1986. Pass several campsites here. Unless the weather is foul, continue on to scenic sites beyond. Before long the trail will divide. For the best camping, continue straight ahead. One mile beyond the old cabin site the trail ends at the Coleman Glacier Overlook. Small campsites may be found 500 feet west of the overlook in a band of scraggly trees.

The best skiing lies west of the overlook, separated from it by a series of steep, slide-prone gullies. Ski up the open ribs from the overlook, bearing right. Reach a broad bench at about 6,500 feet, then continue to aim west over rolling Heliotrope Ridge. Try out some of the steep slopes and bowls beyond.

Many skiers find the long open slopes leading to the summit of Mount Baker extremely alluring. Do not attempt to ski the higher reaches of the mountain without climbing gear, as deep crevasses lie hidden under the smooth snow.

2 NORTH FORK NOOKSACK

Open to: nonmotorized
Surface: forest road
Rating: easiest
Round trip: 5 miles
Skiing time: 2 hours
Elevation gain: 400 feet
High point: 2,600 feet
Best: January–mid-March
Avalanche potential: low
Map: *Green Trails* Mt. Shuksan #14

It is unclear whether it is the nearly level terrain, the outstanding scenery, or the closure to snowmobiles that makes this such a popular area. Whatever the reason, the North Fork Nooksack River Road draws novices and experts alike.

Access: From Glacier, drive Highway 542 east for 12.5 miles. Just before the highway crosses the North Fork Nooksack River, go left on Hannegan Road. Park in the small space provided (2,200 feet). If the parking area has not been plowed, continue on Highway 542 for 0.1 mile to the Salmon Ridge Sno-Park.

The Tour: Hannegan Road follows the North Fork Nooksack River upstream along the valley floor, open and level. Views start immediately, Mount Shuksan gleaming in winter white, Mount Sefrit and Ruth Mountain standing out along Nooksack Ridge.

At 1/2 mile, enter the forest. Several spur roads branch off; stay left at all junctions. At 1 1/2 miles the road splits. Hannegan Road

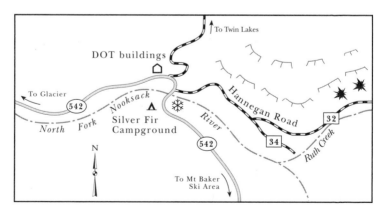

No. 32 goes left, up Ruth Creek for 4 miles to the road's end at Hannegan Campground. Avalanche hazard is high after the first mile and winter travel is not recommended. From the split, go right on North Fork Nooksack River Road No. 34. The road skirts the north side of the valley for a long mile to the turnaround point at the washed-out Ruth Creek bridge. ·

Mount Shuksan towering over the North Fork Nooksack River

3 SALMON RIDGE SNO-PARK

Open to: skis only
Surface: groomed
Rating: easiest to most difficult
Round trip: up to 10 miles
Skiing time: 5 hours
Elevation gain: up to 1,200 feet
High point: 3,400 feet
Best: mid-December–February
Avalanche potential: low
Map: *Green Trails* Mt. Shuksan #14

In the North Cascades, hillsides sweep up from the river bottoms to the glaciated summits in a near-vertical fashion, leaving very little terrain for rambling ski tours. However, with a lot of determination and hours of backbreaking work, the Nooksack Nordic Ski Club created a groomed ski-touring area in the heart of these perpendicular mountains. With set tracks, a wide skating lane, and several steep, non-groomed backcountry roads, this area has challenges for all types of cross-country skis and skiers.

Despite all the effort to keep the trails in good shape, the capricious weather is the true arbitrator of the skiing conditions here. Trailhead elevation is moderate and the quality and quantity of snow varies radically throughout the winter. Do not be surprised if you arrive in midwinter to find little or no snow. Always come with an alternate plan in mind.

Access: From Glacier drive Highway 542 east for 12.8 miles. Five hundred feet after crossing the North Fork Nooksack River, turn left into the Salmon Ridge Sno-Park (2,200 feet).

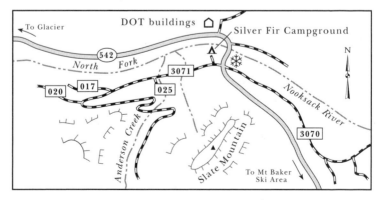

Anderson Creek Road and North Fork Nooksack River valley

Razorhone Road No. 3070: This popular tour begins at the east end of the parking area. The groomed road heads east toward the Nooksack River for a few hundred feet before turning southeast to follow the river upvalley. Several trails branch off on either side. Trails on the right loop through the rain forest. To the left, trails head through the brush to the edge of the river.

Razorhone Road climbs away from the river at 1/2 mile, then descends back to the valley floor to cross a lively creek at 1 1/2 miles. Another climb is followed by yet another descent, which leads to a crossing of Bagley Creek. Shortly beyond is a steep hill. At the crest, a trail (not groomed) branches off to the right. Beyond the intersection the road descends into a basin, where it passes a second spur road before, at 2 miles, coming to an end at the edge of the Nooksack River.

Anderson Creek Road No. 3071: To begin the tour, carefully cross to the west side of Highway 542. Two roads start here. Stay to the left, on Road 3071. (The road on the right leads to some circular skiing around Silver Fir Campground.) The first portion of the tour is a gradual descent down the North Fork Nooksack River valley. Then, just before the 2-mile marker, the road makes an abrupt turn and begins climbing.

At 2 1/2 miles is an intersection (2,200 feet); stay left and continue the climb. Near mile 4 the scene changes as the road crosses Anderson Creek again (3,000 feet), makes a steep switchback, and enters a hanging valley (the natural sweep of the valley was cut off when the Nooksack Glacier scoured out the North Fork valley many millennia ago). Shortly after passing the 5-mile marker, the road ends in a clearcut at the Anderson Creek trailhead, an abandoned trail that goes on up the valley another mile to nowhere in particular.

4 ARTIST POINT AND COLEMAN PINNACLE

Artist Point
Open to: nonmotorized
Surface: trail
Rating: backcountry
Round trip: 5 miles
Skiing time: 3 hours
Elevation gain: 1,100 feet
High point: 5,220 feet
Best: December–May
Avalanche potential: low
Map: *Green Trails* Mt. Shuksan #14

Coleman Pinnacle
Open to: nonmotorized
Surface: trail
Rated: mountaineer
Round trip: 11 miles
Skiing time: 6 hours
Elevation gain: 2,080 feet
High point: 6,200 feet
Best: December–May
Avalanche potential: high
Map: *Green Trails* Mt. Shuksan #14

It's not possible to come away from a visit to Artist Point with any doubts about the source of its name. Located between the vertical massif of Mount Shuksan and the (restlessly?) slumbering dome of Mount Baker, you can spend hours at Artist Point photographing, painting, or just contemplating the view. The scene is further embellished after nearly every winter storm by hardy trees plastered with wind-driven snow like so many lonesome statues. However, most winter visitors show more interest in cutting turns in the famed powder than watching the clouds drift around.

Beyond Artist Point beckon the excellent slopes below Coleman Pinnacle. This sharp spike in the long spine of Ptarmigan Ridge reigns over excellent powder bowls with runs that descend more than 1,000 vertical feet. The tour to the pinnacle passes through several avalanche-prone areas and is unsafe unless the snow is quite stable. Be sure and talk with the Forest Service snow ranger at the ski area before heading out.

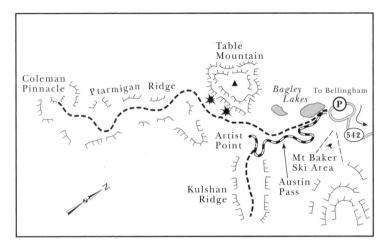

Access: Drive Highway 542 east from Bellingham 55 miles to its end, at the upper Mount Baker Ski Area parking lot (4,120 feet). (On Mondays and Tuesdays the road is not plowed.) Park in the upper lot with the downhill skiers and head out. There has been some attempt by the ski area to collect a parking fee from cross-country skiers. The area owners can charge a fee for parking in their lot, but they cannot charge for parking along the road.

Artist Point: From the south end of the upper parking lot, head along the edge of the ski area, following the summer road to Austin Pass (unmarked). Stay out of the path of the alpine skiers. Follow the road along the west side of a beginner chairlift to a broad bench at the ski area boundary. Here folks with climbing skins will zip past their herringboning and kick-turning comrades. Stay to the right of the road until you reach the ridge crest at Austin Pass (4,700 feet). Bear right along the ridge. Skiers with climbing skins can take the quick route, straight up the next hill. Others will contour east on the road to gentler slopes, then head right and climb the rolling terrain to the crest of Kulshan Ridge (4,900 feet). Be wary of the drop-off on the far side—don't let enthusiasm for the view draw you beyond the trees that mark the edge of the ridge. Artist Point is the large snow-covered parking area and summer trailhead.

Coleman Pinnacle: From Artist Point, climb to the right. Near the base of Table Mountain, ski over the side of Kulshan Ridge and drop nearly 200 vertical feet in a single swoop down the south side, then traverse along the lower edge of the open slope below Table Mountain to a 5,000-foot saddle. This is an area of extreme avalanche danger.

Do not attempt to cross below Table Mountain when the snowpack is unstable.

Once beyond Table Mountain, descend to contour below the first hump on Ptarmigan Ridge. Once safely beyond the rocky cliffs, head up the ridge and ski along the crest. Following the route of the summer trail, stay on the southeast side as much as possible. Coleman Pinnacle is an obvious rocky spur and the fourth major high point encountered along the ridge. Ski east around the pinnacle, then head down the bowl on the west side. Snow remains powdery here for much of the season, and the run is outstanding.

To return, ski well to the west of the steep slopes of Ptarmigan Ridge.

Telemarking the open slopes below Coleman Pinnacle

5 HERMAN SADDLE

Open to: nonmotorized
Surface: trail
Rating: backcountry
Round trip: 5 miles
Skiing time: 4–6 hours
Elevation gain: 1,060 feet
High point: 5,300 feet
Best: December–April
Avalanche potential: moderate
Map: *Green Trails* Mt. Shuksan #14

The Herman Saddle tour offers some of the finest downhill cross-country skiing in the western Cascades. The snow is frequently powdery and the slopes are often smoother than most groomed ski areas. Views of Mount Shuksan and Mount Baker are huge beyond Table Mountain—and the entire tour is in plain view of lift skiers on Panorama Dome.

Note: Avalanches are always a possibility on this route. Do not ski this run after a heavy snowfall or during times of unseasonably warm weather. In addition, the route is easily lost in times of poor visibility. Always consult the snow ranger at the ski area before setting out.

Access: Drive Highway 542 east from Bellingham 55 miles to its end, at the Mount Baker Ski Area (4,120 feet), and park in the upper lot.

The Tour: Follow the road along the edge of the ski area for 1/4 mile. When you reach the steep hill below Austin Pass, go right and

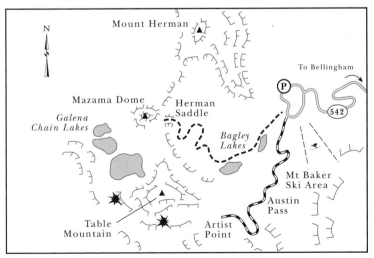

drop to the summer Information Center. This small log building overlooking Bagley Lakes was once used as a warming hut for skiers. From
the old warming hut, descend left along a sloping bench to its end. A
couple of quick turns will bring you to the white plain below, where
the two Bagley Lakes lie hidden under a blanket of snow.

Cross the basin and head for Herman Saddle, the lowest and most
obvious pass in the circle of peaks between Table Mountain and
Mazama Dome. As the basin bends west, the ascent begins. Skiers with
climbing skins will be glad; for those without, there commences a
long series of switchbacks. Stay to the right, on the flanks of Mount
Herman, well away from the basin headwall. Near the top, at around
5,100 feet, head left (south), contouring below Mazama Dome to reach
the saddle at 5,300 feet. On the way up, plan your descent. Decide
which slopes you want to mark with graceful figure eights (or sitzmarks)
for lift skiers on Panorama Dome to admire and envy (or laugh at).

Skiers descending the open slopes below Herman Saddle

6 PARK BUTTE

Open to: all uses
Surface: open slopes
Rating: backcountry
Round trip: up to 18 miles
Skiing time: 1–3 days
Elevation gain: 3,100 feet
High point: 5,000 feet
Best: March–May
Avalanche potential: moderate
Maps: *Green Trails* Lake Shannon #46 and Hamilton #45

By spring, a single day is ample time to reach the snow-covered meadows of Park Butte and return to the car before dark. However, a single day is not enough time to ski each and every inviting slope at the Butte and on the adjoining flanks of Mount Baker. Carry camping gear to ensure your opportunity to ski all the snow-covered meadows, then climb a hill to watch the sun set over Twin Sisters.

Sad to say, these wide-open spaces attract snow machines like a picnic does ants. Until the Forest Service recognizes that this spectacular area is the wrong place for a motorized rodeo, skiers will be happier if they visit late in the season or on a weekday.

Access: Drive Highway 20 east from Sedro Woolley 14.5 miles and go left on Baker Lake Road. At 12.5 miles, just after crossing Rocky Creek, turn left on Loomis-Nooksack Road No. 12. The road is drivable throughout the winter for 3.5 miles to a sno-park at the junction of Loomis-Nooksack Road and Schriebers Meadow Road No. 13 (1,900 feet). Hopefully you will be able to drive on up Road No. 13. The

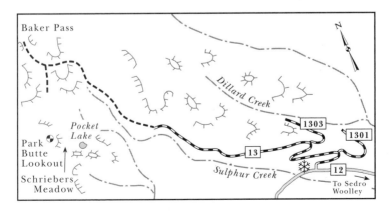

Rolling hills and open bowls await skiers at Park Butte

ideal time to ski is when you can drive 4 of the 5 miles to the trailhead.

The Tour: Five miles from the sno-park, Road No. 13 ends at the Park Butte trailhead. Follow the well-signed, heavily traveled snow-mobile track across Sulphur Creek and stick with it for the next 1/4 mile into Schriebers Meadow (3,263 feet).

When you come to Sulphur Creek a second time, turn right and follow the water course north to the upper end of the meadow. Continue to use the creek as a guide as you head up the open slope between two lateral moraines, deposited by the currently receding Easton Glacier. About halfway up the first rise you will be faced with at least one creek crossing; use caution during the spring melt season.

Continue climbing up the middle of the valley to the last tree. You should now be opposite the highest point of the moraine on your right. Go left and traverse the relatively gentle slope to the top of the moraine (climbing skins are handy if you have them). Follow the crest of the moraine for 100 feet, then ski through trees to a small gully, which, when followed to the top (4,500 feet), gives views over the entire area.

On a clear day you will see the endless slopes here and to the east; enjoy.

Park Butte Lookout is maintained by the Skagit Alpine Club. The building is open throughout the year and available to visitors on a first-come basis. No system for preregistration was available during research, so an alternate shelter should always be carried. Reservations may be required in the future; check with the Sedro Woolley Ranger Station for more information. The final approach to the lookout is steep and dangerous when icy.

7 KENNEDY HOT SPRINGS

Open to: nonmotorized
Surface: trail
Rating: backcountry
Round trip: 10 miles from road end
Skiing time: 8 hours
Elevation gain: 2,300 feet
High point: 3,300 feet
Best: February–March
Avalanche potential: high
Maps: *Green Trails* Sloan Peak #111 and Glacier Peak #112

Hot springs and snow are a seductive combination, so it's not surprising that Kennedy Hot Springs is a popular winter destination. A long soak in the hot springs after a day of skiing soothes the back and takes the boredom out of winter camping.

There is no best time to make a winter visit to Kennedy Hot Springs. If the snowfall has been heavy, skiing may start long before you reach the end of the 11-mile access road up the White Chuck River valley. When the snowfall has been light, the road may be drivable right to the trailhead, and then you may have to walk some or all of the trail.

Access: Drive to Darrington and follow the "Mountain Loop Highway" signs south. The county road turns into Forest Road No. 20 at the edge of town. Take the second road on the left immediately after crossing the Sauk River bridge. White Chuck River Road No. 23 is 11 miles long and ends at the trailhead (2,300 feet).

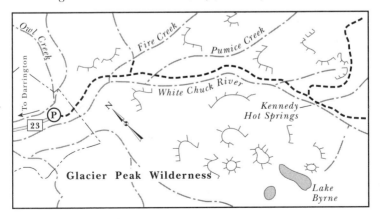

The Tour: The trail travels upriver, tunneling through thick brush and around tall trees for 3/4 mile before traversing a steep hillside above the river. At 1 1/2 miles, descend to cross Fire Creek, where the intersection with Meadow Mountain Trail is passed. The next checkpoint is Pumice Creek, which is crossed at 2 miles. The trail then descends to the river and traverses a beach area covered with boulders freshly dislodged from the hillside above. Do not linger in this hazardous area.

Shortly beyond, the trail crosses a steep, slide-prone bank that rarely holds snow. When the trail is snow-free, take off your skis and walk across the bank. If there is snow on the trail here it is going to slide soon, so retreat 100 feet or so and scramble up a broad slope to the top of the terrace. Cross over the top of the slide area, then return to the trail. A little farther on there is a second hazardous bank. This one must be crossed. Take off your skis and walk.

A solitary switchback provides a notable landmark at 4 miles. Beyond this single twist the trail enters an open flood plain, cut by several creeks. Kennedy Creek, at the far end of the plain, is the final creek. After crossing, go right along the base of a forested hill to reach the guard station, at 5 miles (3,300 feet). The best camping is located in this area.

The hot springs pool is located on the opposite side of the White Chuck River and is reached by a bridge. Cross with caution, as the only handrail, located on the upriver side, is frequently hidden under a mound of snow.

Once across, go left 50 feet to the steaming pool, which is fairly warm through the winter (it does cool off during the spring snowmelt).

Don't just stand there, hop in.

Kennedy Hot Springs

8 SCHWEITZER CREEK LOOP

Open to: all uses
Surface: forest roads
Rating: most difficult
Round trip: 14 miles
Skiing time: 8 hours
Elevation gain: 1,800 feet
High point: 2,800 feet
Best: January–February
Avalanche potential: low
Map: *Green Trails* Silverton #110

Day trips, overnight trips, side trips, and loop trips—they're all here. Take as much time as you can spare to fully explore this area, or plan to come back several times.

The Schweitzer Creek Road system attracts a full complement of winter users: snowshoers, hikers, dogsledders, three-wheelers, four-wheelers, snowmobilers. Weekend visitors should come with a spirit of adventure; the parade of winter explorers can be entertaining. To enjoy winter's peace, visit midweek.

Note: The 1/4-mile connector trail that completes the loop has not been maintained for many years. The route is overgrown and some of the markers have disappeared. If you are unfamiliar with this area, you may have trouble following the trail. First-time visitors should

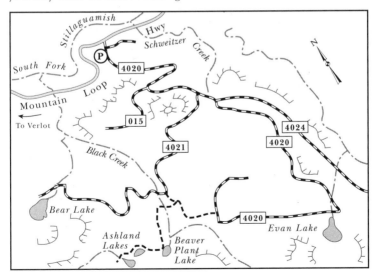

approach this loop with a sense of adventure. Do not be afraid to turn back if you become confused.

Access: Drive east 11 miles from Granite Falls on the Mountain Loop Highway to the Verlot Forest Service Information Center. Check your odometer and continue on another 3.9 miles. Find Schweitzer Creek Road No. 4020 on the right (1,200 feet) and park.

The Tour: The road starts off with an intersection. Stay to the right and begin the climb out of the rain forest environment of the valley floor. Several spur roads are passed before reaching the intersection that marks the beginning of the loop portion of the tour, at 2 3/4 miles (2,150 feet). Go left, continuing straight ahead on Road 4020.

Occasional views enliven the journey as the road traverses the brushy hillside. Look for Big Four Mountain, as well as Vesper, Sperry, and Three Fingers. Near 5 miles, the road rounds a steep switchback. As soon as the road levels off, pass the Evan Lake trailhead. The small lake is located a few hundred feet from the road in a dense grove of trees (2,751 feet). No campsites. The tent sites at Boardman Lake, a mile farther up the trail, are difficult to access in the winter, so if you are looking for a campsite at this point, consider pitching your tent in the trailhead parking area.

To continue the loop, follow Road 4020 on up the hillside. The road levels off at 2,800 feet (5 1/2 miles), then gradually descends for 1 mile through a brushy clearcut. Continue on for 1/8 mile after the road returns to the trees, then watch on the left for a blue diamond and, maybe, a sign marking the very faint connector trail. Head left through the grove of venerable old trees to a clearcut. Continue straight ahead to reach the Ashland Lakes Trail in 1/4 mile.

The Ashland Lakes Trail offers you another choice. To the left, south, you may follow the trail for 1 1/4 miles to campsites at Beaver Plant Lake, or continue 1/2 mile farther to Ashland Lakes. This is a reasonable option when there is enough snow to cover the exposed rocks and roots along the way. To continue the loop, head right, north, on the Ashland Lakes Trail 1/4 mile to the trailhead and road. Go left for a short, steep descent to reach Road 4021 at 7 miles (2,400 feet).

Road 4021 offers another chance for a side trip. Just 1 3/4 miles to the left is the Bear Lake trailhead (2,600 feet), where a 1/4-mile trail leads to the forested lake and more campsites.

The loop follows Road 4021 to the right, north, contouring around the flat-topped ridge to views of Three Fingers and Mount Pilchuck. At 9 1/4 miles, Road 4021 rejoins Road 4020, closing the loop portion of the tour. Go left and descend back to the Mountain Loop Highway at mile 12.

Overnight campsite near Beaver Plant Lake

9 DEER CREEK ROAD

Open to: nonmotorized
Surface: forest road
Rating: more difficult
Round trip: 9 miles
Skiing time: 6 hours
Elevation gain: 1,500 feet
High point: 3,100 feet
Best: January–March
Avalanche potential: low
Map: *Green Trails* Silverton #110

Deer Creek is the one and only road in the Verlot area reserved for nonmotorized sports. Beyond the throngs of enthusiastic snow-players, skiers and snowshoers will find peaceful forests, snow-shrouded clearcuts, and awesome views of knife-edged peaks.

Access: Drive the Mountain Loop Highway east from the Verlot Forest Service Information Center for 12.1 miles to Deer Creek Road No. 4052. Park in the large lot on the left, if plowed, or along the edge of the road (1,600 feet).

The Tour: Taking care to dodge exuberant and sometimes out-of-control sledders, head up Deer Creek Road, climbing steeply through dense forest to a small knob. In the first 1/2 mile, two unsigned spur roads branch off; stay left at both. At 1 mile (2,000 feet), the sadly overgrown Double Eagle Road heads east. Continue left on Deer Creek Road, climbing steadily northwest, heading deeper into

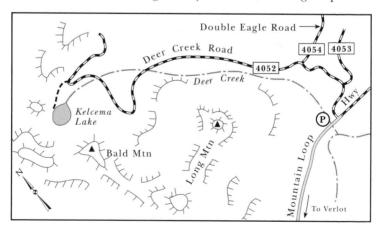

Deer Creek

the long, narrow valley. Ahead, Bald Mountain, majestic in its cloak of snow, dominates the skyline.

By 1¼ miles, the views are impressive and, amazingly, by 2¼ miles, the views have expanded to include Big Four and the jagged summits of the Monte Cristo group. Near 3½ miles, the road crosses Deer Creek and soon after turns abruptly north to ascend along the base of Bald Mountain. Deer Creek is recrossed at the 4½-mile point and, immediately after, you will pass the Kelcema Lake trailhead (3,100 feet). The road continues up through another old clearcut. The return is a long, fun glide.

If you enjoy a little challenge and adventure, head up the trail to Kelcema Lake. The lake is located a scant ½ mile from the road and is easily negotiable by snowshoers and experienced skiers. If you lose the trail, simply follow Deer Creek to the lake. Several sheltered campsites are located on the east shore.

10 BIG FOUR AND COAL LAKE

Open to: all uses
Surface: forest roads
Rating: easiest to more difficult
Round trip: 5–16 miles
Skiing time: 3 hours–2 days
Elevation gain: up to 2,160 feet
High point: up to 3,880 feet
Best: January–February
Avalanche potential: moderate
Map: *Green Trails* Silverton #110

When the snow level is low, the Mountain Loop Highway makes a splendid tour. The road tunnels through a lush forest of moss-hung trees, along the edge of the snowbound Stillaguamish River, and on each side of the valley sheer walls rise to superbly scenic glaciated summits.

When the snow level climbs above the valley floor, skiers can explore the very scenic road to Coal Lake. This road offers grandstand views of the surrounding mountains as well as opportunities for weekend outings.

As with all popular areas, the Mountain Loop Highway has its own set of problems and challenges. This is a multiple-use area and, in midwinter, the multiples arrive in force: dogsledders mush, snowshoers web, hikers slog, skiers glide, snowmobilers roar, and ATVs skid. If you are not comfortable with the crowds, try a weekday tour instead.

Access: Drive the Mountain Loop Highway east from the Verlot

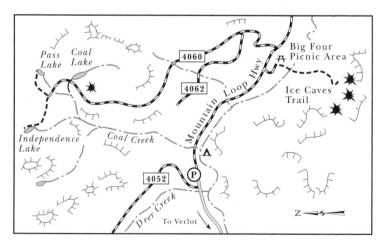

Forest Service Information Center 12.1 miles to Deer Creek Road No. 4052. Park along the lefthand side of the highway (1,600 feet). If there is not enough snowcover, follow the crowds and drive on. The road makes a good tour no matter where you start.

The Tour: From the parking area, head east up the paved road. Skiing should start at the roadblock that may or may not stop the traffic from continuing up the valley. The Big Four Picnic Area, located on the right at 2½ miles, is a natural turnaround point, and the adjacent meadow, the site of a hotel until 1949, makes an excellent snow-play area. Big Four Mountain dominates, tall and cold, and when it is touched by the sun, it roars with avalanches.

The 1-mile trail to the ice caves is a popular winter walk. The trailhead is located near the Coal Lake Road No. 4060 turnoff. If you choose to do this walk, please remember the roaring avalanches mentioned at the end of the last paragraph. The ice caves are formed, in part, by these avalanches, and they are common occurrences, so stop your walk at the edge of the trees.

When not chopped up by machines, Mountain Loop Highway makes a good 8-mile tour, from the Big Four Picnic Area to Barlow Pass.

When the snowcover is insufficient to ski Mountain Loop Highway, or if you simply wish to escape the crowds, try Coal Lake Road No. 4060. The start is located just east of the Big Four Picnic Area. The road begins by climbing gradually to vistas of the Stillaguamish Valley and surrounding peaks. Eyes are naturally drawn to the massive north wall of Big Four, but other mountains are also impressive. A spur road branches off to the right at ½ mile, and a second heads off to the left ¼ mile beyond. From this point, the route is straightforward, without routefinding difficulties. Avalanche hazard is low until the road crosses a steep, open slope at 6¼ miles. Cross only if the snow is stable. At 6¾ miles, pass the Coal Lake Viewpoint. Continue on for a final ¼ mile. Just before the outlet creek, go right to find the lake and campsites a short ⅛ mile from the road (3,420 feet).

Meadow at Big Four Picnic Area

11 MILLER RIVER

Open to: nonmotorized
Surface: forest road
Rating: easiest
Round trip: 4–14 miles
Skiing time: 3 hours–2 days
Elevation gain: up to 2,100 feet
High point: 2,200 feet, at road's end
Best: mid-December–January
Avalanche potential: low
Map: *Green Trails* Skykomish #175

Moss-draped trees, rivers, waterfalls, and mountain goat viewing ensure an interesting tour on a motor-free route up the narrow Miller
River valley. The tour follows an old logging road through rain forest-
like vegetation up a steep-sided valley, with fascinating views of Cascade
Mountain and Maloney Ridge. Backcountry-equipped skiers may continue on from the end of the road for a 1½-mile trail adventure to
Lake Dorothy.

Access: Drive Highway 2 to the Money Creek Campground sign
(located at the entrance of the tunnel 2.7 miles west of Skykomish).
Turn south at the campground sign on the Old Cascade Highway and
follow it for 1 mile before turning right on Miller River Road No.
6410. Continue straight for 2.1 miles to the end of the plowing at
Miller River Campground (1,040 feet). (The road is plowed on a low-
priority basis, so always carry a shovel and tire chains.)

The Tour: From the parking area, head up Miller River Road.
Using the honor system rather than a gate, this road has been reserved

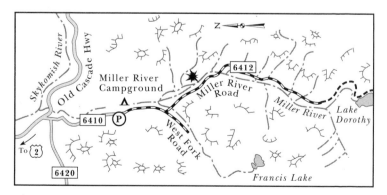

Frost-painted tree along the edge of the Miller River Road

for skiers, snowshoers, and hikers. Some car and truck drivers don't seem to quite grasp this system, so don't be surprised if you have to ski around tire ruts for the first 1/2 mile or so.

The road heads through dense timber along the edge of the Miller River for 1 1/2 miles, passing nearly overgrown West Fork Road and crossing the West Fork Miller River (1,300 feet). A short 1/8 mile beyond the bridge, pass a turnout on the left side of the road, which serves as the first of the two mountain goat viewing spots. Look across the valley and watch the cliffs for little snow patches that walk.

The second mountain goat viewing site is on the East Fork Miller River Bridge, crossed at 3 miles (1,450 feet). The road then makes its one and only switchback of the tour before heading on up the valley for another 2 1/2 miles to reach the Lake Dorothy trailhead, at 5 1/2 miles (2,100 feet).

Continuing on to Lake Dorothy requires backcountry skis and skills to follow the snow-covered trail. If the lake is your goal, ski to the far right end of the parking area. The trail is easy to find for the first mile. Once across the confluence of Camp Robber Creek and Miller River (2,480 feet), ski straight up into a basin, then contour west around the headwall to the crest. Once up top, stay on the snow-covered trail as it winds through the trees, climbing steadily northwest to the Lake Dorothy outlet (3,058 feet).

12 SKYLINE RIDGE

Open to: skis and snowshoes
Surface: ungroomed slopes
Rating: backcountry
Round trip: 4 miles
Skiing time: 3 hours
Elevation gain: 1,200 feet
High point: 5,200 feet
Best: January–March
Avalanche potential: low
Maps: *Green Trails* Stevens Pass #176 and Benchmark Mtn. #144

Years before there were specially designed skis for the backcountry, refugees from the mobs, or what passed for mobs sixty years ago, at the Stevens Pass Ski Area fled across the highway to the untracked slopes of Skyline Ridge (then called Heather Ridge). Though the long, south-facing ascent rarely offered the far-famed "Stevens powder," and explorers were burdened by heavy mountaineering outfits, they returned time and time again.

Nowadays Skyline Ridge is an extremely popular tour for backcountry skiers. The reason is the same now as it was then—untracked slopes to sculpt unhurried turns, and views over miles and miles of snow-clad peaks.

Access: Drive Highway 2 to the summit of Stevens Pass and park across the road from the downhill ski area, or wherever there is room (4,050 feet).

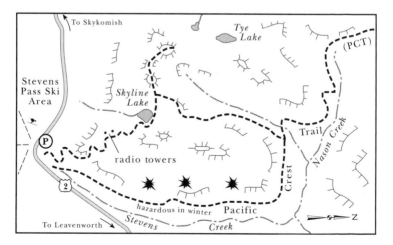

The Tour: Starting at the parking area at the summit across Highway 2 from Stevens Pass Ski Area, walk west to find a cat track heading uphill. Pass several cabins tucked in the trees. Stay with the track as it angles across the ridge to a telephone relay station at the foot of the open slopes.

To the right of the telephone relay station, a primitive road, obscured by snow, heads steeply up. Climbing skins are very helpful. A quarter of the way to the ridge top, the road fades away. Continue upward; in unstable conditions stay to the left (west) side of the open slope.

At 4,900 feet, the radio relay shed is passed and the hard climbing ends. Mount Hinman and Mount Daniel come into view. However, the really big picture awaits above. Just below the heavy timber, ski northwest, then turn uphill in thinning forest to the snowy plain that is Skyline Lake (5,092 feet). Continue to the base of a rock knob on the ridge crest. Unless equipped with an ice ax, do not try for the top; be satisfied with the superb view from the saddle, which includes Glacier Peak to the north and Mount Stuart to the southeast.

Warm up on the short slopes around Skyline Lake, then head northwest. Ski into the trees, then plunge over the edge of the north side of the ridge and telemark your way into some of the finest powder bowls around. You may descend as much as 1,300 feet, until a west-to-east–running drainage is reached (approximate location of the Pacific Crest Trail). At this point, your best course of action is to slap on your climbing skins and head back to Skyline Lake. (If you look at your map and feel tempted to follow the Pacific Crest Trail back to the parking area, be forewarned that it crosses several active avalanche chutes. If the conditions are not entirely stable or your avalanche savvy is not excellent, you could end up taking an eternal nap under a pile of snow.)

Skyline Ridge near Skyline Lake

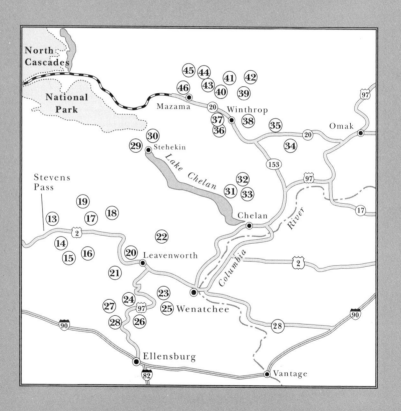

North Cascades: East Side Region

Characterized by fine snow and beautiful weather, the east side of the North Cascade Mountains can justifiably be called a cross-country skiers' paradise. These perfect conditions have resulted in the development of world-class resorts catering to the needs of the cross-country skier. The town of Leavenworth sponsors the grooming of ski trails in three locations around the metropolitan area. On an even more massive scale, the Methow Valley community has developed a system of trails that lace across the entire valley floor for more than twenty miles and climb the rolling foothills in the Loup Loup, Sun Mountain, and Rendezvous areas.

Most of the cross-country skiing on the east side of the Cascade Mountains is done on immaculately groomed trails at resorts or sno-parks, making it an excellent area for skating. The near-perfect trail conditions make it an ideal location for first-time skiers to learn the basic skills of cross-country skiing.

With the light snow and groomed tracks comes a preference for the lighter, narrower performance skis and boots. Serious east-side skiers tend to choose waxable instead of no-wax skis. Skating is very popular and visitors will be able to find rental equipment at the resorts.

The snowfall on the east side of the Cascades is noticeably less than on the west side. The sparseness of the snow accumulations at the cross-country skiing areas from Blewett Pass north tends to discourage off-trail explorations. Before heading off-trail to cut some turns on an open slope, check to be sure there is a solid base.

13 SMITH BROOK AND LAKE VALHALLA

Smith Brook
Open to: nonmotorized
Surface: forest road
Rating: more difficult
Round trip: 3¹/₂ miles
Skiing time: 2 hours
Elevation gain: 800 feet
High point: 4,000 feet
Best: January–March
Avalanche potential: high
Map: *Green Trails* Benchmark Mtn. #144

Lake Valhalla
Open to: nonmotorized
Surface: open slopes
Rated: backcountry
Round trip: 7¹/₂ miles
Skiing time: 4 hours
Elevation gain: 1,900 feet
High point: 5,100 feet
Best: January–March
Avalanche potential: high
Map: *Green Trails* Benchmark Mtn. #144

Smith Brook is unique. This moderately high-elevation tour has snow all winter and is always a safe bet when the snow is chancy at lower elevations. The gradually climbing road makes for easy touring and is heavily used by beginners and family groups. Best of all, neither a sno-park permit nor a trail pass is needed to ski here.

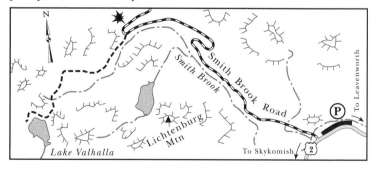

Since the Forest Service turned over the entire Mill Creek Sno-Park to commercial interests, many skiers have looked to Smith Brook Road as an alternative. Unfortunately, Smith Brook is not the snow-play paradise that Mill Creek was. Parking is the first challenge encountered. The only legal parking is 1/8 mile east of Smith Brook Road. Probably the worst feature of this tour is the extreme avalanche danger beyond the 2-mile point. Unless you are backcountry equipped and have a sound understanding of avalanche hazards, you must be satisfied with a short tour.

Access: Smith Brook Road lies 4.7 miles east of Stevens Pass on a divided section of Highway 2. If approaching from the west, it is necessary to drive 6 miles beyond Stevens Pass to the Mill Creek U-turn. Head back west toward the pass 1.2 miles to find the parking area (3,200 feet). *Note:* Improperly parked cars will be towed. Properly parked cars, if left overnight, are also occasionally towed.

The Tour: Walk up Highway 2 for 1/8 mile or, if the snow is clean, ski the road bank. No matter which way you go, you will have to claw your way up a wall of snow, which can be 10 to 15 feet high, to reach the road. Once on Smith Brook Road, begin a gentle climb through alternating forest and clearcuts. At 1 3/4 miles, the road makes a broad switchback in a large clearcut before reentering the trees. This is the turnaround point for those skiers who are not heading on to Lake Valhalla.

Backcountry skiers continuing on to Lake Valhalla should ski up to the 1 3/4-mile point, then look for a crossing of Smith Brook. Once on the opposite side, parallel the road until it switchbacks. If there is not enough snow to allow an early crossing of the creek, stay on the road to the corner of the switchback, then continue straight off the road into a meadow (4,000 feet). *Do not* attempt to follow the summer trail, which traverses across the most hazardous section of the avalanche slope.

About 400 to 500 feet beyond the meadow, turn left and ski to the hillside, then climb to the right over rolling slopes. At about 4,500 feet the forest cover thins. Ahead is an avalanche-prone hillside on the flank of avalanche-prone Lichtenberg Mountain; swing to the right and continue climbing to an open bowl.

Looking straight ahead, southwest, is a saddle. That is the goal. Ski to the northwest, then head southwest for a climbing traverse across a hillside cut by deep gullies. The 5,100-foot saddle is reached at 3 1/2 miles from Highway 2.

Lake Valhalla lies 400 feet below the saddle. To ski the lake, angle down to the right; slopes to the left could slide. If the climb back out from the lake is too intimidating, try heading up to the top of the 5,700-foot knob above the saddle for some exhilarating skiing down lightly timbered slopes.

View from ridge over snow-covered Lake Valhalla

14 STEVENS PASS CROSS-COUNTRY

Open to: skis and snowshoes
Surface: groomed roads
Rating: easiest to most difficult
Round trip: up to 15 miles
Skiing time: 5 hours
Elevation gain: up to 1,220 feet
High point: 3,920 feet
Best: mid-December–March
Avalanche potential: low
Map: area handout

This cleverly designed cross-country ski area is molded into the restrictive confines of the shoe-box–shaped Mill Creek valley. The creative designers of this stepchild of the Steven Pass Resort have developed a railroad theme for the valley and, consequently, given it a life of its own.

The Stevens Pass Nordic Center offers rental equipment, lessons, excellent grooming, and even a 1¾-mile-long snowshoe trail. The center is open 9:00 A.M. to 4:00 P.M., Fridays, Saturdays, Sundays, and holidays. The upper parking lot closes at 4:00 P.M., but skiers parking in the lower lot can use the trails at any time, on any day. In 2001, trail passes were only required when the center was open. A sno-park permit is not required.

Access: Drive Highway 2 for 5.8 miles east of Stevens Pass, to Mill Creek Road (2,800 feet); a U-turn road gives access for westbound traffic. If you think you might leave later than 4:00 P.M., or if you ski here on a weekday, park in the first lot.

The Tour: Once on the tracks, you have an interesting series of

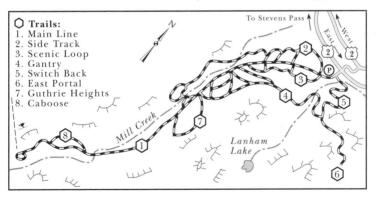

Trails:
1. Main Line
2. Side Track
3. Scenic Loop
4. Gantry
5. Switch Back
6. East Portal
7. Guthrie Heights
8. Caboose

To Stevens Pass

Mill Creek

Lanham Lake

options to choose from. The Main Line trail heads up the valley 4.5 miles to end at the base of Southern Cross and Jupiter Chairs on the backside of Stevens Pass. This trail gives access to all the other trails in the system and is rated *easiest*. The benches and picnic tables located along the trail are particularly nice on sunny days.

For a little more challenge, try the forested Side Track and Side Track Spike trails, which are rated as *more difficult*. For a few more thrills, give the rolling Scenic Loop a try. This 3/4-mile trail runs through the forest, but the constant hills make it very fun.

For the best scenic views and the most challenging skiing, head up to the Gantry. With descents that should require either seatbelts or parachutes, this trail, as well as its various access trails, is very deserving of its *most difficult* rating. And for a great workout, be sure to ski out the East Portal to the areas' 3,920-foot high point overlooking the Nason Creek valley.

Ice- and snow-covered fir needles

15 LANHAM LAKE AND JIM HILL

Lanham Lake
Open to: skis and snowshoes
Surface: trail
Rating: backcountry
Round trip: 3½ miles
Skiing time: 4 hours
Elevation gain: 1,283 feet
High point: 4,143 feet
Best: December–March
Avalanche potential: none
Map: *Green Trails* Benchmark Mtn. # 144

Jim Hill
Open to: skis and snowshoes
Surface: open slopes
Rating: mountaineer
Round trip: 8 miles
Skiing time: 6 hours
Elevation gain: 3,805 feet
High point: 4,200 feet
Best: February–May
Avalanche potential: moderate
Maps: *USGS* Labyrinth Mountain, Stevens Pass, Mount Howard, and
  Chiwaukum Mountains

Two destinations, a beautiful subalpine lake and a scenic mountaintop make this one of the most classic backcountry skiing areas in the Cascades. Lanham Lake, a short but rather difficult tour, is an excellent midwinter destination. Jim Hill is at its best in the spring, after the snow stabilizes. Once you have pieced the maps together, Jim Hill is likely to become an annual event for all telemark enthusiasts.

Both trips require a covering of at least three feet of snow to be fun. Heavy brush makes skiing nearly impossible when snowcover is insufficient.

Access: Drive Highway 2 to Mill Creek Road (2,800 feet), 5.8 miles east of Stevens Pass; a U-turn road gives access for westbound traffic. The large parking area here is for the Stevens Pass Nordic Center. This is a groomed area, and fees are charged to use the trails on days

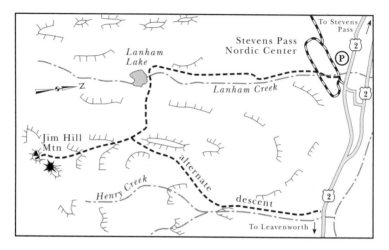

when the center is open. Park in the first lot; the upper parking area is blocked off after 4:00 P.M.

Lanham Lake: Backcountry skiers will find an immediate trail access right at the start of the groomed road. You must leave the road at the Lanham Lake trailhead and head up the steep hillside on the narrow trail. Many skiers walk the first section. You are not allowed to use the roads, which provide easier access to the powerlines, without buying a trail pass *when the center is open* (see Tour 14). When the center is closed, ski up Mill Creek Road for about 1 mile, then follow a route that currently goes by the name of Chuga Chuga. This groomed trail climbs up and to the east, intersecting the Lanham Lake Trail under the powerlines at the edge of the drop-off overlooking Lanham Creek. Go right and head uphill into the trees. The trail parallels Lanham Creek through alternating forest and old clearcuts and across several old logging roads. Keep left, staying approximately 500 feet from the creek.

The valley narrows. Continue straight ahead on a climbing traverse. A scant 1/2 mile of steep climbing leads to Lanham Lake (4,143 feet). Nestled in the trees, this serenely frozen lake offers many fine picnic and camping sites, with views up to the icicled ramparts of Jim Hill Mountain.

Jim Hill: Ski to Lanham Lake, then head east, across the outlet. When you reach the hillside, begin a climbing traverse south. Find a shelf and follow it back to the northeast, to the 5,650-foot saddle on the crest of a very narrow ridge.

Climb south along the crest of the ridge until it divides at 6,200 feet, then ski up a small basin. Continue up to a small dip on the summit. This is an avalanche-prone area, so be sure the snow is stable before making the final ascent.

For the descent, head back down the way you came, as far as the saddle. The safest, least avalanche-prone route is the ridge crest. Watch for cornices and unstable snow. From the 5,500-foot saddle, you have two choices for descending. You may follow your ascent route back or drop down the Henry Creek drainage (recommended). Stay to the west of Henry Creek. You should intersect Highway 2 no more than 1½ miles below Mill Creek Road. Hitchhike or walk up the road to return to the start.

Lanham Lake and Jim Hill Mountain

16 CHIWAUKUM MOUNTAINS (SCOTTISH LAKES)

Coulter Ski Trail
Open to: skis and snowshoes
Surface: forest roads
Rating: most difficult
Round trip: 13 miles
Skiing time: 6 hours
Elevation gain: 2,800 feet
High point: 5,000 feet
Best: January–February
Avalanche potential: low
Maps: *Green Trails* Wenatchee Lake #145 and Chiwaukum Mtns. #177

Scottish Lakes
Open to: skis and snowshoes
Surface: trails and ungroomed slopes
Rating: backcountry
Round trip: 20 miles and more
Skiing time: 1–4 days
Elevation gain: 100–2,000 feet
High point: 7,000 feet
Best: January–April
Avalanche potential: moderate
Maps: *Green Trails* Wenatchee Lake #145 and Chiwaukum Mtns. #177

The Scottish Lakes area of the Chiwaukum Mountains is a perfect mixture of rolling hills, snow-covered alpine lakes, open meadows, forests,

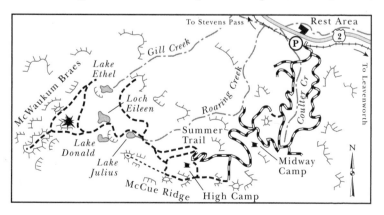

and outstanding views. Backcountry skiers have the option of carving turns on open slopes or through forest. If the telemark turn has somehow eluded you, this country is equally good for touring. Best of all, the weather here tends to be just a little bit better than at Stevens Pass or Lake Wenatchee.

The Scottish Lakes tent cabins are currently operated by Scottish Lakes High Country Adventures, Inc. You may contact them at High Country Adventures, P.O. Box 2036, Leavenworth, WA 98826, or on the web at *www.scottishlakes.com.*

Although the Scottish Lakes are in the Alpine Lakes Wilderness and are open to everyone, visitors who attempt to completely disassociate themselves from the commercial concession will be plagued with access problems. The trailhead is on private land and parking is nonexistent. Independent visitors must be prepared to either park at one of the Lake Wenatchee Sno-Parks, or park in Leavenworth and hitchhike back to the start. Under current management, parking comes with the price of having your packs or yourself carried by Sno-Cat to the wilderness boundary (a good deal), where the independent-minded could head out to camp in a secluded spot.

The Coulter Ski Trail is the best route to use if you decide to ski into the Scottish Lakes. The trail involves considerable climbing through old clearcuts, is moderately scenic, and requires a large expenditure of energy. Skiing is at its best when there is a minimum of 2 feet of snow at the parking area.

Access: Drive Highway 2 east 17 miles from Stevens Pass. Just opposite the rest area, turn right onto the Coulter Creek road system (2,200 feet). Park in the area reserved for camp patrons.

Coulter Ski Trail: Starting at the railroad tracks, walk the roughly plowed road for the first 1/4 mile to a signed junction, and turn right on the Coulter Ski Trail. Another 1/4 mile brings a left turn at a large Y (2,300 feet). As the way climbs, stay left at the next intersection, then go right at the two following intersections. At 1 3/4 miles, enter the base of a clearcut. Ascend to the left, avoiding the cliffs. After gaining 200 feet, head up the clearcut, aiming for the upper right side. Crest the ridge at 3,900 feet to find a road and tremendous views of the Chiwaukums and Nason Ridge. Bear left, losing a few hundred feet, to a three-way intersection at 3 miles.

Turn up, following the cat tracks past Midway Camp and marked ski trails. At 6 1/2 miles is High Camp (5,000 feet) and the end of the Coulter Ski Trail. Either stay at High Camp or follow the ridge toward Lake Julius and choose from among the numerous campsites

Overlook of Coulter and Nason Creek

along the ridge, in the Roaring Creek valley below, or at Loch Eileen.

Scottish Lakes: A number of trails radiate out from High Camp, designed for all degrees of skill and energy. Serious backcountry skiers will be unable to resist the formidable all-day trip up the McWaukum Braes. From the end of the Coulter Ski Trail, follow the Summer Trail along the ridge above Roaring Creek for 1½ miles, then descend to the valley. Head east up the valley ½ mile to Lake Julius, which is passed on the north. Shortly beyond the lake, follow the valley as it makes an abrupt turn to the north. Climb 500 feet in 1 mile to Loch Eileen.

Above Loch Eileen, head east, climbing steeply. This short section has the only avalanche potential in the area and should not be crossed in unstable conditions. At the top of the narrow ledge, go right, skiing above 5,900-foot Lake Donald. From here, the skiing is open to the top of any of the three braes.

McCue Ridge is another excellent run. The trip through forest and meadows is marked for the whole 2½ miles of ridge crest and along several access trails. It can be skied in all weather conditions, but is best on sunny days when views from a 6,258-foot crest extend for miles over the whole Chiwaukum Range.

17 LAKE WENATCHEE STATE PARK

Open to: skis only
Surface: groomed
Rating: easiest
Round trip: up to 14 miles
Skiing time: 1–6 hours
Elevation gain: up to 430 feet
High point: 2,300 feet
Best: January–February
Avalanche potential: none
Map: *Green Trails* Plain #146

If you love diagonal striding or skating, it is hard to find a better place to ski than on the beautifully groomed trails at Lake Wenatchee State Park. All the elements for a fun ski day are provided: The trails are neatly groomed for all abilities, there are heated bathrooms, a sledding hill, a camping area with a covered cooking shelter, and space to sculpture an igloo or a snowman.

Most of the trails at the park are exactly what you would expect— short loops with moderate climbs and moderate descents. There are a couple of trails that are significantly different: the Backwoods Loop, with its carnival-style descents and climbs, and, most noteworthy of all, the long and winding 14-mile round trip to Nason Ridge View. This extensive trail takes you cruising across the Kahler Glen Golf

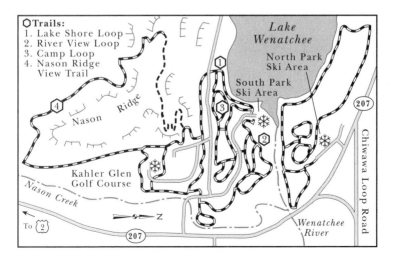

Course, then through a checkerboard of Longview Fibre forest plantation and U.S. Forest Service lands.

The trails at Lake Wenatchee State Park are groomed Thursdays through Sundays. Grooming on the upper 4 miles of the Nason Ridge Trail is not done as often. A sno-park permit with a Special Groomed Area sticker is required. Sno-park permits may be purchased from the Parkside or Midway groceries, located north of the park entrance, or at Beverly's Restaurant, open on weekends, at the golf course.

Access: Drive Highway 2 east 19 miles from Stevens Pass, and at Coles Corner, turn left on Highway 207 and go 3.6 miles. Turn left again at the "South Entrance Lake Wenatchee State Park" sign. Cross Nason Creek, then stay right as the road splits and park at the lakeshore sno-park (1,900 feet). To reach Kahler Glen Golf Course, stay left when the road splits and drive for 0.3 mile, then go left again and drive 0.4 mile to the sno-park. The North Unit of the State Park is accessed by following Highway 207 north for another mile.

South Unit–Wenatchee State Park: Take time to study the signboard and map before you start. There are loops within loops throughout the park. Loops average between ³/₄ mile and 1¹/₄ miles in length. Connect a couple of these short loops and you will quickly create a 4- to 6-mile-long tour. Lake Shore Loop takes you right along the edge of the lake, where Poe and Nason Ridges and Dirtyface Peak reflect in the crystalline waters. River View Loop heads over to the Wenatchee River, and Camp Loop runs through the campground.

Kalher Glen Golf Course: A large sno-park is located at the golf course. Skiers may cruise the trails around the condominiums and out across the fairways, or use the parking area as a starting point for an extended tour on the Nason Ridge View Trail. The golf course is still in the developing stages, and routes of the skiing trails are constantly changing as dictated by construction and the creation of new roadways.

Nason Ridge View Trail: On a clear day this is an amazingly scenic tour, first with views of expensive homes, followed by scenic glimpses of farms along Nason Creek. Begin at the golf course parking area. After 3 miles, the trail starts to climb through clearcut and burns from the 1995 and 1996 forest fires. Views of the Chiwaukums and Stuart Range expand as you make your gradual ascent. At 7 miles, the groomed trail reaches the crest of Nason Ridge and ends. Straight ahead is a full view of Dirtyface Peak, as well as a glimpse of Lake Wenatchee. To the northeast is Fish Lake, where, on clear days, you can see the snowmobiles buzzing across the frozen waters like busy worker ants.

Snow-covered trees along the banks of the Wenatchee River in Lake Wenatchee State Park

At the turnaround point, you will see signs for the Nason Ridge Trail. Tired skiers, even ones with blisters, should avoid the temptation to descend by this route. The trail is narrow, often icy, frequently cut by creeks—your basic backcountry, metal edge, cable-binding experience. This hiking trail is rated as *most difficult* to ascend. Descent is considered off the scale. If you must do the loop, it is best to start off the first time by climbing up the Nason Ridge Trail from the trailhead located just outside the northwest corner of the golf course area. The trail climbs to 3,160 feet, then intersects the groomed trail.

North Unit–Lake Wenatchee State Park: The North Unit of Lake Wenatchee State Park has fewer trails, less parking, and less skier use than the South Unit. It does have an excellent view of Nason Ridge and the Glacier Peak Wilderness from the lakeshore. It does have a play area for the kids near the lakeshore, where, despite the usual thick covering of snow, children tend to gravitate. The 3½-mile loop should be skied clockwise to avoid the plunge down an amazingly steep section of trail.

18 CHIWAWA SNO-PARK

Open to: skis and snowshoes
Surface: groomed and trails
Rating: easiest to most difficult
Round trip: up to 15 miles
Skiing time: 2–8 hours
Elevation gain: up to 680 feet
High point: 2,590 feet
Best: January–February
Avalanche potential: none
Map: *Green Trails* Plain #146

Looking for solitude, searching for adventure, or just trying to find an excellent place to ski? Variety is the one commodity that the Chiwawa Sno-Park has in abundance.

Access: Drive Highway 2 east 19 miles from Stevens Pass, then turn left on Highway 207 at Coles Corner and follow it for 4.6 miles. Shortly after crossing the Wenatchee River, the road divides. Stay to the right, on the Chiwawa Loop Road, for 1.5 miles to the Chiwawa Sno-Park (1,970 feet). A sno-park permit with a Special Groomed Area sticker is required.

The Tour: A large information board and map at the parking lot will help to orient you to the ski trails (three) and the snowmobile trails (endless).

Squirrel Run Trail is a 4-mile round trip and is technically the *easiest* of the three trails to ski. This ungroomed trail starts at the southwest

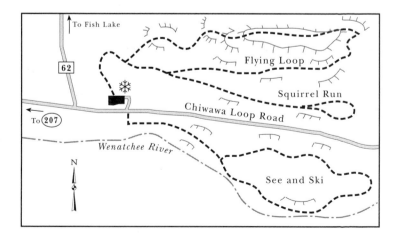

corner of the sno-park and climbs gradually on a wide logging road. After 1/4 mile, cross a groomed snowmobile trail. At the 1/2-mile point, cross a second snowmobile trail and then head steeply up the hillside, leaving the machines behind. At 3/4 mile, The Flying Loop Trail branches off to the left and Squirrel Run levels off for a gently rolling traverse through the forest. After a mile, the trail starts a 1/2-mile loop that gradually turns you back the way you came. (Despite the *easiest* rating, this trail is best noted for solitude and not for ease of skiing. Don't be surprised if you have to break your own trail.)

See and Ski Trail begins across the road from the sno-park. This 5-mile loop is groomed twice a week as long as there is sufficient snow-cover. It is also the most scenic of the three trails. The route takes you through the forest for 1 1/2 miles, then makes a sweeping loop along the edge of the Wenatchee River before heading back. When the snow is soft, this is an excellent tour for everyone. When icy, only skiers who are comfortable with *more difficult* trails should attempt it.

The Flying Loop Trail (named for the most common mode of descent) is the most challenging of the three trails, and is often used by snow-shoers. The first 3/4 mile of this ungroomed loop is skied in conjunction with the Squirrel Run Trail. Once the two trails part, there is a stiff 1 1/2-mile climb to the ridge top, followed by a challenging 1/2-mile traverse of the ridge crest, and finally a steep mile-long plunge back down the forested hillside to intercept the Squirrel Run Trail. When the snow is soft, this 5-mile trail is recommended only for those who have the skills required for skiing *most difficult* trails. When the snow is icy, strap on the snowshoes instead.

View of the Wenatchee River from the See and Ski Trail

19 LITTLE WENATCHEE RIVER ROAD

Open to: all uses
Surface: forest road
Rating: easiest
Round trip: 5 miles
Skiing time: 2 hours
Elevation gain: none
High point: 1,960 feet
Best: January–February
Avalanche potential: none
Map: *Green Trails* Wenatchee Lake #145

Little Wenatchee River Road is ideal for skiers who prefer solitude to crowds. The road follows the valley bottom and rolls just enough so that you are always either going slightly up or gradually down. For scenery, the buttress-like ramparts of Nason Ridge dominate the skyline above the trees.

This is a multiple-use area that rarely sees too many multiples of anything on any given day. Although you may see snowmobiles, they rarely will pass more than once during a trip. Snowshoers and skiers are the most common users of the road. At the time of this writing, no permits were required to ski or park here. Occasional winter logging operations may close this area. Check with the Ranger District office before making the long drive to road's end.

Access: Drive Highway 2 to Coles Corner, located 19 miles east of Stevens Pass, then head north on Highway 207. Follow the road around Lake Wenatchee for 10.9 miles. At the north end of the lake the road divides; stay left, on Little Wenatchee River Road No. 6500, and drive the final 1.5 miles to the gate and turnaround area (1,960 feet).

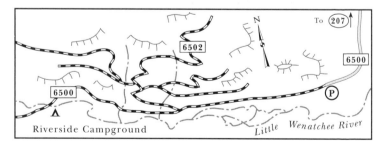

Skiers on the Little Wenatchee River Road

The Tour: Little Wenatchee River Road tunnels through the forest along the base of Wenatchee Ridge. At the end of the first nearly level mile, the Little Wenatchee River swings over from the north to the south side of the valley and is occasionally visible from the road. Views expand over the open river channel to Nason Ridge and Mount Mastiff.

The river swings back to the south side of the valley near 2 1/4 miles, and 1/4 mile beyond, Spur Road 6502 branches off on the right, marking a good turnaround point for groups with novice skiers.

Anyone continuing on will find that Little Wenatchee River Road remains nearly level until it divides at 4 1/2 miles. Go left and descend to the Riverside Campground for river access and views.

20 LEAVENWORTH

Open to: skis only
Surface: groomed
Rating: easiest
Round trip: 9 miles
Skiing time: 1–2 days
Elevation gain: 200 feet
High point: 1,500 feet
Best: January–February
Avalanche potential: none
Map: *Green Trails* Leavenworth #178

Ski immaculately groomed tracks along the banks of the Wenatchee River, roller-coaster up and down through ponderosa pine forest at the base of Tumwater Mountain, or skate right into town for a hot lunch. If you like your skiing mixed with all the amenities of life, then Leavenworth is the ideal place.

An active cross-country ski club in Leavenworth keeps trails groomed in three separate areas around town; a moderate donation

is asked to help keep the grooming machines running. No sno-park permit is required.

Note: Leavenworth lies at the relatively low elevation of 1,200 feet. Insufficient snowfall can be a problem. If uncertain about snow conditions, inquire at the Leavenworth Ranger Station, or by calling their office: (509) 548-6977.

The Golf Course: The most popular skiing area at Leavenworth is The Golf Course. At the western end of town, go south off Highway 2 on Icicle Creek Road. Drive 0.6 mile to Golf Course Road, then turn left and drive 0.1 mile.

The 12 kilometers (7.5 miles) of trails cruise over rolling terrain,

Meadow Loop on the Icicle River Trail

with excellent views of the surrounding mountains and the Wenatchee River. There are two main loops: Lazy River Trail, rated *easiest,* circles the golf course in about 2 miles, and Tumwater Loop, rated *more difficult,* is 1 mile longer and requires good control to avoid embarrassing yourself on the descents. From the golf course you may ski to Leavenworth on the Waterfront Park Trail for a quick meal at a downtown restaurant.

Icicle River Trail: Drive south from Highway 2 on Icicle Creek Road for 2.6 miles. Leave the main road where it takes a 90-degree bend and go straight on CYO Road. Take the first left, to find a large parking area and ticket booth.

The Icicle River Trail is made up of two loops, each approximately 2½ miles long. The Ned Kuch Loop tours the nearly level ground between the parking area and the irrigation canal. The Meadow Loop is located on an island between the canal and Icicle River and has several interesting hills to navigate.

Leavenworth Ski Hill: Near the west end of town, turn north on Ski Hill Drive. Drive for 1.5 miles through orchards to the winter sports area. Just inside the gate is the start of a 1¼-mile loop, which is lighted at night. A second, 2-mile loop climbs to a viewpoint and is the most challenging in the Leavenworth trail system.

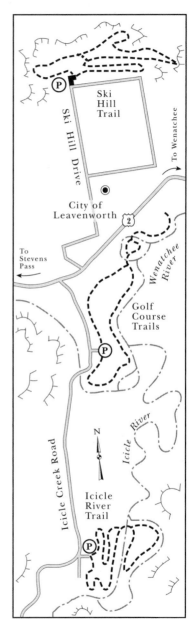

21 ICICLE CREEK ROAD

Open to: all uses
Surface: forest road
Rating: easiest
Round trip: 9 miles
Skiing time: 4 hours
Elevation gain: 780 feet
High point: 2,080 feet
Best: January–mid-March
Avalanche potential: low
Maps: *Green Trails* Leavenworth #178 and Chiwaukum Mtns. #177

A narrow valley, flanked by stunning mountains and sliced by a rushing creek that lives up to its icy name, provides a very scenic backdrop for this easy tour up Icicle Creek valley.

The Icicle Creek valley is very narrow and the surrounding mountains very steep. In midwinter, these two factors combine to keep the valley floor shaded and cool, a place where the snow lingers after it has melted from the groomed trails in the Leavenworth resort area (Tour 20).

This is a "shared" road, which means you can expect to see snowmobiles. The most conspicuous are the machines of the homeowners who live upvalley and commute to work and school.

Access: Drive Highway 2 to the western end of Leavenworth, then turn south on Icicle Creek Road. After 4 miles the road ends at a gate. The large Snow Lakes trailhead does winter service as a sno-park. A Leavenworth groomed trail pass is not required to ski Icicle Creek Road; however, your Northwest Forest Pass must be prominently displayed on your windshield.

The Tour: The first thing you will notice as you start up the valley

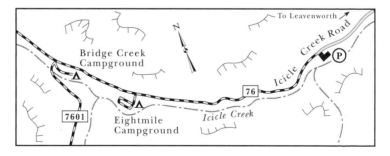

Icicle Creek

is the scenery; from the serrated mountaintops thousands of feet above to the enchanting snow mushrooms covering the rocks in the river below, this area is beautiful. The next thing to notice is the presence or absence of the snowmobiles that are usually parked in a neat row just inside the gate. These snowmobiles belong to the families who live up the valley. The presence, or absence, of the snowmobiles should serve as a reminder that you are sharing your road with other users. Be on the lookout for machines at all times; however, these local commuters are some of the most polite and conscientious snowmobilers around, so do not be afraid to take the kids with you.

From the moment you leave the car, the scenery is a distraction. Do not be tempted to leave the road in search of a better view of the creek; walls of snow overhang the river and are dangerous. At 4½ miles, go left to Bridge Creek Campground (2,080 feet). This sparsely forested camp area makes an excellent lunch spot and turnaround point. Bridge Creek also marks the end of most snowmobile travel. If you wish to continue upvalley, you will probably have to break trail.

77

22 VAN CREEK LOOP

Open to: all uses
Surface: some snowmobile grooming, and forest roads
Rating: more difficult
Loop trip: 7¼ miles
Skiing time: 4 hours
Elevation gain: 1,135 feet
High point: 3,140 feet
Best: January–February
Avalanche potential: low
Maps: *Green Trails* Leavenworth #178 and Cashmere #179

Although a perfect dry-side loop for skiing and exploring, this ideal area has long been overlooked by skiers. Maybe, just maybe, if someone includes it in a guidebook along with words such as "fun, views, loops and more loops, explorations," and "challenge," then maybe, just maybe, more skiers will consider giving this tour a try.

Parking at Van Creek is very limited. Fifteen vehicles will fill the area and overflow must go elsewhere. On weekends the lot fills with trucks and snowmobile trailers. Do not be discouraged; although the entire area is open to snowmobiles, after the first mile they are rarely seen.

Access: At the east end of Leavenworth, turn north off Highway 2 on Chumstick Road and head toward Plain. At 2.1 miles, go right on Eagle Creek Road; there is a big sign to Eagle Creek Ranch at the turnoff. Head up the narrow valley for 5.7 miles, a potentially challenging drive after a snowfall. The plowing ends at the intersection of

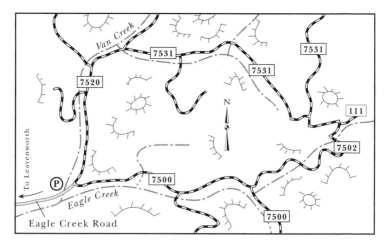

Van Creek and Eagle Creek Roads (2,005 feet). Park off the road in the space provided. No parking or access stickers are required.

The Tour: Unless it is very icy, the recommended direction for the loop is clockwise. Ski north up Van Creek Road No. 7520. This road receives some attention from the snowmobile groomer, and the majority of the machines head that way, accessing the 180 miles of groomed roads in the Lake Wenatchee/Entiat trail system. At the 1 1/4-mile point, pass Road 7805 on the left, offering the first of several invitations to depart from the planned loop and head out to the ridge tops.

At 1 1/2 miles, the loop route takes a right on East Van Creek Road No. 7531 (2,327 feet). Road 7531 climbs steadily for the next 1 3/4 miles, passing several interesting spurs on the right before arriving at the ridge top intersection at 3 1/4 miles (3,140 feet). Continue straight ahead on Road No. 7502. (Road 7531 stays to the left and continues climbing. Long-distance skiers can follow Road 7531 until it loops back to Road 7520 for a 20-mile loop.)

Back to the loop: Road 7502 continues to climb for the next 1/4 mile, then, after passing Spur 111, begins a 1 3/4-mile descent into Eagle Creek valley. At 5 1/4 miles, go right on Eagle Creek Road No. 7500 and settle in for a 2-mile glide back to the start.

Skiing Road 7531

23 TRONSON MEADOW LOOPS

Open to: skis and snowshoes
Surface: forest roads
Rating: more difficult
Round trip: 1–10 miles
Skiing time: 3 hours–all day
Elevation gain: 500 feet
High point: 4,400 feet
Best: January–February
Avalanche potential: low
Map: *Green Trails* Liberty #210

Deep in the heart of Blewett Pass snowmobile country, the Forest Service has reserved a small area for travelers powered solely by bread, cheese, energy bars, and enthusiasm. Although this area is not large, it is criss-crossed with so many trails that you can easily explore for several days without covering them all.

This is undoubtedly the best-developed, nongroomed area set aside for nonmotorized use in the northern half of the Washington Cascades. The Forest Service and local ski clubs deserve considerable approbation for the project, which includes marking of trails and the placement of numerous trail maps.

Access: Drive Highway 97 to the Tronson Meadow Sno-Park, located 0.8 mile north of the Blewett Pass summit. Alternate sno-park parking is available at the Blewett Pass summit (4,102 feet), Upper Tronson Meadow Road, Tronson Campground, and a couple of small turnouts near the summit.

The Tour: The loops in Tronson Meadow and the trails around Blewett Pass are all candidates for *more difficult* or *most difficult* ratings. Some of the steeper trails might even be rated as most appropriate for *backcountry* skiers. The only *easiest* tour for skiers is a loop through Tronson Campground.

The two main loops starting at the

Tronson Meadow

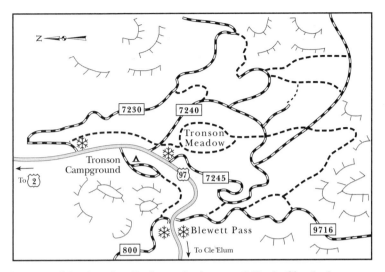

Tronson Meadow Sno-Park are both *more difficult.* Check the map, then ski up Road 7240 for a mile to a major intersection (4,160 feet). To ski the east loop, go left and continue the steady climb through forest, with an occasional peek-a-boo view of the Stuart Range. At 1½ miles (4,400 feet), the road ends and the loop continues on trail for ½ mile. When you reach Road 7230, ski to the left and head back 1¾ miles. Just before reaching Highway 97, find a trail on your left and follow it back to Road 7240. Go right and return to the sno-park at 4 ¼ miles.

Equally enjoyable is the west loop around Tronson Meadow. From the sno-park, ski up Road 7240 for 1 mile to the major junction, then go to the right and follow the road on a wide loop across the top of Tronson Meadow. At 2¼ miles, go right on Road 7245 and descend toward Highway 97. Just before reaching the highway, go right and ski the trail back to the 7240 road.

The Tronson Meadow snowmobile closure area extends to the north side of the highway, where several *most difficult* trails and routes can be found. The main access to this less-developed area is from the sno-park on the north side of Blewett Pass summit. Ski up Scotty Creek Road for 500 feet to the first corner, then go straight, leaving snow-mobile country for the nonmotorized area. Follow the old road 500 feet, to an unmarked intersection where the road divides. If you go straight, you will plunge down a broad, clear-cut bowl. For a looping traverse of a rounded knoll with twisted trees and views of the Stuart Range, go left from the intersection and head down the overgrown road. When the road splits a second time, go left.

24 WENATCHEE RIDGE

Open to: nonmotorized
Surface: forest roads
Rating: more difficult
Round trip: 6 miles
Skiing time: 4 hours
Elevation gain: 458 feet
High point: 4,560 feet
Best: January–February
Avalanche potential: low
Map: *Green Trails* Liberty #210

Ridge after ridge, gleaming and snow-covered, roll south and north like white waves, giving this top-of-the-world ski route along Wenatchee Ridge a sense of space and grandeur.

Access: Drive Highway 97 to Blewett (formerly Swauk) Pass (4,102 feet) and park in the north side sno-park. A large information board and map helps skiers orient themselves before heading out on the maze of forest roads.

The Tour: Head east from the information board on a groomed snowmobile route. Although most snowmobiles stay to the south side of the pass, expect to see a few in the first ¹/₂ mile. After 150 feet, the road swings left (north). Ignoring the skiers' trail (Tour 23) that heads off to the right, follow the main road up the hillside. After skiing ¹/₂ mile, reach a small saddle and junction (4,320 feet). Turn left on Wenatchee Ridge Road and leave the snowmobiles behind. (Scotty

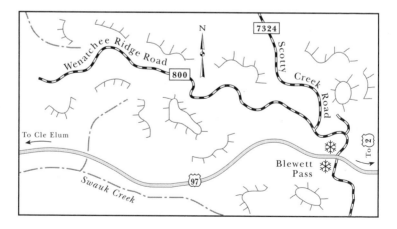

View of the Stuart Range from the Wenatchee Ridge Road

Creek Road descends straight ahead into snowmobile country.)

Thanks to some energetic clearcutting, there are unobstructed views for most of the ridge tour. The road rolls, dropping from the ridge crest to contour around the higher peaks, then returning to the crest. Small knolls can be scenic lunch spots as well as fun ski hills. Backcountry-equipped skiers will find clear-cut slopes of various steepness to challenge their turning abilities.

Just before the 3-mile point, the road splits. Climb the upper fork to the top of a small knoll for a final overlook of Red Top Mountain, the Swauk Valley, and the lowlands beyond.

25 HANEY MEADOW

Open to: skis and snowshoes
Surface: trails
Rating: backcountry
Round trip: 10 miles
Skiing time: 8 hours
Elevation gain: 1,860 feet
High point: 5,960 feet
Best: January–February
Avalanche potential: moderate
Map: *Green Trails* Liberty #210

Excellent terrain, surprising views, and great powder bowls make the trip to Haney Meadow a backcountry adventure that is worth repeating.

Access: Drive Highway 97 to the Blewett Pass Summit Sno-Park and park on the south side of the road (4,102 feet).

The Tour: There are two routes to Haney Meadow. The easiest route follows the groomed snowmobile roads for 10 comparatively gentle miles. Keep this option in mind in case you need to use it on the way back or if the trail is ice hard or the snowpack is unstable.

The peaceful choice is the steep, narrow, challenging, but well-marked trail that reaches the meadow in 5 miles. From the upper end of the sno-park, head uphill for 1/2 mile on a road shared with snow-mobiles. The Haney Meadow Trail, marked only by a small metal sign

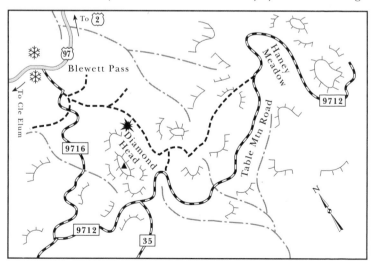

Tronson Ridge from Haney Meadow Trail

on a tree at the turnoff, is the second trail branching off on the lefthand side of the road.

The trail starts with a climbing traverse across a wide clearcut, followed by a short descent and more climbing. At 1 1/2 miles (4,500 feet), a trail from Tronson Meadow joins in on the left. The Haney Meadow Trail continues straight ahead, settling into the serious work of climbing a narrow valley on the east side of Diamond Head. Two avalanche chutes are crossed. If the snow-pack is unstable (and it will be after most major snowfalls), detour off the trail and ski though the trees below.

The trail ascends around the head of the valley, then climbs open slopes on the far side. A tall, lone tree near the top, at 4 miles, marks another intersection (5,840 feet). The trail to the right is an escape route to Table Mountain Road if the lower section of the Haney Meadow Trail is deemed unskiable on the way back. The Haney Meadow Trail continues straight ahead to the forest edge and then turns right, to climb up and over an open knoll.

At 4 1/2 miles the trail splits (5,960 feet). Both forks lead to the meadow; the left is best for views. Follow the left trail up to the ridge for a broad panorama of the Cascades, featuring the Stuart Range. This is the proper turnaround for day tours. The right fork traverses around the ridge to rejoin the left. The united way drops 1/2 mile to the end of an old spur road, which continues to descend another 100 feet to Table Mountain Road. Turn right for the final drop to Haney Meadow (5,502 feet). The meadow itself is a broad sloping plain, ringed by forested hills, and on weekends it is buzzing with snowmobiles.

Are you camping? Include these in your day trips: Mount Lillian, Upper Naneum Meadows, Mission Ridge Ski Area via Road 9712, and Lion Rock via Road 35.

26 PIPE CREEK SNO-PARK

Open to: skis and snowshoes
Surface: forest road
Rating: most difficult
Round trip: 5 to 9¹/₂ miles
Skiing time: 3 or more hours
Elevation gain: 550 and up
High point: 4,350 to 4,958 feet
Best: mid-December–mid-March
Avalanche potential: low
Map: *Green Trails* Liberty #210

The Pipe Creek Sno-Park is like a breath of fresh winter in the center of one of the busiest freeways (for snowmobiles, that is) in the state of Washington. The area accessed from the Pipe Creek Sno-Park is snowmobile-free, and skiers who come here can be assured of the chance to explore winter's tranquility in peace. Parents can bring their families without fear. Beginners can practice their skills with safety and dignity.

From the sno-park, skiers have a choice of two trails: No. 141, which heads toward Blewett Pass, and No. 140 (Pipe Creek Trail), which climbs steeply to views. Both of these trails can be turned into loops.

Access: From the west, leave Interstate 90 at Exit 85 and head toward Wenatchee on Highway 970. Turn north on Highway 97 and

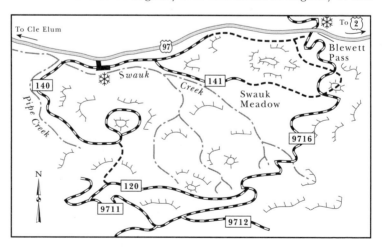

drive 13.1 miles to Pipe Creek Road. The sno-park is on the right (3,500 feet). If coming south from Highway 2, drive Highway 97 to the summit of Blewett Pass. Check your odometer and head downhill for 1.7 miles to find the sno-park on your left.

Trail 141: Heading north, then east, from the sno-park, this trail is rated easiest. It follows a logging road that parallels Highway 97 through forest and clearcuts. At the end of the first 1/2 mile, the road divides; to the left, a road (*more difficult*) continues to parallel Highway 97 for the next 2 miles to the Blewett Pass Sno-Park (4,102 feet). Along the way, the road and grooming end and the final ascent is made on a narrow trail. To the right, Road 141 (*most difficult*) heads up to Swauk Meadow, where you leave the road and continue the climb to Road 9716 on a trail marked with occasional blue diamonds. Once up on Road 9716, a *most difficult* trail may be followed to Blewett Pass for a 5 1/2-mile loop, or you may connect the two trails by skiing Road 9716 (groomed for snowmobiles) north to Blewett Pass, where you rejoin the skier trail.

Pipe Creek Trail: The reason that this trail is rated *most difficult* is immediately apparent. The tour begins with a steep 1/8-mile descent. After crossing Swauk Creek the road sweeps uphill, threading its way through the Pipe Creek canyon.

After a 2-mile climb you will reach a saddle and an intersection (4,300 feet). To the left is the Diamond View Loop, a mile-long trail that circumnavigates a forested knoll and passes several fine viewpoints of Diamond Head and the Stuart Range.

The Pipe Creek Trail continues on from the saddle, heading to the right (south). Before long your blue diamond–marked trail leaves maintained forest roads and heads out over skid roads and clearcuts. Although well marked, the trail's unexpected twists and turns make it difficult to follow. At the end of a mile you will reach an intersection (4,720 feet) with Road 120, called the Dunning Ranch Trail.

If you have had enough exploring, this is an excellent point to turn around and head back down. If you are looking for more adventure, go left (east) on the Dunning Ranch Trail and follow it for 1 mile to Road 9716 (4,690 feet). Road 9716 is a nearly level and rather boring snowmobile raceway that can be used to create several loops. If you go left (north) on Road 9716, you can loop back to the Pipe Creek Sno-Park via Swauk Meadow or Blewett Pass, for a total trip mileage of 8 1/2 or 9 1/2 miles, respectively.

If you head right (south) on Road 9716, you can cruise with the

Skiers ascending the Pipe Creek Road

motorized sleds for 1/2 mile to a three-way intersection (4,958 feet).
Go straight, toward Liberty, on Road 9712 and descend for 1/4 mile,
then take a right on Hurley Creek Road No. 9711. Descend for another
1/2 mile and then head to the right on Road 120 (the Dunning Ranch
Trail). Ski across the open hillside for 1/8 mile to reconnect with the
Pipe Creek Trail. Total trip mileage is 8 3/4 miles.

27 OLD BLEWETT PASS HIGHWAY

Old Blewett Pass
Open to: all uses
Surface: groomed for snowmobiles
Rating: more difficult
Round trip: 8 miles
Skiing time: 4 hours
Elevation gain: 1,030 feet
High point: 4,064 feet
Best: January–March
Avalanche potential: low
Map: *Green Trails* Liberty #210

Skiers' Trails
Open to: skis and snowshoes
Surface: forest roads and trails
Rating: more difficult
Round trip: 2 miles and more
Skiing time: 1 1/2 hours
Elevation gain: 250 feet
High point: 3,300 feet
Best: January–February
Avalanche potential: none
Map: *Green Trails* Liberty #210

This is a tale of a name that would not die. When Highway 97 was
built across the mountains from Ellensburg to Wenatchee, it was given

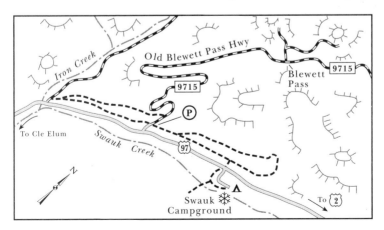

the name of Blewett Pass Highway, in recognition of the narrow dip in the hills that allowed the road to make its way through the rugged wall of mountains. The highway was narrow, with steep, sharp switchbacks, and driving was hazardous.

Forty years ago, Highway 97 was rerouted from Blewett Pass to Swauk Pass. The new road was wider, straighter, and totally free of the pesky switchbacks that plagued the old road. Despite the Swauk Pass sign at the summit, people continued to refer to the road and the pass it crossed as Blewett. Finally, in the late 1990s, the highway department gave in to years of tradition and changed the name of Swauk Pass to Blewett Pass.

This tour has two options. When the snowmobiles are not parading, skiing along the old Blewett Pass Highway to the authentic and original Blewett Pass is not only a lot of fun, but it is also extremely scenic. When the snowmobiles' marching band is on the loose, the skiers' loop through the open forest along Highway 97 is the more enjoyable option.

Skiers' Trail traversing a ponderosa pine-covered hillside

Access: Drive north on Highway 97 from Ellensburg or on Highway 970 from Cle Elum. At 7 miles from the junction of Highways 97 and 970, pass Mineral Springs Resort. In 3 miles more find the old Blewett Pass Highway on the left (3,048 feet), with parking for up to eight cars.

Blewett Pass: Three trails start at the parking area, two for skiers and one for snowmobilers. The snowmobile trail goes to the old Blewett Pass; the blue-diamond skiers' trails do not. To reach the old Blewett Pass, head straight up from the parking area, following the orange diamonds. After 30 feet you will reach an obvious road. Go right and ski along the left side of a narrow clearing. Soon the timber closes in and the route is evident.

The grade is gentle but steady. As elevation is gained, Red Top Mountain Lookout can be seen to the southwest, with the flat top of Table Mountain to the southeast. At 1 mile the road divides; stay left and begin to switchback up the hillside.

At 4 miles, reach the 4,064-foot summit of the original Blewett Pass. Nothing is here now, but there used to be a small restaurant and, in the late 1930s, a rope-tow ski lift.

At the summit you are just a short distance from good views. Go left (west) and ski up a rough logging road, passing two spurs on the right. Stop at the edge of a long, open hillside and gaze down on the old highway below.

Skiers' Trails: If there are too many snowmobiles on the old Blewett Pass Highway, these two trails may save your day. Both trails are fun romps through the forest, gaining very little elevation throughout their 2- and 2 1/3-mile courses. Best of all, both trails make loops, so you won't have to keep dodging oncoming skiers.

The 2-mile trail begins on the righthand side of the old Blewett Pass Highway. The first half of the trail parallels Highway 97. The trail winds a bit from one old skid road to another, so pay close attention to the blue diamonds marking the route. The second half of the loop is considerably more challenging than the first. The return trip starts by wandering through the forest on a narrow trail, then climbs up an old streambed to an abandoned logging road. The route follows the logging road down.

The 2 1/3-mile loop connects the old Blewett Pass Highway with Iron Creek Road. Begin your loop by skiing up the old Blewett Pass Highway for 0.1 mile, then go left and switchback up to the crest of a forested ridge. The trail dodges trees down to Iron Creek then returns, paralleling Highway 97.

28 IRON CREEK

Open to: nonmotorized
Surface: forest road
Rating: easiest
Round trip: 6 miles
Skiing time: 3 hours
Elevation gain: 700 feet
High point: 3,600 feet
Best: mid-December–mid-March
Avalanche potential: low
Map: *Green Trails* Liberty #210

Ironically, in an area where snowmobiles are the dominant life form, Iron Creek Road provides a scenic sanctuary from the iron herd.

Access: Drive 8.8 miles north along Highway 97 from the intersection of Highways 97 and 970 (or 7.8 miles west from Blewett Pass Summit) to Iron Creek Road No. 9714. Park at a small pullout on the north side of the highway (2,900 feet).

The Tour: Three tours start at this parking area. A 2 1/3-mile marked ski loop heads east, paralleling Highway 97, to the old Blewett Pass Highway, then makes a looping return. Another tour takes you a couple of peaceful miles up the Hovey Creek drainage. However, the best family and beginners' tour lies up the Iron Creek drainage, described here.

Begin the tour by skiing north up Iron Creek Road. The road parallels Iron Creek as it winds its way along the floor of the deep, forested valley. During the middle of winter, the sun rarely makes it to

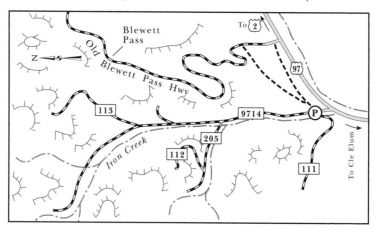

Iron Creek Road

the floor of the valley, ensuring an excellent quality of snow and a slight chilliness to the air. Near the end of the first mile, the road crosses the creek and enters a broader section of the valley. At noon, when the sun sneaks over the hillcrests, this is an excellent spot for a picnic.

Continuing up the valley, Iron Creek Road wanders along the creek, traversing small bands of trees. If the cold at the valley floor starts to get to you, consider heading up West Fork Road No. (9714) 205, which branches off on the left at the 1-mile point. (To find the sunshine, if there is any, ski West Fork Road for 1 1/3 miles to Spur Road (9714) 112, then go right and head steadily up to views and warmth on the ridge above.) Iron Creek Road passes Spur Road (9714) 113 on the right at the 2-mile mark. (If looking for some hard climbing, you can follow the spur road for 2 miles to a narrow, 4,000-foot pass located 1 mile west of the old Blewett Pass.) Iron Creek Road enters a clearing at 2 3/4 miles and for the first time the end of the valley is visible. The road ends 1/4 mile beyond at the base of a steep, avalanche-prone hillside that rises all the way to the crest of Teanaway Ridge.

Turn around and enjoy the glide back down the valley.

29 STEHEKIN VALLEY TRAILS

Open to: nonmotorized
Surface: groomed
Rating: easiest
Round trip: 5 miles
Skiing time: 2 hours–all day
Elevation gain: 40 feet
High point: 1,250 feet
Best: mid-December–February
Avalanche potential: none
Map: *Green Trails* Stehekin #82

The community of Stehekin lies nestled at the base of ice-clad mountains at the head of 50-mile-long Lake Chelan. It has the faintly exotic appearance of being out of time with the rest of the world. And indeed it is: Accessible only by boat or airplane, Stehekin is the kind of place you read about in books. The community lacks supermarkets, shopping malls, and most of the other common attributes of our hyperactive society. Even cell phones won't connect to the outer world.

Stehekin Valley is not an area of endless skiing opportunities; the mountains are too steep and avalanche prone to be tackled by anyone other than an expert mountaineer skier. However, for skiing at a leisurely pace, there are two groomed areas that vie for your attention. This tour describes the valley area near town. The second area is described in Tour 30.

Access: Just getting to Stehekin is a trip in itself. You may fly from Chelan or ride the *Lady Express* from either Chelan or Fields Landing. (See the Introduction for more information about the boat, as well as lodging and camping opportunities.) From Stehekin you may walk or

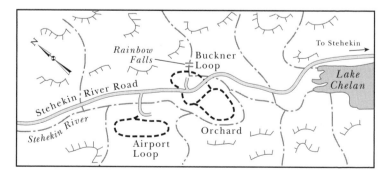

Rainbow Falls emerging from a heavy coating of snow and ice

pay for a van ride up Stehekin River Road 3 miles to the trailhead at Rainbow Falls or 4 miles to the Airport Loop.

Buckner Loop: Two areas in the lower valley are groomed on a regular basis. The Buckner Loop is the longer and more interesting of the two, as it loops through the forest and then passes the historic displays at the old Buckner Farm. From the trailhead at Rainbow Falls, check out the ice-covered water at the falls, then don your skis and follow the marked trail along the falls access road. Cross Stehekin River Road, then head out through the forest on a groomed trail. At the first intersection, go straight. After crossing Buckner Farm Road, the trail cruises along the edge of the Stehekin River to the historic Buckner Orchard, where elk and deer are often spotted. The loop then parallels Rainbow Creek back to the start. Plans are in the works to turn this loop into a figure-eight that will wind back to the falls.

Airport Loop: Take the van upvalley for 4 miles from the boat dock. Go left at the intersection and cross the Stehekin River. Where the road divides again, go left again. In 2000, the Airport Loop was a mile-long, level circuit around the airport runway. The grooming is outstanding, with two lanes for diagonal striding and a skating lane. This is a great area for young skiers, with an almost-level track for easy skiing and small hummocks to climb and descend. The scenery is excellent. The Airport Loop will probably be expanded in the future. Also in the plans are a 2-mile river trail and a 7-mile valley trail.

30 STEHEKIN RIVER ROAD

Open to: skis and snowshoes
Surface: groomed
Rating: easiest to more difficult
Round trip: up to 16 miles
Skiing time: up to 8 hours
Elevation gain: up to 780 feet
High point: 2,200 feet
Best: late-December–mid-March
Avalanche potential: moderate
Map: *Green Trails* McGregor Mtn. #81

No winter trip to Stehekin is complete without a tour on Stehekin River Road. It is there that you will see winter at its best: trees trimmed in snow and gleaming with lacy crystals, a roaring river made peaceful by knots of ice and snow, massive icicles streaming off the rocky valley walls, and mounds of fluffy powder snow.

This winter paradise results from long months of sun deprivation. High mountains line both sides of the valley, and throughout December and January the sun never rises high enough to reach the valley floor. The result is as beautiful as it is chilly. Dress warmly when you head out to spend a day viewing winter's finest.

Stehekin River Road is groomed to Dolly Varden Camp, a wonderful 8½-mile round trip. Beyond Dolly Varden Camp the road is cut by several avalanche chutes. A bypass trail has been created on an old wagon road that is too narrow for grooming, a situation that may change in the future.

Access: The tour begins at the end of the plowed portion of Stehekin River Road (1,420 feet). In 2002, the skiing started 8½ miles from the boat dock. You may arrange for a ride to the road end with

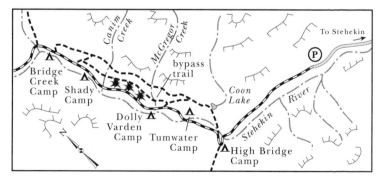

the North Cascades Lodge; see the Introduction for information.

The Tour: From road's end, follow the groomed tracks upvalley through a narrow tunnel of snow-laden trees. The trail leads you across several nearly level terraces, left eons ago by the river. Views range from brief glimpses of snow-plastered mountains to occasional looks at the river.

At 2½ miles, the road begins a short climb to the High Bridge Ranger Station (1,620 feet). Just beyond the buildings, the aptly named High Bridge takes the road across the Stehekin River. Deep packed snow hangs over both sides of this railingless bridge; please avoid the temptation of peering over the edge.

Beyond High Bridge, the road heads into a series of switchbacks and begins climbing with gusto. At the second switchback, look right for a short spur road leading to High Bridge Camp, which has a three-sided shelter and a pit toilet. Skilled backcountry skiers can join the Pacific Crest Trail here, and follow it uphill to Coon Lake or all the way to Bridge Creek Camp. The trail has a variety of markers ranging from orange-painted can lids to official cross-country ski markers.

Views are limited as the road continues upvalley through the forest. The next point of note is a spectacular bridge crossing at 3½ miles, just beyond Tumwater Camp. The snow hangs over the edges; it would be easy to slip off if you strayed too close to the sides.

Beyond the bridge the scenery becomes positively dramatic. Icicles hang from rocky cliffs right along the road's edge. Below, the river weaves around large rocks topped with pillars of snow, looking like old pioneers dressed in bed caps. Views extend to the towering ridge crests. At 4 miles (1,920 feet), Old Wagon Road, a connector trail, branches off on the right. Skiers continuing upvalley to Bridge Creek Camp should leave the main road here to avoid the avalanche chutes beyond Dolly Varden Camp, which is just ¼ mile ahead. Old Wagon Road is followed for the next 2¼ miles. At 6¼ miles from the start, find a spur trail on the left, which leads back to the main road for the final mile-long cruise into Bridge Creek Camp.

Stehekin River

31 ECHO VALLEY

Open to: skis only
Surface: groomed
Rating: easiest to most difficult
Loop trip: 5 miles
Skiing time: 2 hours
Elevation gain: 400 feet
High point: 3,200 feet
Best: mid-December–February
Avalanche potential: none
Map: *USFS* Chelan Ranger District

Echo Valley Ski Area is patronized by hordes of young kids. Laughing and screaming are the main forms of communication as they zoom up rope tows and zip back down the short, steep slopes. A few feet away from the scene of all this unbridled enthusiasm is a series of elegantly organized cross-country ski trails. Located so near the scene of such high-spirited pandemonium, the silence of the Nordic trails is almost deafening.

The Echo Valley Nordic Trails are supported by donations. No sno-park permit is required to park or ski. Please leave a donation in the box at the trailhead to help defray the cost of grooming.

Access: From downtown Chelan, drive north, then west, on Highway 150 (North Shore Road) for 4 miles, then turn right on Boyd Road. Following the signs to Echo Valley Ski Area, head up through the hillside residential area and orchards. At 3.4 miles, turn right on Boyd Loop Road, and after another 1.2 miles, go right again on

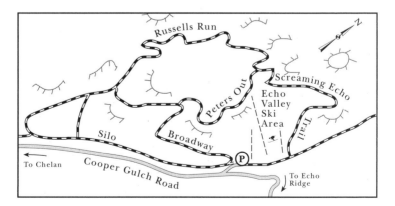

Russells Run

Cooper Gulch Road. At 7.4 miles from Highway 150 you will arrive at Echo Valley Ski Area. Park at the lower end of the lot (2,800 feet).

The Tour: From the lower end of the parking lot, start your skis on a wide trail groomed for both skating and diagonal striding. This trail is called Silo and is rated *easiest.* Stay left at the junction with Broadway Trail and glide downvalley for 1 mile to an unmarked intersection near an old wooden silo. Go right, and head uphill for about 150 feet to a second junction. Once again stay to the right and continue on uphill (the trail to the left loops back to the silo). After skiing another 200 yards, reach a third intersection. Go left, and head out for adventure on Russells Run. This twisting and winding trail soon leaves the pine forest and heads onto open ridges with expansive views and great peacefulness.

At the end of 1½ miles on Russells Run is an intersection. Ski left and head up Screaming Echo Trail, which climbs to views at the area's 3,200-foot high point. Once you have taken in the panorama of snowy hillsides, return to the start in one of three ways.

1: Just beyond the summit are two cat roads. The one on the left is the least-rational return route. This track may or may not be groomed, but is guaranteed to raise screams and is rated *most difficult* or *insane.*

2: From the summit follow the cat track on the right, which is groomed to the top of the ski area. At that point, skiers with telemark proclivities will have an opportunity to descend the steep slope back to the lodge.

3: The most rational choice is to head back down Screaming Echo Trail. At the intersection, continue down on Peters Out, a *most difficult* trail, which will take you to Broadway Trail in 1 mile. Go left on Broadway for the final ½ mile back to the start.

32 THE OUTBACK

Open to: skis and snowshoes
Surface: groomed and open slopes
Rating: most difficult
Round trip: 7.6 miles
Skiing time: 4 hours
Elevation gain: 1,524 feet
High point: 4,324 feet
Best: mid-December–February
Avalanche potential: none
Map: *USFS* Chelan Ranger District

To experience the full smorgasbord of skiing opportunities at Echo Ridge (see Tour 33 for more Echo Ridge tours), you must be prepared to break free of the groomed trails and head to The Outback. This rolling adventure to the backcountry is ideal for the skier with an explorer mentality and a pair of skis that love to break trail.

Access: From the center of Chelan, follow Highway 150 (North Shore Road) toward Manson. After 4 miles, go right on Boyd Road for 3.4 miles. Take a right on Boyd Loop Road and drive 1.2 miles. Go right again on Cooper Gulch Road for 2.8 miles.

The pavement ends at Echo Valley Ski Area. Drive past the ski area and on through the snowmobilers' sno-park. Keep your chains handy, as the road (officially Road 8021, but unsigned) now narrows and heads steeply upward. After 1.4 hair-raising miles you will come to the Zoom Hill parking area, located in a turnout at a sharp switchback (2,800 feet).

The Tour: From the parking area, walk back 75 feet to find Road 8021, better known as the Zoom Cross-Country Ski Trail, on your right.

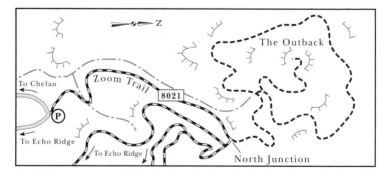

This road is groomed for diagonal striding and skating. The initial mellow climb allows you to warm up. However, before long you are climbing with a purpose.

After climbing for 2 miles, Zoom Cross-Country Ski Trail arrives at North Junction, where you are faced with a confusing gaggle of snowmobile and ski trails. A large information board with a map will help you to orient yourself (3,320 feet). From the junction, look to your left to find the blue diamond and the "Skier Only" sign that mark the entrance to The Outback. At this point you leave the groomed trails and start on the adventure.

The designated route heads northwest from the pass, following an old road 1/2 mile to a T intersection at 3,520 feet. You may go left or right to circumnavigate the large bald hill in front of you on a series of old roads in 2 1/2 miles. If looking for views and a slope for some turns, ski straight through the T intersection and continue climbing for another 1/2 mile, to the 4,324-foot summit of the hill. Once you have absorbed the view, choose a slope with the best snow coverage and see how many turns you can carve. End your day with a quick zoom back to the start.

On the Outback Trail

33 ECHO RIDGE

Open to: skis only
Surface: groomed
Rating: more difficult
Round trip: up to 13 miles
Skiing time: 5 hours
Elevation gain: up to 625 feet
High point: 3,825 feet
Best: mid-December–February
Avalanche potential: none
Map: *USFS* Chelan Ranger District

Echo Ridge Sno-Park is the result of hard work on the part of the Lake Chelan Nordic Club and the personnel of the Chelan Ranger District. This sno-park provides skiers with a machinefree area where they can enjoy the excellent scenery of the southern Sawtooth Mountains while experiencing the excitement of skiing on beautifully groomed trails.

Access: From the center of downtown Chelan, drive north, then west, on Highway 150 (North Shore Road) toward the town of Manson. At 4 miles, go right on Boyd Road, following signs to Echo Valley Ski Area for 3.4 miles. Turn right on Boyd Loop Road and, after another 1.2 miles, go right again on Cooper Gulch Road. At 7.4 miles from Highway 150, the paved road ends at the downhill ski area. Pass the resort and a snowmobile sno-park, then continue up on a steep, narrow forest road (unsigned) for 2.6 miles to its end, at Echo Ridge Sno-Park (3,400 feet). **Note:** The final 2.6 miles can be very hazardous when icy. Drive cautiously and always carry chains.

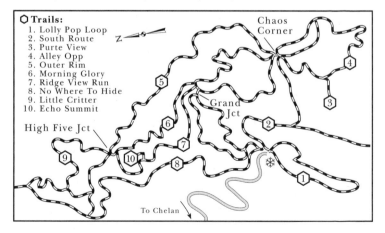

Trails:
1. Lolly Pop Loop
2. South Route
3. Purte View
4. Alley Opp
5. Outer Rim
6. Morning Glory
7. Ridge View Run
8. No Where To Hide
9. Little Critter
10. Echo Summit

Chaos Corner

High Five Jct

Grand Jct

To Chelan

The Tour: Purte View (say it out loud) is a delightful destination. With only a moderate expenditure of energy and a large expenditure of fun, you can ski to one of the best views in the area. Begin your tour by skiing up Chickadee Trail, located at the upper lefthand corner of the parking lot. After an initial steepish climb, the trail mellows into an easy traverse. Pass the Upsy Daisy Trail, then continue on for 1 mile. At Grand Junction (3,550 feet), go right on Windsinger Trail and traverse southeast 3/4 mile through a young tree plantation to Chaos Corner (3,480 feet). Once again take the trail on the right and glide out on the west arm of the Alley Opp Trail for 1/2 mile.

At 2 1/4 miles from the start, find the Purte View Trail (ungroomed) on your right. Head up a low, open hill for a 1/8 mile to the crest of a knoll (3,425 feet). From this viewpoint/lunch spot, you can look down Purtteman Gulch to Lake Chelan, fog permitting, and on to the Chelan Mountains.

On the return trip, add to your fun by looping back to Chaos Corner on the Alley Opp Trail. This trail has a couple of short, steep descents and at least two rather tight turns, making it very challenging when icy. From Chaos Corner, try the ridge-hugging Zippidy Do Da Trail to Grand Junction. Return to the parking lot on the Upsy Daisy Trail.

For a longer tour, check out the very scenic Outer Rim Loop. This tour is a compilation of several loops that takes you over and around the entire Echo Ridge area. Begin your loop by following Chickadee Trail for 1 mile from the parking lot to its end at Grand Junction (3,550 feet). Go left on Ridge View Run and watch for the Stuart Range to the south, the Chelan Mountains to the west, and the rolling hills of the Sawtooth Mountains to the north. At 1 1/2 miles from the sno-park, take a short side trip to the crest of 3,825-foot Echo Summit. This 1/8-mile-long trail is not groomed but is easy to ski, and the views from the top are outstanding.

Back on Ridge View Run, continue north to reach High Five Junction at 2 miles. Head left on Little Critter Trail, which will return you to High Five Junction at the 3 1/4-mile point of your loop.

From High Five Junction, ski down the Outer Rim Trail. The descent lasts for a mile, so zip up your jacket and pull your hat over your ears. Once down, you will spent the next mile in an easy climb to reach Chaos Corner, 5 1/4 miles from the start. At this point you can go left on Alley Opp Trail, a loop that will add an extra 1 1/2 miles to your day, or you can head back to Grand Junction on Zippidy Do Da. At Grand Junction, go straight for a couple hundred feet, then take a right on Upsy Daisy and follow it back to the parking area.

Panoramic vista from crest of Echo Ridge

34 LOUP LOUP—SOUTH SUMMIT SNO-PARK

Open to: skis only
Surface: groomed, trails, and open slopes
Rating: easiest to most difficult
Round trip: up to 13 miles
Skiing time: 1 to 5 hours
Elevation gain: up to 700 feet
High point: 4,659 feet
Best: December–mid-March
Avalanche potential: none
Map: *Green Trails* Loup Loup #85

At the summit of Loup Loup Pass is a little-known, groomed cross-country ski area. With only an occasional clearcut offering an escape from the trees, the views are of the peek-a-boo variety, making the sheer exhilaration of skiing the chief attraction here. Joined together, these trails create a dizzying number of loops. In short (and please excuse the pun), you can loop loop to your heart's content.

The grooming at South Summit Sno-Park is done in various styles according to the terrain and base, as follows: Mainline trails follow logging roads and receive the attentions of the groomer; secondary logging roads receive only occasional grooming; and skid roads and open slopes are left in a pristine state. Skaters and diagonal striders can take their pick between gently rolling terrain and radical runs with steep descents and equally steep climbs. Backcountry and

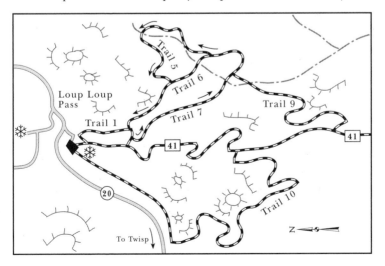

Trails traverse the forested hillsides from the South Summit Sno-Park.

telemark skiers will find trails and open slopes for cutting turns.

Visitors to the South Loup Loup area need a sno-park permit. A Methow Valley Sport Trails Association (MVSTA) pass is not required.

Access: Drive Highway 20 east from Twisp 12.5 miles to the summit of Loup Loup Pass. Turn south on the South Summit Sno-Park Road and descend 0.5 mile to the parking area (3,950 feet). If the snowplow has not been by recently, you may need to park near the highway and ski into the sno-park.

The Tour: No specific loop is recommended here. Or, to put it another way, we recommend trying all the loops. Before you head out, study the map at the south end of the parking area. Choose a loop that looks interesting and get set to explore. Check the little box below the sign for an area map. If the map box is empty, you may want to make a sketch map of your proposed route, including all the intersections you will pass along the way.

All the trails are clearly marked with identification numbers and difficulty ratings. Beginner skiers can make an enjoyable loop by combining trails 1, 7, 5, and 6 (in that order). The more adventurous and skilled can make a day of it by looping out on the 7 1/2-mile-long No. 9 Trail. Telemarkers and other powder junkies can drop knee a few times on the F Trails that link several loops, or cruise around the 7 1/2-mile-long Powerline Trail (No.10), which has several steep sections.

When you finish one loop, try another one, then another, then another, and another, and another. . . .

35 LOUP LOUP SKI AREA—BEAR MOUNTAIN

Open to: skis only
Surface: groomed
Rating: easiest to backcountry
Round trip: up to 20 miles
Skiing time: 2 hours to all day
Elevation gain: 1,230 feet
High point: 5,450 feet
Best: mid-December–mid-March
Avalanche potential: low
Map: *Green Trails* Loup Loup #85

Virtually unknown to the skiing community of the state of Washington is a gem of an area at Loup Loup Pass. The area, operated by the Loup Loup Ski Resort, has fun intermixed with thrills and spills for all cross-country skiers. It is a place where your skis are always appropriate, be they narrow skating skis or metal-edged telemark specials. Diagonal striders with traditionally narrow skis will find the beautifully groomed tracks diversified enough to be fun for beginners as well as experts. Casual tourers, gliding along on their wider skis, will find the friendly atmosphere and views to be exhilarating. Backcountry and telemark skiers, with their heavy boots, metal edges, and reduced cambers, have use of groomed trails that are designed with them in mind, with steep slopes for carving turns.

The Loup Loup Ski Area trails are operated on a fee basis. Fees, incredibly minimal when compared to charges in the valley, are

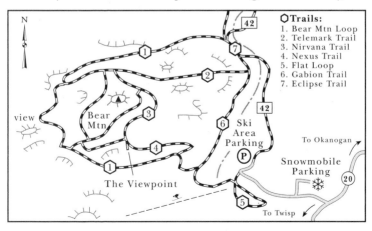

collected when the ski area is operating or when there is someone at the office. Grooming occurs only on days of operation, which are Saturdays, Sundays, and Wednesdays. A sno-park permit is not required.

Access: From the intersection of Highways 153 and 20, located just east of Twisp, drive 12.5 miles east on Highway 20 to Loup Loup Pass. At the summit take the first left. Pass the North Summit Sno-Park, then continue on 1.2 miles to the ski area (4,080 feet). If the ski area is not operating, the road will be gated 0.2 mile from the parking area. A small space along the edge of the road is plowed for parking. Do not block the gate.

The Tour: Beginners can get the feel of their skis by trying out the Flat Loop, located just south of the ski lifts. This loop, actually a figure eight with an optional shortcut, is 3 miles long and runs through meadows and forest. The youngest skiers may also enjoy the 1½-mile Short Loop, which has just enough of a slope to excite the age five and under crowd. Both of these trails are rated *easiest.*

If you are looking for scenery, try the Nexus Trail, which climbs to views on Bear Mountain. After steadily gaining elevation for a mile, the trail reaches The Viewpoint (4,800 feet). You then have a choice of trails: Nexus, Nirvana, or Bear Mountain Loop. For Bear Mountain Loop, you may ski around the rolling Bear Mountain summit, then follow Nirvana back to Nexus for a 5-mile trip. Of course, you can easily expand the tour by skiing down Bear Mountain Trail to Eclipse Trail (4,400 feet). At this point, you may follow either Eclipse Trail (*most difficult*) or Road 42 (groomed for snowmobiles). Eclipse Trail ends after a long ¾ mile at the Telemark Trail, where you are faced with a short but extremely challenging descent to the Gabion Trail. Most days, the ¾-mile-long road cruise with the snowmobiles is the lesser of the two evils. The Gabion Trail ends at the parking lot. This extended loop is about 7 miles long.

The Telemark Trail is the only trail that actually crosses over the crest of 5,450-foot Bear Mountain. This challenging trail is a wide, hard-packed swath that heads straight up to the rolling summit, then descends in a similar fashion. If you stay on the hard-packed trail you will need climbing skins to ascend and controlled, linked telemarks to descend. You may prefer to do most of your climbing either on the Nexus or the Bear Mountain Trail. On the descent you may cut wider turns on the lightly forested slopes next to the trail rather than in the narrow track.

Bear Mountain Loop

36 METHOW VALLEY COMMUNITY TRAIL

Open to: skis only
Surface: groomed
Rating: easiest to more difficult
One way: 17 1/2 miles
Skiing time: 1 hour–3 days
Elevation gain: 400 feet
High point: 2,110 feet
Best: late-December–February
Avalanche potential: none
Map: *MVSTA* Rendezvous

From Winthrop to Early Winters, the Methow Valley Community Trail tours the entire valley, making it the *pièce de résistance* of the Methow Valley Sport Trails Association (MVSTA) trail system.

You do not need to ski the entire distance in one day; the trail is designed to be skied in comfortable day trips starting and ending at convenient parking points. Groups with two cars can arrange one-way adventures. The most exotic and delightfully decadent method is to ski from inn to inn along the trail.

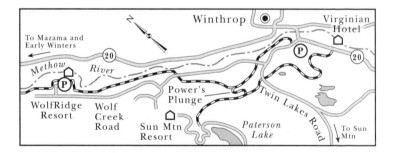

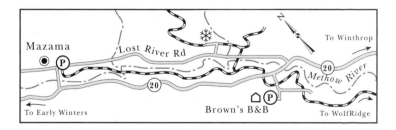

Winthrop to WolfRidge Resort: On this very scenic 6-mile, *easiest* section of trail (12 miles round trip), you'll ski past barns and across open fields with excellent views of the valley. From Winthrop, the trailhead is accessed by driving south on Highway 20. Cross the Methow River bridge and take an immediate right on Twin Lakes Road. After a couple hundred yards, just before the school, look for the turnoff to the trailhead parking area, on the right.

From the trailhead parking, follow the immaculately groomed trail west across the valley floor, where it swoops and winds across the open fields, then loops out and around private dwellings and farm buildings. Following the crossing of Wolf Creek Road at 1¼ miles, the trail continues its wide swing toward the west side of the valley and an intersection with Power's Plunge Trail from Sun Mountain at 2¼ miles. Continue straight on the Methow Valley Community Trail.

The wide trail now heads north upvalley, crossing more fields and then heading into the trees to cross Wolf Creek and recross Wolf Creek Road. After jagging and jogging around private dwellings, the trail descends to WolfRidge Resort at 6 miles. The warming hut at the edge of the practice loop is open for day use. Go in and eat your brown-bag lunch by the fire or buy yourself a muffin and some tea from the self-service tray.

WolfRidge Resort to Brown's Bed and Breakfast: This very enjoyable 5-mile section of the trail (13 miles round trip) is rated *more difficult.* Along the way you will ski past farms, fields, and houses while meandering through forest and meadows along the edge of the Methow River. To reach WolfRidge Resort, go south from downtown Winthrop on Highway 20. Cross the Methow River bridge, then take an immediate right on Twin Lakes Road. After 1.3 miles, go right on Wolf Creek Road and follow it for 4.4 miles, to the resort entrance. From the day-use parking area, ski north. The trail parallels Wolf Creek Road to the end of the plowing, then heads up the center of the road as it leaves the houses and enters the forest. This is a very straightforward section of trail, with the River Overlook Loop being the only optional variation on the route. The River Overlook Loop begins near the 1-mile point and swings east for a closer look at the Methow River, before returning to the main trail ½ mile north.

Brown's Bed and Breakfast to Mazama Country Inn: This section of the trail is 6½ miles long (10 miles round trip) and is rated *easiest.* To reach the start of the tour, drive west from Winthrop on Highway 20 for 9.1 miles. At Wolf Creek Road, go left for 0.1 mile. The day-use parking area is located on the right. The tour begins with an easy

Skiers near WolfRidge Resort

ramble around a farm field, followed by a walk across Highway 20. Back on skis, the trail takes you into the trees and along the edge of the Methow River, which is crossed at 3 miles on a suspension bridge. The trail takes on various names at this point, such as Post Loop Road and River Run Trail. Where River Run Trail ends, you should be directly across the road from the entrance to Mazama Country Inn.

37 SUN MOUNTAIN

Open to: skis only
Surface: groomed
Rating: easiest to most difficult
Loop trip: nearly 37 miles
Skiing time: 3 hours–all day
Elevation gain: 1,387 feet
High point: 3,987 feet
Best: January–February
Avalanche potential: low
Map: *MVSTA* Sun Mountain

From its perch 1,000 feet above the Methow Valley floor, Sun Mountain Lodge has an ample supply of scenic overlooks and dramatic views. Whether novice or veteran, skaters and diagonal striders will appreciate the diversity of the skiing opportunities as well as the excellent scenery. Most trails at Sun Mountain are groomed for skating as well as diagonal striding.

Access: From Twisp, drive Highway 20 north 5.3 miles. Turn left on Twin Lakes Road for 1.8 miles, then go left on Patterson Lake Road and drive for 5.6 more miles to Sun Mountain Lodge. Stop by the ski shop for a map, equipment rentals, trails information, and a ski pass (required for all trail users). Parking at the lodge itself is for guests, but 0.6 mile below the lodge is a day-use area, located just off Thompson Ridge Road (2,700 feet). A sno-park permit is not required.

The Tour: The day-use area is a delightful starting point. At the parking lot are outhouses and a warming hut. On weekends a woodstove

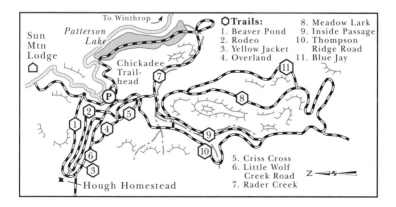

Warming hut at the day-use area of Sun Mountain Resort

heats the hut, and food and warm drinks may be purchased here.

If this is your first visit, start your explorations by heading uphill from the parking area to Thompson Ridge Road. Go right and descend to Beaver Pond Trail, then follow it through aspens to reach the old Hough Homestead and shelter at 1.5 miles. For your return, complete your loop around the Beaver Pond area by following the roly-poly Yellow Jacket trail or the well-graded Little Wolf Creek Road back to Thompson Ridge Road. A left turn will take you back to the warming hut at 3 miles.

For scenery as well as exercise, Thompson Ridge Road is a sure bet. Stay with the groomed road for 4 miles, over a pass and down the other side, to a major intersection (3,480 feet) with Meadow Lark Trail. Follow Meadow Lark to Blue Jay. The Blue Jay Trail winds through the forest, passing several scenic overlooks, before it returns to the Meadow Lark Trail 2 miles later. Continue on Meadow Lark Trail until it meets Upper Inside Passage and ends. At this point you may choose to either return to Thompson Ridge Road or add a few thrills to your trip with a 1 1/2-mile descent down the *most difficult* Lower Inside Passage, to rejoin Thompson Ridge Road 1/2 mile above the day-use area. The entire loop is 10 1/2 miles long.

Adventure seekers should make a loop down to Patterson Lake. From the day-use parking area, ski up Thompson Ridge Road 1/2 mile, then go left on Lower Inside Passage. After a short distance you will arrive at a four-way intersection. Go left for an exhilarating descent down Rader Creek. At the bottom, go left again and follow the trail across Patterson Lake (check at the Sun Mountain ski shop for the condition of the ice before you start). At the far end of the lake, go left again and follow Patterson Resort Trail uphill to Chickadee. At this point, take either a left or a right for the final 1/2 mile back to the warming hut. The loop is 5 miles long and has a *most difficult* rating.

38 PIPESTONE CANYON

Open to: all uses
Surface: forest road
Rating: most difficult
Round trip: 10 miles
Skiing time: 5 hours
Elevation gain: 750 feet
High point: 2,900 feet
Best: January–February
Avalanche potential: low
Map: *Green Trails* Twisp #84

Not far above the town of Winthrop is a scenic lake and an exotically beautiful canyon. The lake lies in a fold in the open, rolling hillsides and is easily accessible by skis, snowshoes, and snowmobiles. Beyond the lake is a narrow canyon, with steep walls and intriguing rock formations. Best of all, the canyon lies in a wildlife preserve, where snowmobiles are not allowed and skiers can enjoy the scenic wonders in relative peace and quiet.

Skiing in this area requires neither a sno-park permit nor a ski trail pass. Snowmobiles are rare except on weekends.

Access: Coming in to the south end of Winthrop on Highway 20, drive across the Methow River bridge and take an immediate right on Twisp-Winthrop Eastside Road. In 0.2 mile, go left on Center Street and then, in a few yards, right on Castle Avenue. Drive south 1.6 miles and turn left on Bear Creek Road. Head uphill 1.8 miles to the pavement's end. Park in a small plowed area on the right side of the road (2,150 feet).

The Tour: Ski up Lester Road. The climb is steady and even steep

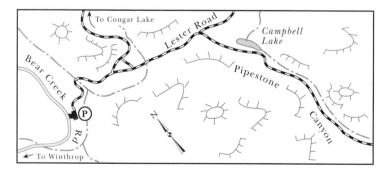

in sections. The two spur roads passed on the left lead north around Bowen Mountain to Cougar Lake. At 3½ miles the road enters a broad meadow (2,900 feet). Once you are in the meadow, leave the road and ski to the right. You may have to hunt around a bit to find the windswept road to Campbell Lake. The way descends, passing the lake, to reach the entrance to Pipestone Canyon and the wildlife preserve at 4¾ miles. Cross the fence and continue on the road, heading down the canyon ¼ mile to the pipestone formation. If time allows, ski the entire 2-mile length of the canyon, losing only 480 feet in elevation. Rounded hills at the lower end offer good skiing. The quiet visitor may see deer or coyotes.

From Lester Road, the views extend over the Methow Valley into the heartland of the North Cascades.

39 BLUE BUCK MOUNTAIN

Open to: all uses
Surface: forest roads
Rating: more difficult
Round trip: 4 miles to Cougar Lake, 10 miles to road's end
Skiing time: 2–4 hours
Elevation gain: 800 feet to lake, 3,400 feet to road's end
High point: 5,400 feet
Best: mid-December–mid-March
Avalanche potential: low
Map: *Green Trails* Twisp #84

Neither an expensive trail pass nor an expensive sno-park permit is required to ski this tour and, in the Methow Valley, that is truly unusual. Most enticing of all, this excursion takes you through the Methow Valley Wildlife Recreation Area, a scenic masterpiece with views over the valley into the glacier-clad heartland of the North Cascades.

Of course, because no fee is charged to ski here, you are likely to find yourself all alone and you may even have to break your own trail. The Methow Valley Wildlife Recreation Area is closed to motors from October 1 to December 31, while the deer are migrating from the high mountains to their wintering grounds along the Columbia River. The rest of the winter you may have to share the road with a snowmobile or two.

Access: From the center of Winthrop, leave Highway 20 where it makes an abrupt turn to recross the Methow River and continue straight, following the main street north. As it bends and heads uphill

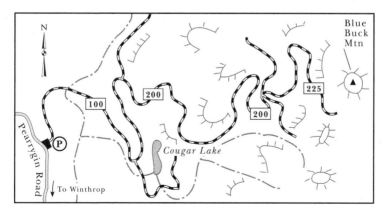

Blue Buck Road

it becomes Bluff Street. After 1.6 miles, go right on Pearrygin Road. Head up until the road levels off at 5.3 miles, then watch for Road 100 on the left. Park out of the way of local traffic (2,000 feet).

The Tour: Views begin almost immediately as you ski up Road 100. Pass two side roads to the left and two to the right before arriving at the first switchback and an intersection at 1½ miles (3,120 feet). To reach Cougar Lake, go right for ¼ mile, then left for an ⅛ mile (3,200 feet). However, if views are your goal, stay left at the intersection at 1½ miles and continue the climb. After ½ mile, go right on Road 200 to the National Forest Boundary (3,400 feet), at 2½ miles from the start. From here, numerous side roads diverge, but, provided the signs are not buried, there should be little trouble following the main road. In another mile there is a four-way junction; go straight through, on Road 225. At 5 miles from the plowed road where you parked (5,400 feet), the road ends. Trees make it impractical for all but *backcountry* skiers to continue to the top of Blue Buck Mountain, but the descent back down the road is exhilarating.

40 RENDEZVOUS PASS HUT

Open to: skis only
Surface: groomed
Rating: more difficult
Round trip: 10 miles
Skiing time: 1–4 days
Elevation gain: 1,345 feet
High point: 3,985 feet
Best: mid-December–February
Avalanche potential: none
Maps: *Green Trails* Doe Mtn. #52 and Mazama #51

Anyone who has ever spent a long winter night in a tent will immediately recognize the appeal of hut-to-hut skiing. The system of six interconnected huts in the Rendezvous Pass area can go a long way toward taking the sting out of winter camping.

Other than the huts, the Rendezvous Pass area offers excellent touring and skating on groomed trails, as well as backcountry exploring and outstanding slopes for telemarking.

The Rendezvous Pass area is part of the Methow Valley Sport Trails

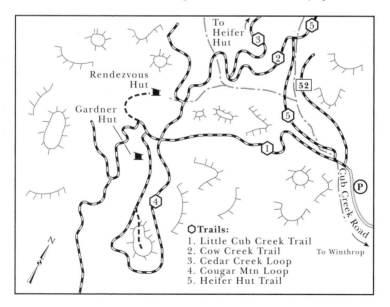

Trails:
1. Little Cub Creek Trail
2. Cow Creek Trail
3. Cedar Creek Loop
4. Cougar Mtn Loop
5. Heifer Hut Trail

Association and a pass must be purchased, available in Twisp and Winthrop, before skiing the trails. Reservations and hut information can be obtained by calling Rendezvous Outfitters, Inc., at (800) 422-3048. Gear-hauling services are also available.

Tours to Rendezvous Pass start near Mazama, at the Goat Creek Sno-Park (Tour 43) or, as described here, from the east at Cub Creek. The Cub Creek access is the shortest and the best for day trips.

Access: Drive Highway 20 west 0.1 mile from Winthrop. Turn right on West Chewuch River Road and follow it for 6.6 miles. At Cub Creek Road, turn left and drive 2.1 miles to the end of the plowed road. Go right up a narrow lane for the final ascent to the parking area (2,635 feet).

The Tour: Ski up Cub Creek Road (now called Road 52). After 1/4 mile, the road divides. Follow the left fork 1/8 mile down to Cub Creek, then take the first road on the left and cross the creek. Ski up this road 300 feet to another fork and go right on the Heifer Hut Trail (the left fork is the Little Cub Creek Trail, one of two alternate return routes).

The route heads upvalley through alternating forest and meadow for 2 miles. Except for two steep climbs, the trail is nearly level until it meets the Cow Creek Trail. Turn left here and ski uphill into the South Fork Cow Creek Valley.

Four miles from the start, Spur Road 400 branches off on the right. This road is part of the Cedar Creek Loop, which leads to Banker Pass and the Heifer Hut (the second of the two alternate return routes). Continue on up Cow Creek Trail. Pass the upper end of Little Cub Creek Trail at 5 miles. After another 200 feet, the Cougar Mountain Loop Trail takes off on the left; continue straight.

Forested Rendezvous Pass is reached at 5 1/2 miles (3,985 feet). For views, ski to the left a few hundred feet up a small knoll. To reach Rendezvous Hut, ski over the pass about 300 feet, then follow the trail markers to the right (off the road), through the forest, for 1/2 mile.

For those staying at the hut, there are miles of marked trails to explore, such as the 4-mile groomed track around Cougar Mountain, a 13-mile ungroomed round trip to Fawn Peak, or a long descent to the Methow River Valley past Gardner Hut, Cassal Hut, and Fawn Hut.

The easiest way back to the start is to return the way you came. The Little Cub Creek alternate is a steep 4 1/2-mile trail that is *difficult* when icy. Cedar Creek Loop is a meandering 10-mile *moderate* ski from the pass to the parking area. The trail is not steep and the views of Buck Mountain make this an excellent tour if you have time.

Rendezvous Hut

41 HEIFER HUT

Open to: skis only
Surface: groomed
Rating: more difficult
Round trip: 10 miles
Skiing time: 5 hours
Elevation gain: 1,365 feet
High point: 4,000 feet
Best: mid-December–mid-March
Avalanche potential: none
Map: *MVSTA* Rendezvous

Heifer Hut is one of six winter getaways in the Rendezvous Hut system. The hut is reached by a peaceful ski tour through open pine and spruce forest and has a delightful tree-framed view of Buck Mountain.

If you don't happen to be lucky enough to be making an overnight stay, the hut is still a great destination for a day trip. Hut courtesy requires that you do not enter the hut if another party is already inside. If you light up the woodstove, please leave a donation for the wood.

The well-signed trail to the hut is groomed for diagonal striding and skating. A MVSTA trail pass is required; however, a sno-park permit is not necessary. For hut information and reservations, contact Rendezvous Outfitters, Inc., at (800) 422-3048.

Access: Drive to the Cub Creek trailhead parking area (see Tour 40).

The Tour: From the parking area, ski across the field to intersect Cub Creek Road and then head upvalley ¼ mile. Where the road divides, follow the groomed trail to the left. Immediately after crossing Cub Creek, the trail forks again. Go right, following the signs to Heifer Hut and Cow Creek Trail. (The left fork is the groomed Little Cub Creek Trail to Rendezvous Pass.)

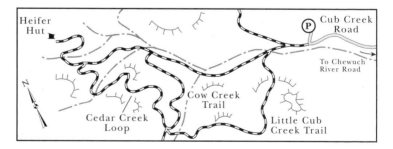

The ascent is generally gradual as you glide through forest and clearcuts. However, a couple of short descents serve to keep you alert, and two very steep climbs will certainly help to keep you warm.

At 3 miles, Heifer Hut Trail meets Cow Creek Trail (3,200 feet). Stay right. After another 1/4 mile you will ski past a sheep-loading ramp. At this point, the trail makes a sharp bend and begins to climb steeply and steadily. Watch out for descending skiers who are having so much fun that they either cannot or do not want to stop.

The next junction is reached at 4 1/4 miles (3,900 feet). To the left is Cedar Creek Loop, an alternate return route. For now, stay right on a nearly level trail that meanders into the Heifer Creek drainage, crosses the creek, and then wanders back out again. At 4 3/4 miles you will encounter the steepest climb of the tour. This final 1/4-mile push to the hut, at 4,000-feet, is breathtaking.

Interior view of Heifer Hut

42 BUCK LAKE

Open to: all uses
Surface: snowmobile groomed
Rating: most difficult
Round trip: 6 miles
Skiing time: 3 hours
Elevation gain: 1,080 feet
High point: 3,200 feet
Best: mid-December–February
Avalanche potential: low
Map: *Green Trails* Doe Mtn. #52

Buck Lake lies on a wide bench below Buck Mountain, west of Doe Mountain, east of Fawn Peak, north of Blue Buck Mountain, and not far northwest of yet another Buck Mountain. Despite the overworked name, Buck Lake makes a delightful destination for a short day tour.

Access: Drive to Winthrop on Highway 20. Where the highway makes a 90-degree turn in the center of town, leave the main road and continue straight (north) between the rows of western-style buildings. Before long, the road bends uphill and then heads up the Chewuch River valley. After 6.8 miles, cross the Chewuch River. Go right on West Chewuch River Road, which soon turns into Forest Road 51. Continue upriver another 2.5 miles to Eightmile Sno-Park (2,120 feet), located just opposite Eightmile River Road No. 5130.

The Tour: Eightmile River Road is a groomed snowmobile route. Luckily, throughout the week and on most weekends, few machines use it. The road immediately starts to climb, making a few switchbacks before reaching the Buck Lake turnoff in a short mile (2,360 feet).

Go left on Buck Lake Road No. 100 and continue the steep climb, which promises a fast descent on the return trip. At 1½ miles, pass a

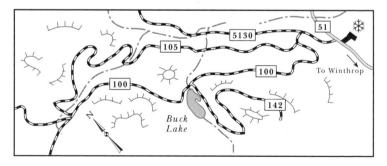

semi-abandoned logging road on the right and continue to climb. Around 2 miles, the road straightens and traverses northwest through logging cuts. Across the valley you'll see the rocky walls of Paul Mountain.

At mile 3, the road divides again. The left fork leads to a boat ramp at the south end of Buck Lake, then on up Spur Road 142 to the summit of a low hill overlooking the lake in about a mile. The right fork heads past the lake, then past a small, forested campground with tables for picnicking.

If more exercise is desired, 4 extra miles may be added to the tour by skiing rarely used logging roads in a long loop. Starting at Buck Lake, ski to the right, past the campground, for 1 1/2 miles. The first time the road divides, stay right on Road 100. The next time it divides, go right on Road 105. Stay on this road as it loops east, then bends south, returning to Buck Lake Road 1 1/2 miles from the sno-park. Few views or snowmobiles bless or curse this loop.

Snow-covered Buck Lake Campground

43 FAWN HUT AND BEYOND

Open to: skis only
Surface: groomed
Rating: most difficult
Round trip: 7½ miles or more
Skiing time: 4 hours to all day
Elevation gain: 1,380 feet
High point: 3,460 feet
Best: December–February
Avalanche potential: moderate
Map: *Green Trails* Mazama #51

It's like a little piece of Norway, with open vistas, mountain huts, and well-groomed ski trails. The major difference between this location and Norway is this area is maintained by the Methow Valley Sport Trails Association. A trail pass is required. Hut reservations and information can be obtained by calling Rendezvous Outfitters, Inc., at (800) 422-3048. Gear-hauling service to the hut is available.

Access: Drive west from Winthrop 8.5 miles on Highway 20. Just before crossing the Methow River, turn right on Goat Creek Road and head toward Mazama. After 3.4 miles, turn right again on Goat Creek Forest Road No. 52 and follow it for 0.4 mile to the sno-park (2,080 feet). Parking here requires a sno-park permit. If you do not have a permit, you may use the day-use lot at the entrance to Mazama Country Inn. If you're doing an overnighter, let the inn staff know you will be leaving your car for several days. Parking at the inn means

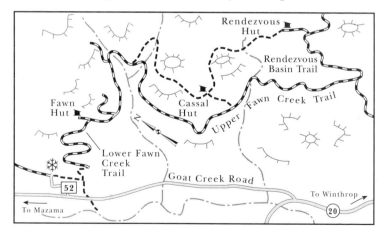

you will be skiing an extra 3 miles (one way) just to reach Fawn Hut.

The Tour: From the south end of the Goat Creek Sno-Park, follow the groomed ski track on a winding and rolling course through the forest. After 20 yards, pass a junction with the trail from Mazama Country Inn. Continue straight ahead for 1/4 mile to reach a second intersection. Go left on the Lower Fawn Creek Trail for a steep climb up the forested hillside. At 3/4 mile from the sno-park, the Lower Fawn Creek Trail joins a wide logging road and broadens to include two sets of tracks for diagonal striding as well as a wide skating lane (2,400 feet). For the next 2 1/2 miles the trail climbs relentlessly, gaining elevation with a couple of long switchbacks. Views expand at every corner.

At 3 3/4 miles from the parking lot, a groomed spur road branches off to the left, heading uphill to Fawn Hut (3,460 feet), where you will be rewarded with a delightful view of Gardner Mountain to the west and Rendezvous Mountain to the south. Day skiers are welcome to enter the huts as long as no other group is already in residence. If you do use the hut, please leave it clean, and if you light a fire, leave a donation to cover the cost of the wood.

If you are not stopping at Fawn Hut, continue straight ahead for an easy glide into the Fawn Creek drainage on Upper Fawn Creek Trail. The trail remains nearly level for the next 2 miles, then gradually dips to the West Fork Fawn Creek drainage. Once over the creek there begins an easy descent into Rendezvous Basin. At 2 1/2 miles from Fawn Hut the Upper Fawn Creek Trail ends. Continue on the Rendezvous Basin Trail for a gradual climb through the gentle basin between Rendezvous and Grizzly Mountains. In this section you will twice intersect the Cassal Creek Trail, which loops out from the Cassal Hut.

Rendezvous Pass (3,985 feet), reached at 6 3/4 miles from Fawn Hut, is buried in trees, but, by following the signs to the hut (1/8 mile northwest), you'll snag views of Gardner Mountain and the surrounding countryside.

Fawn Creek Trail

44 GOAT MOUNTAIN ROAD

Open to: all uses
Surface: snowmobile groomed
Rating: more difficult
Round trip: 3–14 miles
Skiing time: 1–6 hours
Elevation gain: 240 feet to 2,640 feet
High point: up to 4,800 feet
Best: mid-December–March
Avalanche potential: low
Map: *Green Trails* Mazama #51

Just because your 3-day pass has expired is no reason to leave the Methow Valley. If you have a sno-park permit, you have all that is required for an outstanding tour with typical, outstanding Methow Valley scenery and better-than-west-side weather. You may even start to wonder why you wasted so much time skiing on the valley floor.

Goat Mountain Road is part of an extensive groomed snowmobile trail system. Expect some mechanical competition on weekends and holidays. On weekdays you may have the entire road system to yourself.

Access: The tour begins at the Goat Creek Sno-Park (2,080 feet). Drive west from Winthrop 8.5 miles on Highway 20. Just before crossing the Methow River, turn right on Goat Creek Road and head toward Mazama. After 3.4 miles, turn right again on Goat Creek Forest Road No. 52 and follow it for 0.4 mile to the sno-park (2,080 feet). Parking here requires a sno-park permit.

The Tour: From the Goat Creek Sno-Park, follow Road 52 north. Skiing is easy, especially if the groomer has been by recently. The climb starts gradually, allowing plenty of time to warm up. A short descent at 1/2 mile leads to a crossing of Goat Creek, followed by an easy,

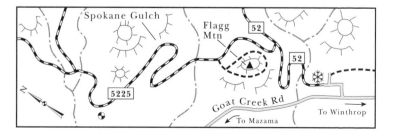

Spectacular North Cascades scenery from Goat Mountain Road

mile-long climb to an excellent viewpoint located at the first switch-back (2,420 feet), the first of many turnaround points.

Beyond the viewpoint, the rate of climbing increases as Road 52 heads up the Goat Creek valley to reach a major intersection at the 2-mile point (2,800 feet). Go left on Goat Mountain Road No. 5225 and begin a steady climb up the forested hillside. If this seems like a lot of work, just think how fun the descent will be. After a mile of climbing, the road levels briefly (3,400 feet). Note Spur Road 050 on the left. This road may be followed 1 mile to the 4,004-foot crest of Flagg Mountain.

Road 5225 continues its steady ascent, soon rewarding your efforts with views across the valley to Driveway Butte. Views continue to expand to include Sun Mountain, Sandy Butte, and a host of glaciated North Cascades summits. Before long the road switchbacks, and at 6 miles, shortly after passing Spokane Gulch, you will pass another excellent viewpoint. At 7 miles (4,800 feet), a sharp bend to the northeast marks a final turnaround point for day trips.

45 MAZAMA AND WILSON RANCH

Open to: skis only
Surface: groomed
Rating: easiest to more difficult
Loop trip: 7 miles
Skiing time: 3 hours
Elevation gain: 200 feet
High point: 2,150 feet
Best: late-December–mid-February
Avalanche potential: none
Map: *MVSTA* Mazama

Diagonal striders or even the more aerobic skate skiers will find plenty of room to roam on immaculately groomed trails in the Mazama area of the Methow Valley. With plenty of trails to choose from, it is easy to pick a route that is perfect for your group.

As with most tours in the Methow Valley Trail System, you can lengthen or shorten your trip by choosing a slightly different route through the intertwining network of looping trails. A sno-park permit is not needed for this tour; however, you must have a MVSTA trail pass.

Access: From Winthrop, drive west on Highway 20 for 14.6 miles. At Lost River Road, go right and head across the valley to a four-way intersection. Go straight through the intersection to the Mazama Country Inn access road. A few feet beyond the intersection look for the day-use parking area on the right (2,150 feet). Ski rentals and accessories are available at the inn.

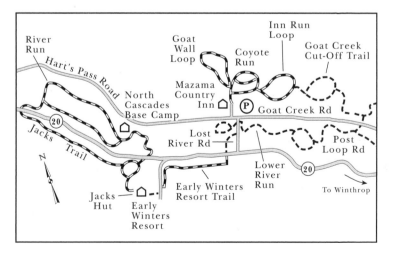

River Loop: From the day-use parking area, carry your skis back to the four-way intersection, then cross the road. Start your loop on Lower River Run Trail, located on the left (south) side of Lost River Road.

For the next 2 miles your skis will take you through small meadows along the river's edge. At the end of River Run Trail, stay left on Post Loop Road, which heads across Goat Creek and over a plowed road to reach the Goat Creek Cut-Off Trail at 2 3/4 miles. Leave Post Loop Road here and go left for the hardest climb of the tour. When icy this ascent is murderous and best walked. Once up, the trail crosses Goat Creek Road to intersect Lower Fawn Creek Trail. Go left and head back upvalley.

Ski through the forest on a trail that rolls with the terrain. At 3 3/4 miles the trail divides again. Following the signs to Mazama Country Inn, stay left. The trail crosses the Goat Creek Sno-Park access road, then heads into several short but steep descents before crossing Goat Creek on a sturdy bridge.

At 4 3/4 miles the trail leaves the forest and heads across level fields, soon to divide again. At the first intersection, go right on Flagg Mountain Loop. When the two legs of the Flagg Mountain Loop come back together, go straight ahead on Inn Run Loop Trail for 3/4 mile, then take a right and, shortly after a second right, reach Coyote Run Trail for a short hill-climbing adventure and a view. At 6 1/4 miles, stay to the right on Goat Wall Loop and complete your tour with a scenic cruise along the base of Goat Wall. Walk the inn access road back to the day-use parking area to return to your car at 7 miles.

Wilson Ranch Trail: This valley bottom cruise, with views of snow-plastered mountains and sheer rock walls, is an idyllic, easy trip for diagonal striders or skaters. The heated warming hut at the turn-around point, where snacks and hot drinks may be purchased, is a rather nice incentive, too.

From the day-use parking area at Mazama, grab the skis and walk west, heading straight toward Highway 20. Pay attention to traffic, of which there is very little. Walk over the Methow River bridge, then, shortly after, look for a road on the right. Walk down this lane a few feet to find the start of Wilson Ranch Trail, on the left.

The trail heads out over the snow-covered fields, often winding for no particular reason. Head through a small stand of trees, then go back into the fields. At 1/2 mile, the trail dips under Highway 20 and continues north, on the west side of the road. At 1 1/4 miles, cross the Wilson Ranch Road. Continue straight another very short 1/4 mile to reach Jacks Hut, located to the left of the main trail. The hut is a busy place, open from 9:00 A.M. to 4:30 P.M. The first floor has a small food concession, ski rentals, restroom, and visitor's information; the second floor is the office for a heli-skiing service.

Groomed trail through the open fields at Mazama

46 EARLY WINTERS—BASE CAMP

Open to: skis only
Surface: groomed
Rating: easiest to more difficult
Loop trip: up to 10³/4 miles
Skiing time: 5 hours
Elevation gain: 600 feet ˙
High point: 2,800 feet
Best: late-December–February
Avalanche potential: none
Maps: *MVSTA* Mazama and *Green Trails* Mazama #51

Great scenery, old ranch houses, numerous looping trails, easy rolling terrain, and two warming huts make this a great area for skiers
young, old, and in-between.

Early Winters is part of the Methow Valley's system of ski trails,
and you'll need a trail pass to ski here. Parking is free. **Note:** Some of
the trails in this area cross private land. Please behave accordingly.

Access: From Winthrop, drive west 16.6 miles on Highway 20 to
the end of the open road at the Early Winters Campground (2,240
feet). You may also access these trails from the North Cascades Base
Camp, reached by driving 14.4 miles west from Winthrop, then turning right on Lost River Road. Cross the valley to Mazama, then go left
on an unsigned road. After 2.2 miles, go left on the Base Camp road.
Park in the day-use area.

The Tour: Numerous possibilities await—short loops or long loops,

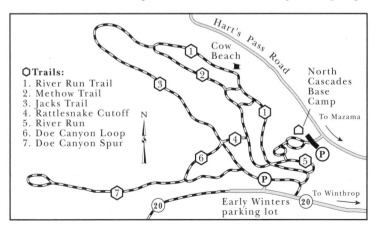

○**Trails:**
1. River Run Trail
2. Methow Trail
3. Jacks Trail
4. Rattlesnake Cutoff
5. River Run
6. Doe Canyon Loop
7. Doe Canyon Spur

take your pick. For a short loop, try skiing the River Run/Methow Trail Loop. This loop is only 5 1/4 miles long and incorporates the best of the area. The easiest access is from North Cascades Base Camp. Descend from the parking area to cross the Methow River, then go right and climb to an intersection of the River Run and Methow Trails. Go straight and ski upvalley on the Methow Trail. Glide or skate past old farms with dramatic views of ice-coated Goat Wall. Return to your starting point on River Run Trail. If you get cold on your way back, take a rest stop at the tiny Cow Beach warming hut.

For a longer loop, combine Methow Trail and Jacks Trail. These two trails form a nearly level, 6 1/2-mile loop around the Early Winters area that is ideal for beginning skaters. The warming hut at Cassal Ranch is a great place to stop for a snack. The shelter is actually someone's home, so please treat it with great respect. The parking area at Early Winters provides the most convenient access for this loop.

If you would like to do a bit of climbing, followed, of course, by a descent, try the Doe Canyon Spur. This is a *more difficult* trip. A well-used bench marks the top of the climb. The run back is fast and fun as long as you have a good grasp of the basic principles of stopping. Early Winters is also the most convenient access point for this trail.

Skier near Base Camp

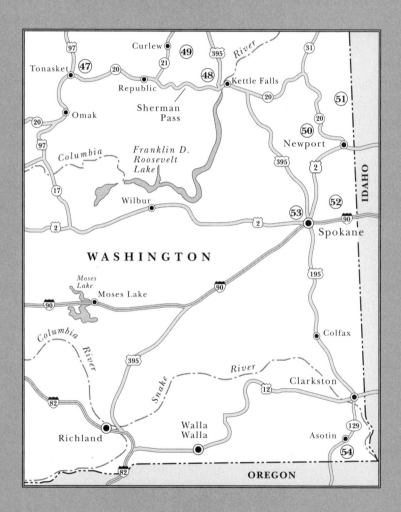

The Inland Region

With a remarkable disdain for geology, many people consider the volcano-studded Cascades to be Washington State's only mountain range, and the only place to find cross-country skiing. Nothing could be farther from the truth. The Kettle Range has some of the best skiing in the state. In Washington's northeast corner, the Selkirk Range is almost as excellent. And along the southeastern border, the rolling terrain of the Blue Mountains makes for ideal ski touring.

With the exception of Mount Spokane State Park, most of the ski areas in this region are isolated from the state's major population centers. Cross-country skiers may go for an entire day without seeing other groups, creating wonderful opportunities to experience the peace and delicate beauty of the winter landscape.

One of the most unique ski areas is located in Spokane, where the city's parks and recreation department sponsors two groomed cross-country ski areas. City residents can ski groomed trails just a few miles from their doorsteps.

Weather in the Inland Empire tends to be very variable. Extreme cold alternates with sudden warming trends, making it essential that skiers carry water-resistant gear on all extended trips.

47 HIGHLANDS SNO-PARK

Open to: skis only
Surface: groomed
Rating: easiest to most difficult
Round trip: up to 10 miles
Skiing time: 1–5 hours
Elevation gain: up to 1,000 feet
High point: 4,850 feet
Best: January–February
Avalanche potential: low
Map: *USGS* Havillah

Peaceful, scenic, and a whole lot less commercial than the neighboring Methow Valley—these are just some of the reasons for visiting Highlands Sno-Park. This little-known area is well designed with a wide variety of challenges, making it an ideal area for every cross-country skier. Pick from trails with wide skating lanes, narrow trails snaking through the open forest, or ungroomed slopes that are steep enough to make the most experienced telemarkers hike back up for a second run. Best of all, for the social members of the skiing community, there are trails with two diagonal striding lanes located side by side, so that skiers can comfortably converse as they glide along.

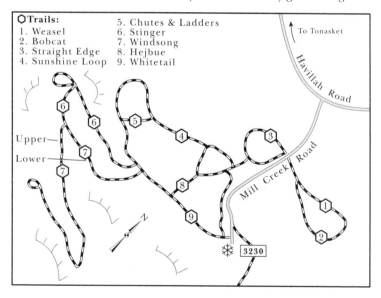

○Trails:
1. Weasel
2. Bobcat
3. Straight Edge
4. Sunshine Loop
5. Chutes & Ladders
6. Stinger
7. Windsong
8. Hejbue
9. Whitetail

To Tonasket

Havillah Road

Upper
Lower

Mill Creek Road

N

❄ 3230

A snowy day at the Highlands

Access: Drive Highway 97 to the north end of Tonasket. Go east on Havillah Road. Even if you miss the small road sign, you will certainly see the larger Sitzmark Ski Hill sign. Head toward Havillah for 15.4 miles, then go right on Mill Creek Road No. 3230. After heading up hill for 0.5 mile, pass the lower Highland Sno-Park parking area. The main parking area is located another 0.5 mile up the road. Go right at the intersection and park in the main parking area (3,831 feet). A sno-park permit is required.

The Trails: Before you start skiing, be sure to sign the trail register. The number of skiers' signatures helps determine the amount of funding the area receives. Also note that the parking area is shared with snowmobilers who will be heading up the Forest Service road. Skiers often use the first 11.5 kilometers (7 miles) of the groomed road as a skating area.

Once you have checked the map, head out and enjoy the glide. From the main parking area, you can choose to head down to the Hejbue to Straight Edge to practice your skating in the field loop, or start out on a woodland adventure with Ida's Ford to the Bobcat/ Weasel loop. One of the most popular trips is a loop that starts from the parking area and follows Whitetail to Lower Windsong, then goes right on Stinger for a wild descent to the viewpoint, followed by an easy return on Whitetail, for a total of 6 kilometers (3 3/4 miles).

48 SHERMAN PASS SNO-PARK

Open to: nonmotorized
Surface: open slopes and trails
Rating: most difficult to backcountry
Round trip: 3–6 miles
Skiing time: 2–8 hours
Elevation gain: up to 1,000 feet
High point: 6,600 feet
Best: January–March
Avalanche potential: high
Map: *USGS* Sherman Peak

Your backcountry skiing, routefinding, and snowpack awareness skills should be well honed before you do any skiing in the Sherman Pass area. If your skills are not top-notch, make sure that someone in your party is well versed in routefinding, avalanche avoidance, and avalanche rescue techniques.

Despite the dire warnings, this is a spectacular skiing area. The generally excellent eastern Washington snow, combined with the open slopes along the summits of Kettle Crest, has created an elite cadre of local telemarkers who carve their turns with speed and aplomb. Do not be afraid (if you can) to corner one of these local experts to learn where the hazards are.

Access: Sherman Pass Sno-Park is located on Highway 20, about halfway between Republic and Kettle Falls. The sno-park is on the north side of the highway, at the Kettle Crest trailhead (5,570 feet).

The Tour: The most popular destination, or at least the most

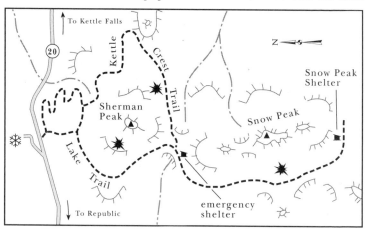

talked-about trip, is to the Snow Peak Shelter. This rough cabin is located south of the pass, 4 miles from the sno-park if you ski the ridge crest route and closer to 6 miles if you follow the somewhat circuitous Kettle Crest Trail. Also on the south side of the pass are excellent telemark slopes on the side of Sherman Peak. To reach the south-side trailhead, walk back up the sno-park access road, cross Highway 20, then head left (east) down the road 25 yards. The trailhead is on the right, marked by a signboard and an orange pole.

A few feet away from the highway, the trail divides. To the right, the Lake Trail heads steeply uphill to the telemark slopes. This is also the most direct way to the shelter, and is marked with orange tape to guide you to your destination. To the left, the Kettle Crest Trail begins its unmarked journey through the White Mountain burn of 1988. This massive fire destroyed 20,000 acres of forest and left new slopes for telemarking and avalanching. The summer trail is cursed with numerous switchbacks that have acutely tight corners, requiring fast reflexes in good conditions and lightning ones in icy conditions.

Following the Lake Trail, and using your climbing skins, head uphill. The "lake" is passed, probably unnoticed, after 1/2 mile of climbing. Following the tape and other tracks, ski around the west side of Sherman Peak then down to the 6,390-foot saddle. An emergency tent with a wood-burning stove is located here. Now ski around the west side of Snow Peak to reach the shelter (6,270 feet).

Reservations are required to stay at the shelter. In 2000, reservations could be placed starting December 1 by calling (509) 775-7419. The price was reasonable. Call the Republic Ranger Station for current snowpack conditions and weather reports before starting out.

If you are not a dedicated backcountry skier, you may prefer to try the mile-long descent from the sno-park to the campground. The trip begins at the parking area and ends when you reach the road or the campground. You may also follow the Kettle Crest trail to the north, up the Columbia Peak area. Again, watch the snow conditions. As more trees fall in the burn areas, slopes that have previously been stable may slide. Always err on the side of caution.

For more information, write: Republic Ranger District, P.O. Box 468, Republic, WA 99166. Or you may call: (509) 775-3305.

Skiers' trail near Sherman Pass

49 BOULDER DEER CREEK SUMMIT SNO-PARK

Open to: skis and snowshoes
Surface: groomed and nongroomed
Rating: easiest to backcountry
Round trip: up to 32 miles
Skiing time: 2–8 hours
Elevation gain: up to 1,730 feet
High point: 5,800 feet
Best: January–mid-March
Avalanche potential: moderate out of groomed area
Map: *USGS* Mt. Leona

For anyone who has ever skied the crowded sno-parks on the west side of the Cascades, the peace and tranquility of Deer Creek Summit is like taking a trip to a deserted tropical island after not seeing the sun for three months. And not only are you likely to enjoy some very peaceful skiing at Deer Creek Summit—chances are you will see a lot of blue sky, too.

With good trails and miles of snowmobile-free backcountry to explore, you know there must be a catch, and there is. This barely known sno-park is located far away from major population centers, in one of the most forgotten sections of our state.

Access: The sno-park can be reached from Kettle Falls or Republic. From Kettle Falls, drive west on combined Highway 20/395 for 3.1 miles. Stick with Highway 395 when Highway 20 branches left to head

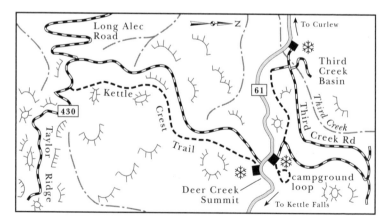

over Sherman Pass. Drive north for another 16 miles, then go left on Boulder Creek Road. This road climbs steeply for 11.8 miles to the 4,640-foot summit of Deer Creek Pass. If coming from the west, drive Highway 20 east from Republic 3 miles to the Highway 21 junction and go north 18.2 miles to Curlew. At the entrance of town, turn right on a road signed "To US 395" and follow it as it climbs above the urban area and becomes Forest Road 61. As you head up to the summit, you will pass several spur roads with plowed parking spaces. These are invitations to explore the non-groomed areas. If you choose to explore these areas, carry a map. At 9.4 miles you will pass a small sno-park at the base of Third Creek Road. If you are planning to ski the Third Creek Loop, this is an ideal location to start, elevation 4,083 feet. Unless you are an excellent skier, plan to do the loop counterclockwise. To reach the summit parking areas, continue on up Road 61 for 1.6 miles. The North Loop parking area is on the left and has a vault toilet. The South Loop parking area is at the summit, along the side of the road.

North Loop: This 5-mile tour has a full encyclopedia of skiing experiences. From the parking area, head up to an intersection with the very easy, 3/4-mile campground loop. Go left and descend on groomed trail, then climb briefly to a second intersection and a choice. The ideal way to enjoy the loop is to head left and descend into Third Creek basin. The descent is on an ungroomed trail that is rated *most difficult,* due to some "thrilling" descents down clifflike drops. These drops can and should be walked when icy.

After descending for 1 1/2 miles, the route reaches the groomed forest roads of Third Creek basin. Go right to a three-way intersection, (4,110 feet), then right again to begin a 2-mile climb to the ridge tops. Views slowly expand, eventually reaching the snow-clad northern Cascades. At the 3 1/2-mile point, Third Creek Road crosses the 4,820-foot crest of the ridge between Rocky Mountain to the west and Dry Mountain to the southeast. The road then descends gradually along the north side of the ridge for 1/4 mile before reaching an intersection. Go right, following the groomed tracks, and climb back to the ridge crest and the ultimate view. From this point it is a speedy, moderate to steep descent back to the parking lot.

South Loop: On the south side of the pass is a very demanding loop that is definitely not for everyone. The lower leg of the loop follows a broad, well-groomed logging road for 2 miles. An ungroomed trail continues on, marked with orange tape, climbing steadily for another 2 miles to an intersection with Long Alec Road (5,390 feet). Go left and continue the steady climb on Road 430. After 200 feet, cross the Kettle Crest Trail. Expert skiers and telemarkers may prefer to return to the start on the trail. Most skiers will do best by following the road for several more miles as it ascends to at 6,082-foot viewpoint on the almost flat-topped crest of Taylor Ridge.

South Loop trail

50 UPPER WOLF TRAIL SYSTEM

Open to: skis only
Surface: groomed
Rating: easiest to more difficult
Loop trip: 2 miles
Skiing time: 1–2 hours
Elevation gain: 30 feet
High point: 2,200 feet
Best: January–February
Avalanche potential: none
Map: none

This is a wonderful urban romp with a city park-type atmosphere. The area is a wooded oasis, bound by houses on two sides and a farm and Highway 20 on the other two sides. The trails, groomed for skating and diagonal striding, are short, and the entire area can be skied in an hour.

In truth, the area is too small to be a destination, but it is ideal for skiers taking a break from traveling to and from other destinations. For Newport residents, it offers a perfect lunch break or afternoon workout.

Access: From Spokane, drive north 46 miles on Highway 2 to the town of Newport. At the town center, go left on Highway 20 and head toward Colville for 0.3 mile. Directly after passing the Newport Ranger District Office, take a left turn on Larch and head uphill for one block. At Laurel-Hurst, go right for 0.5 mile to find the parking area on

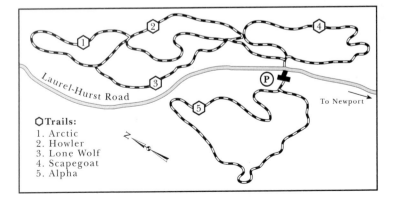

Howler Trail

the left (2,200 feet). The area is closed at dark, precluding all moonlight tours.

The Tour: Trails are located on both sides of the road. On the parking lot side, there is the gently domestic 1.2-kilometer (³/₄-mile) Alpha Loop through the forest. The trail brushes up to a housing development, then edges alongside a farm. Deer tracks, and an occasional deer, can be seen criss-crossing the trail, leaving deep trenches in the soft snow.

Across the road from the parking area are the challenging trails. In this narrow band of forest, the trails dive and fall like a Hammer ride at a neighborhood carnival. When icy, even the *easiest* trails will make your legs shake.

51 GEOPHYSICAL SNO-PARK

Open to: skis and snowshoes
Surface: groomed
Rating: easiest to more difficult
Loop trip: up to 10 kilometers (6 1/4 miles)
Skiing time: 2–6 hours
Elevation gain: 100 feet
High point: 2,500 feet
Best: January–February
Avalanche potential: none
Map: *USGS* Bead Lake

It is the clever twists and turns of the groomed trails that turn a rather commonplace stretch of forest into a fun-filled afternoon on the snow. The Geophysical Sno-Park has an absorbing number of trails that will lure you back again and again.

Access: Drive north from Spokane on Highway 2 for 46 miles, to the town of Newport. Follow Highway 2 east through town, entering Idaho and the town of Old Town. Cross the Pend Oreille River, then take an immediate left and head north on Le Clerc Road for 7.3 miles. At some point you will leave Idaho and reenter Washington—what a crazy border. At Indian Creek Road, go right and drive steeply uphill for a final 1.5 miles. Geophysical Sno-Park and ski trails are on the left.

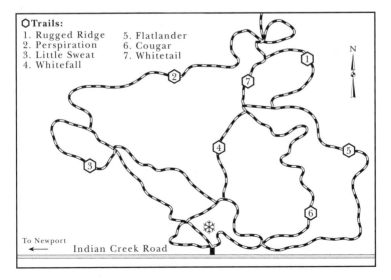

Perspiration Trail

The Tour: From the parking lot you have a variety of trails to choose from. Grooming is sporadic, depending on snowfall. Whitetail, Cougar, Flatlander, and Rugged Ridge are wide and well signed. Trails on the west side of the sno-park are a little more hit and miss. If the trails start to seem monotonous, try the very challenging Perspiration Trail.

This trail is located 1.6 kilometers (1 mile) up Whitetail. Go left (west) from the trail sign and follow the blue diamond–marked route on a squirrelly romp through the forest. Sections at the upper end are steep; however, after the first 0.8 kilometer (1/2 mile), the ground levels and so does the trail. The next 6.4 kilometers (4 miles) are a winding path through one tree plantation after another. When snow covers the trees, the entire area is a winter garden of lace-fringed branches and sparking white meadows. At 8.8 kilometers (5 1/2 miles), Perspiration Trail crosses an unmarked forest road. Shortly after, the trail intersects the groomed Ponderosa and Chipmunk Trails, which soon lead back to the trailhead, completing the 10 kilometer (6 1/4 mile) loop.

52 MOUNT SPOKANE STATE PARK

Open to: skis and snowshoes
Surface: groomed
Rating: easiest to most difficult
Round trip: up to 17 miles
Skiing time: 2–8 hours
Elevation gain: 400 feet
High point: 4,850 feet
Best: January–February
Avalanche potential: none
Map: *USGS* Mount Spokane

With its wide variety of groomed trails, excellent warming huts, and exquisite scenery, Mount Spokane is the best-organized and most expansive sno-park facility in the state. The 17 miles of immaculately groomed trails lead skiers through a fairyland of ice-frosted trees to broad vistas. The trails soar over the hilltops and race along the hillsides. It is no coincidence that you will find a lot of families here; the trails are varied, with enough open areas for snow play or telemarking to keep everyone interested.

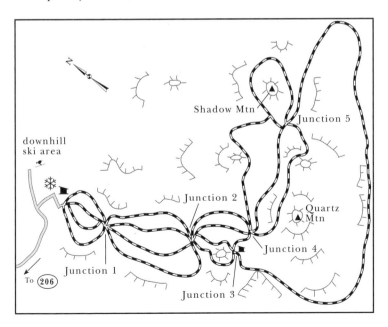

Note: Skiers must have a Special Groomed Area sticker in addition to a sno-park pass. Also, overnighting is not allowed in the State Park. Skiers must exit the area by 10:00 P.M. and cannot return until 8:00 A.M. Parked cars will be towed. The nearest campground in 2000 was a small, private site located at the base of the mountain, 0.1 mile before the entrance gate.

Access: Mount Spokane is located in a massive state park, 25 miles northeast of Spokane. Drive Highway 2 north 10 miles from downtown Spokane. Just past milepost 297, go right (east) on Highway 206 for 15.5 twisting miles to the park entrance. The narrow road heads steeply up for another 3 miles, then levels off. The sno-park is located at the top of the climb, on your right. Drive up through the first parking area, used by snowmobilers, to the skiers' area (4,600 feet).

The Tour: The first thing you will notice is the huge Selkirk Lodge. This is a public facility, with a woodstove for heat, picnic tables, running water, and heated restrooms. The trails start from the right-hand side of the lodge. Four trails head over and around the first knoll, then rejoin on the other side at Junction 1 (4,576 feet). Pick again from the next set of four trails, which take you around or over the next knoll and rejoin at Junction 2 (4,667 feet). Then you have four more trails to choose from, which will take you around or over the next knoll to Junctions 3 and 4 (4,751 feet).

Nova Hut is located at Junction 3. This small shelter is also heated by a woodstove and is a good place for a picnic lunch in inclement weather. From Junction 3 and nearby Junction 4 you have four more choices, including a loop around Quartz Mountain and a challenging dive into a clearcut. Finally, at Junction 5 (4,740 feet), your choices are dropped to three, and if you choose to continue from here, you must make your own trails.

Intersection of trails at Junction 4

53 SPOKANE'S SNO-PARKS

Open to: skis only
Surface: groomed
Rating: easiest to more difficult
Round trip: up to 4 1/2 miles
Skiing time: 1–3 hours
Elevation gain: 200 feet
High point: 459 feet
Best: January–February
Avalanche potential: none
Map: handouts

Two official sno-parks lie within Spokane's city limits, giving residents and visitors alike a wonderful opportunity to enjoy winter's finest offerings without the hassle of a long drive to the mountains. Amazingly, these sno-parks have a secluded, away-from-the-city feel that adds to the fun.

Elevation is the main problem here. Spokane is located at the edge of the snow zone, and some years has several feet of snow that lingers for a month or more. Other years offer a much less cheery picture of winter, and the long, cold months yield insufficient snowfall to even move the grooming machines out of their nice warm garages. Never go to Spokane for skiing without calling ahead to check out the conditions. Your best bet for updated trail conditions is to contact Spokane Parks and Recreation, (509) 625-6200, or try the Chamber of Commerce.

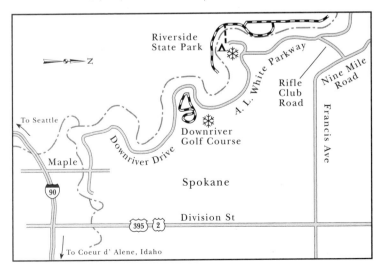

Distinctive rocks in Spokane River at Riverside State Park

Downriver Golf Course: Located on the west end of town near Riverside State Park, the trails loop through open pine forest while touring the fairways of a secluded golf course near the Spokane River. The well-groomed trails are gently rolling, making it an excellent location for practicing the graceful skating flow. The upper and lower loop combine for a total of 5 kilometers (3 miles) of skiing, making it an excellent site for an hour or two of winter exercise.

Downriver Golf Course is located 2.1 miles east of Riverside State Park Campground (see below), off Downriver Drive on Riverview Drive.

Riverside State Park: Deep in a canyon of the Spokane River, 7 miles from the heart of town, is a scenic wilderness. When conditions warrant, Aubrey L. White Parkway West is groomed, and skiers have a chance to skim along the hillside above the river and enjoy winter's finest frost art covering the trees and shrubs.

The start of the 7.2-kilometer (4 1/2-mile) trail can be accessed via several different routes from the center of town. For the out-of-towner, it is easiest to follow the signs off Interstate 90 at Exit 281. Head north, following Highways 2 and 395 through town on Division Street. (Division Street will become Ruby Street for a while; then it will return to Division.) After 4.4 miles, turn left on Francis Avenue and drive 3.1 miles, then go left on Nine Mile Road. Just 0.7 mile beyond, take a left on Rifle Club Road and drive for 0.5 mile. Turn left on Aubrey L. White Parkway East (unsigned) and drive along the river for 1.5 miles to the turnoff to the Bowl and Pitcher and the State Park campground. Descend to the picnic area to park. Carry your skis down to the river and cross the suspension bridge before starting your skiing on the opposite side.

54 FIELD'S SPRING STATE PARK

Open to: skis and snowshoes
Surface: groomed
Rating: easiest to more difficult
Round trip: 1 to 5 miles
Skiing time: 2 to 4 hours
Elevation gain: 430 feet
High point: 4,440 feet
Best: January–February
Avalanche potential: none
Map: *USGS* Fields Spring

This quiet oasis of rounded, forest-covered hills lies on the precipitous edge of some of the most dramatic scenery in the state of Washington. From the open crest of Puffer Butte, the highest point in the park, you can gaze east and allow your eyes to follow the contours of the land as it descends more than 3,000 feet to the canyon of the Snake River. Sharp eyes can catch a glimpse of its glistening waters so far below. To the south, hidden from view by the very steepness of the hillsides, the earth falls away at your feet, plunging with Grand Canyon suddenness to the very dramatic Grande Ronde River. Farther south, the gleaming summits of the Wallowa Mountains and the Eagle Cap Wilderness head to the sky with the same abruptness that the Grande Ronde River shrinks from it.

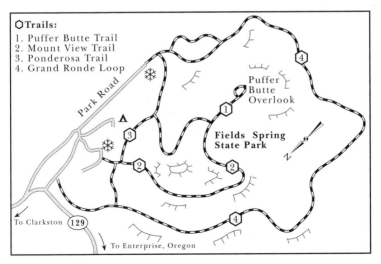

○ **Trails:**
1. Puffer Butte Trail
2. Mount View Trail
3. Ponderosa Trail
4. Grand Ronde Loop

Park Road

Puffer Butte Overlook

Fields Spring State Park

To Clarkston (129)

To Enterprise, Oregon

Field's Spring State Park Sno-Park is a unique area in the southeast corner of the state. Lying amidst a popular snowmobile playground, the well-groomed trails and snow-play area provide a welcome escape for skiers. The tracks follow roads, with plenty of opportunities to head out on your own to cut some turns through the open forest of ponderosa pine, larch, Douglas fir, and grand fir.

Access: From the town of Clarkston, on the Washington-Idaho border, head south 5 miles to Asotin, on Highway 129. Continue to follow Highway 129 as it climbs steeply above the Snake River to the wheat fields on the high plateau above. Cross 3,965-foot Rattlesnake Pass 22.7 miles south of Asotin and descend 0.3 mile before turning left on Park Road. Drive 0.5 mile to the first parking lot. An alternate lot is located 0.5 mile on up the road. Restroom facilities are located at both parking areas. Winter camping is allowed in the somewhat tilting day-use area. The sledding and tubing area is at the lighted slope near the Wo-He-Lo Environmental Learning Center. The park has two environmental learning centers, which accommodate groups.

The Tour: The *more difficult* Puffer Butte Trail is a personal favorite and a definite must for view lovers. The Mount View Trail will take you to the same place with about the same amount of difficulty, and, in combination with the Puffer Butte Trail, makes a great loop. The *easiest* Grand Ronde Loop, when skied in conjunction with the Ponderosa Trail, can take you on a leisurely tour around the State Park.

Pack a good lunch, and on cold days head into one of the heated picnic shelters. On warmer days, head up to the summit of Puffer Butte and uncover the picnic table. As you ski, watch for huge bird tracks in the snow, but before you grab your field guide—the neighboring farm raises wild turkeys.

Puffer Butte Overlook

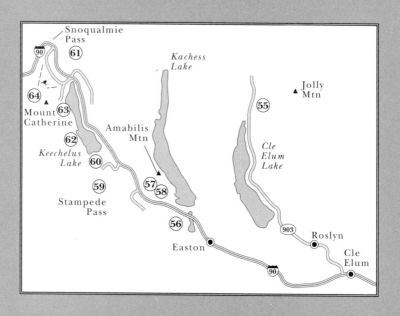

I-90 Corridor: Central Cascades Region

The Central Cascades offer a wide variety of skiing experiences. From immaculately groomed tracks to snow-covered summits, skiers will have no trouble finding excitement and challenges. The aggressive logging practices of the 1970s and 1980s resulted in the creation of miles of roads that make mountain crests and ridge tops considerably more accessible than in the northern regions of the state.

The Central Cascades are strongly affected by Washington's maritime climate. Temperatures can vary by twenty degrees during the day. A typical day during the winter may see snow, rain, and even sunny periods. The extreme variations in temperature make waxable skis about as desirable as a migraine headache, leaving the no-wax varieties as the skis of choice. Skiers should also carry waterproof gear, even on short trips.

The sno-parks and ski resorts in the Snoqualmie Pass area rank among the busiest in the state. The six to eight lanes of Interstate 90 allow relatively easy access from the dense population centers of Puget Sound, and on weekends skiers arrive by the hundreds, filling the sno-parks and creating congestion on the trails. Always plan to arrive at the trailhead by mid-morning to secure a parking spot.

55 SALMON LA SAC SNO-PARK

Open to: skis and snowshoes
Surface: some groomed
Rating: easiest to backcountry
Round trip: 2½–15 miles
Skiing time: 1–8 hours
Elevation gain: up to 4,083 feet
High point: 6,443 feet
Best: January–mid-March
Avalanche potential: moderate
Map: *Green Trails* Kachess Lake #208

This is a stunning area. At the upper end of Cle Elum Lake, the valley narrows to a steep-walled cut between the snow-plastered flanks of Red Mountain, the jagged ramparts of Davis Peak, and the friendly, gleaming dome of Jolly Mountain. Views are excellent.

Sadly, about twenty years ago this potential skiers' paradise was handed over to the snowmobilers to such a complete extent that the very economy of the town of Cle Elum is reliant on the numbers of snowmobilers they can attract throughout the winter. The measures taken to ensure the happiness of the snowmobilers even include grooming a lane alongside the highway for their exclusive use.

On winter weekends, the end of the plowed road at Salmon La Sac literally vibrates with the noise of the machines. The air is putrid with the smell of exhaust. Parking is difficult. Yet beyond the noise, smell, and annoyance, the beauty of the area continues to attract

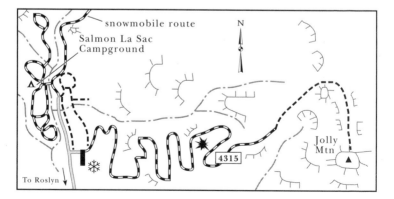

skiers. The Forest Service has taken a second look at some of their policies in this area and is working very hard to attract skiers back to Salmon La Sac. However, if you can ski here on a weekday, you can explore almost machinefree!

Access: From Interstate 90, take Exit 80 and follow the road to Roslyn. Continue upvalley on Highway 903 for 16.3 miles, to the end of the plowed road at Salmon La Sac (2,360 feet). Park either as near to the road's end as is possible, and legal, or go back 0.2 mile and go left on Road 4315, to find a spot in the official sno-park.

Groomed Campground Loops: If you only have a short time to spend, your best bet is to try out the 2 1/2 miles of snowmobile-groomed trails. If you are parked in the sno-park lot, head up to Road 4315 and go right. At the upper end of the plowed area is a skiers' sign. Take the trail on the left and ski into the forest for a *more difficult,* but very fun, run through the trees. After 1/4 mile, the trail divides. The trail on the right climbs 1/8 mile to intercept the Jolly Mountain Trail, and can, when conditions are right, be a very fun run. The trail on the left descends to the corral area, then curves out to cross the main road at the Old Rangers Cabin. Cross the road and ski up it a few feet before going left across the Cle Elum River to find the machine-free loops in the Salmon La Sac Campground. Grooming also extends 1/2 mile upvalley to the trailhead parking area.

Jolly Mountain: This personal favorite remains in the book despite the snowmobile abuse of the area. The tour begins at the end of the plowing at the entrance to Salmon La Sac Sno-Park. Road 4315, up Jolly Mountain, has a "voluntary snowmobile closure" statute. Many snowmobilers do not wish to volunteer for this closure. However, it remains a great area, with fewer snowmobiles than other areas, great views, and, if you get to the top, some pretty nice skiing.

Ski up Road 4315 for 4 miles, to 4,500 feet, then, at a sharp corner, leave the road and head up a steep old cut area to a ridge crest. There is some potential for sliding here, so avoid gullies and open slopes. At 4,920 feet, reach the crest of Sasse Ridge and rejoin the road (safely beyond an exposed slope). Where the road divides, stay right to reach a corniced trailhead parking area at 5 miles (5,400 feet). To continue, head east. Stay just to the right of the ridge crest. At 6 1/2 miles, the ridge rounds to the end of a basin and reaches a 6,100-foot high point. Follow the ridge south, descending to cross a saddle, then ascend the north ridge to the crest of 6,443-foot Jolly Mountain.

Cle Elum River

56 LAKE EASTON SNO-PARK

Open to: skis and snowshoes
Surface: groomed
Rating: easiest
Round trip: up to 5 miles
Skiing time: 3 hours
Elevation gain: 50 feet
High point: 2,230 feet
Best: January–February
Avalanche potential: low
Map: park handout

If you are looking for a lot of scenery and a long day of skiing, this is the wrong area—but short trails and rolling hills make this an ideal area for families and first-time skiers. Young kids will be able to ski all of the park's 5 miles of groomed trails and still have time for some sledding off the banks of Wind Tunnel Way.

Note: With an elevation of only 2,180 feet, Lake Easton lies at the transition zone between rain and snow. Grooming starts later here than at Snoqualmie Pass, and expect the snow to melt earlier in the season. On low snow years, don't expect snow here at all. Of course, it is always best to call the Snoqualmie Pass cross-country skiers' information line to get an update before heading out: (509) 674-2222.

Access: Drive Interstate 90 to the Easton Exit, 70 (located 17 miles east of Snoqualmie Pass). Head east, on the south side of the freeway, for 0.6 mile before making a right turn into the park. Continue straight on the main road for 0.1 mile, then take a right and head back west for

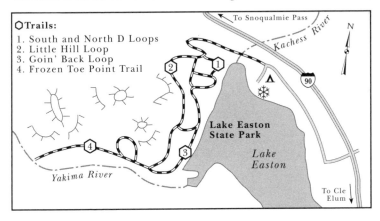

Trails:
1. South and North D Loops
2. Little Hill Loop
3. Goin' Back Loop
4. Frozen Toe Point Trail

To Snoqualmie Pass

Kachess River

N

90

Lake Easton
State Park

Lake
Easton

Yakima River

To Cle
Elum

0.5 mile. Pass the first parking area, which is mainly used by snowmobilers, and park in the second lot, which has the added advantage of being right next to the heated restrooms. A Special Groomed Area sticker is needed, in addition to the required sno-park pass, for parking.

The Tour: The trail starts at the parking lot, in conjunction with a snowmobile trail. In theory, snowmobiles are supposed to stay to the right, where they have their own groomed trail. Skiers stay to the left. This first section is called Wind Tunnel Way. The trail climbs over a low hill, then descends to cross Kachess River at the windblown "Fishing Bridge." A few feet beyond, ski past the best sledding area in the park, then begin a slow but steady climb out of the wind to the S-curves, which generally are kid pleasers; adults seem to prefer the shortcut.

At ³/₄ mile is the first of several intersections. This is also the start of the one-way trail loop. Stay right and ski the forested Little Hill Loop. The name says it all, for the next ³/₄ mile. If you stay right on the groomed trail at all intersections, eventually you will end up on

the Frozen Toe Point Trail. Stay right; the old bridge on the left is very dangerous and a slip could be fatal. The Frozen Toe Point Trail follows the old railroad grade west, passing some old shacks and climbing very gradually past frozen rock walls, where the railroad grade was blasted into the hillside. Frozen Toe Point is located at the bridge over the Kachess River. At the time of this writing, the bridge was gated.

On the way back, you'll follow the forested Goin' Back Loop. Even if you take the extra South and North D Loops, you'll soon find yourself heading back to the parking area and wishing for more.

Frozen Toe Point Trail

57 CABIN CREEK NORDIC SKI AREA

Open to: skis only
Surface: groomed
Rating: easiest to most difficult
Round trip: up to 10 miles
Skiing time: 4 hours
Elevation gain: 200 feet
High point: 2,600 feet
Best: mid-December–March
Avalanche potential: none
Map: *Green Trails* Snoqualmie Pass #207

The title of "most popular" of the Interstate 90 sno-parks could be a bit daunting, if you thought you were heading out to explore the winter's peace and wonders in quiet solitude. On weekends the parking lot fills up, and midday arrivals may have to go elsewhere. For everyone else, the varied terrain and excellently groomed trails guarantee endless fun, challenge, and exercise. Backcountry skiers should keep this area in mind when the avalanche danger on the surrounding hills renders them unsafe for telemarking.

Cabin Creek Nordic Ski Area is a joint venture by the Kongsberger Ski Club and Washington State Sno-Parks. Skiers will see the ski club cabin (please respect their privacy and keep out) on the east side of the road. Approximately four times each winter, some of the trails are closed for races. The schedule is posted in the parking area. Don't

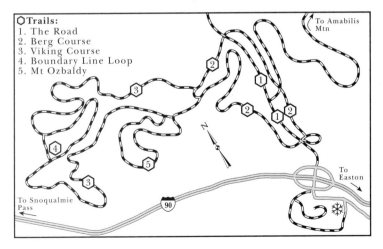

Trails:
1. The Road
2. Berg Course
3. Viking Course
4. Boundary Line Loop
5. Mt Ozbaldy

Skier on Viking Course Trail

worry; there are plenty of places to explore, even on race days.

Access: Drive Interstate 90 to the Cabin Creek Exit 63, located 10.3 miles east of Snoqualmie Pass. Park in one of the two lots on the west side of the freeway (elevation 2,400 feet). Be sure to display your sno-park pass, as well as a Special Groomed Area permit.

The Tour: The main body of trails lies on the east side of the freeway. However, on race days, or if you parked in the lower lot, the 1½-mile Cabin Creek South Trail is a great way to start your day. Along the way you will pass a trail to Stampede Pass Road. This trail is not groomed and is nearly impassable unless there is an abundance of snow. The Cabin Creek South Trail ends at the upper parking area. Take your skis off and walk straight across the overpass to find the main body of trails on the other side.

Trails are all appropriately marked with difficulty levels. Some trails have extremely steep sections. If you choose to walk, please move off the trail. The Road is the *easiest*, with only gently rolling terrain.

The Road is the only trail that is two-way. Please follow the signs; it helps traffic flow and improves the safety for everyone on the steep descents.

On race days, you may wish to explore the Amabilis Mountain trail, which takes off from The Road or the Berg Course. The lower section is occasionally groomed. See Tour 58 for details.

58 AMABILIS MOUNTAIN

Open to: all uses
Surface: ungroomed forest road
Rating: most difficult
Loop trip: 8 miles
Skiing time: 5 hours
Elevation gain: 2,154 feet
High point: 4,554 feet
Best: January–March
Avalanche potential: low
Map: *Green Trails* Snoqualmie Pass #207

Ski the gleaming summit ridge of 4,554-foot Amabilis Mountain to find poster-perfect views of Kachess Lake, Keechelus Lake, Mount Catherine, Silver Peak, and, above all, Mount Rainier, then sweep a few telemarker's signatures on the open slopes before cruising back down the steeply graded roads.

This very popular loop tour over the top of Amabilis Mountain is just one of several favorite trips that bring people to the Cabin Creek Sno-Park by the hundreds on most winter weekends. Tour 57, Cabin Creek Nordic Ski Area, describes the groomed trails. This tour details the land above the crowds. No matter where you are planning to spend the day, arrive early; parking runs out by 10:00 A.M. on weekends. A sno-park pass and a Special Groomed Area permit are required.

Access: Drive Interstate 90 east from Snoqualmie Pass 10.3 miles to Cabin Creek Exit 63. The sno-park is located on the west side of the

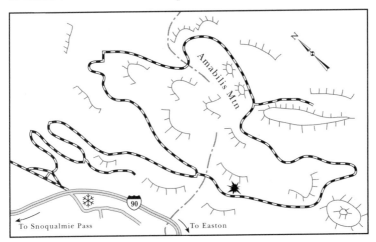

Keechelus Lake from Amabilis Mountain

freeway (2,400 feet). If the upper lot is full, try the lower lot.

The Tour: From the sno-park, walk the overpass to the north side of the freeway and begin your tour on a broad, snow-covered road. Ski straight through the first intersection to find Amabilis Mountain Road a few hundred feet beyond, on the right. The climb starts immediately.

The route switchbacks uphill, passing several old spur roads, first to the left, then to the right. Occasional windows in the forest give glimpses of massive Keechelus Ridge and the Swamp Lake area.

The first major intersection, reached at 2 miles (3,300 feet), marks the start of the loop. You can reach the top from either direction; however, the best views are to the left. In the next mile the road will lead you across a massive clearcut to the north end of the mountain, then turn your skis back to the south with a sweeping switchback. At this point you are on open slopes, just below the long crest of Amabilis Mountain. From here on the road is often windswept and hard to follow. Parallel the ridge crest, climbing steadily.

After 1 3/4 miles of scenic ridge top skiing, you will reach a line of trees. Go right and skirt along the west side of the trees for 1/4 mile. You will first descend, then traverse south, to intersect a major road (4,470).

For the loop return, go straight where you intersect the road and head down a long switchback to close the loop portion of the tour at 6 miles. This leg of the loop crosses a steep avalanche chute and should not be skied when the snow is unstable.

Telemarkers will find possibilities everywhere. Either head back the way you came and pick a likely looking slope, or follow the loop route to more clearcuts on the southern end of the mountain.

59 STAMPEDE PASS

Open to: all uses
Surface: groomed for snowmobiles
Rating: more difficult
Round trip: 10 miles
Skiing time: 4 hours
Elevation gain: 1,300 feet
High point: 3,700 feet
Best: December–March
Avalanche potential: low
Map: *Green Trails* Snoqualmie Pass #207

Miles of roads to climb, high-speed descents through open clearcuts, choice winter campsites, and delightful views combine to make Stampede Pass an enjoyable day or weekend ski tour. The only drawback to this otherwise perfect area is the snowmobile drivers, many of whom appear to need to prove their manhood by rocketing their motors at galactic speeds along the snow-covered roads.

Many of the roads in the Stampede Pass area are groomed for snowmobile use. These wonderfully groomed roads are often very quiet from Monday through Friday, making them ideal midweek diagonal stride and skating areas.

Access: Follow Interstate 90 for 10.2 miles east of Snoqualmie Pass to the Stampede Pass/Kachess Lake Exit 62. Go right and drive past the Crystal Spring Campground. Cross the Yakima River, then

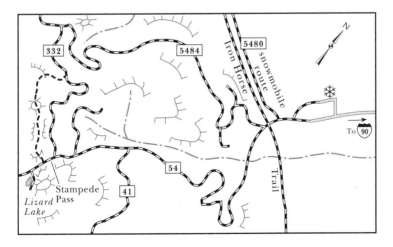

take the first right, into the massive Crystal Springs Sno-Park.

The Tour: Carry your skis to the west side of the parking area and follow the snowmobiles and skiers through the trees to meet the main road at a wide intersection. Encroaching homeowners are keeping the road plowed and attempting to push out the skiers and snowmobilers. Give the homes a wide berth.

Continue straight up Road 54, crossing the groomed Iron Horse Trail at 1/4 mile. Shortly after the road divides, stay left with Road 54 as it swings east, starting the long climb to the pass.

Climb steadily to the powerline clearing at 1 1/2 miles. At this point, the road begins a short series of switchbacks, where you will find excellent views of the Yakima River valley, Amabilis Mountain, and the Keechelus Ridge area. Near the 3-mile mark you will encounter another major intersection, as Road 41 to Easton (popular with snowmobilers) branches left.

Stampede Pass Road heads to the right and carves across the steep, forested walls of Mosquito Creek valley. As you climb, you will pass two roads on the right; the second one, Spur Road 332, connects with Road 5484 and is groomed for snowmobiles. (This spur can be used as a loop back to the start.) At 4 miles the road crests the unpretentious summit of 3,700-foot Stampede Pass.

From Stampede Pass, you can explore miles of connecting roads and open ridge tops. A favorite destination is Lizard Lake, a small, sheltered pond located just 300 feet beyond the pass on the left. Also consider a side trip to the U.S. government weather station, located 1 1/2 miles south (reached by a small road from Lizard Lake). Excellent campsites abound throughout this area.

If you have a map and moderately good navigation skills, you can loop back to the start by either following the route of the Pacific Crest Trail north or descending back to Spur Road 332. To find the Pacific Crest Trail, locate a narrow bench on the north side of the road, about 100 feet on the east side of Stampede Pass. Ski along the narrow bench for about 50 feet, then go right and contour up to the base of a steep slope. (The trail is usually invisible at this point.) Stay in the trees on the left side of the ridge until you reach the ridge crest. Once on the ridge top, follow the path of the Pacific Crest Trail. Using the ridge as a guide, ski along the west side of the crest and follow it over a second hill to a large clear-cut valley.

Continue following the ridge as it meanders in a northwesterly direction to its end, on a hilltop (4,360 feet) overlooking clear-cut Meadow Creek valley. Turn left on the snowmobile-groomed Spur Road 332 and ski the ridge down to a small saddle. Stay right and follow the road on a traverse across the side of a steep hill to a major, but un-signed, intersection. Take a sharp right on Road 5484 for a sweeping descent across a steep hillside. The road swings around a small lake and continues on a steady descent that lasts for 3 miles. The downhill rush ends at Stampede Pass Road. Go left and ski across the old railroad grade at 9 1/2 miles. Return to Crystal Springs Sno-Park at 10 miles.

Ski tracks on slope near Stampede Pass

60 THAT DAM LOOP

Open to: skis and snowshoes
Surface: groomed
Rating: more difficult
Loop trip: 5 miles
Skiing time: 3 hours
Elevation gain: 80 feet
High point: 2,480 feet
Best: mid-December–February
Avalanche potential: low
Map: *Green Trails* Snoqualmie Pass #207

Loops are fun and this one is no exception. Meander through the forest, cross a snow-laced stream, skim over the Yakima River, and ski across Keechelus Lake Dam on a trail perched at the very top. (*Note:* Price Creek Sno-Park and trail across the dam will be closed until the winter of 2003–2004, while the dam is being repaired.)

Access: Drive Interstate 90 east 9.1 miles from the Snoqualmie Pass summit to the *eastbound* Price Creek Sno-Park (2,480 feet). (Note that there is also a westbound Price Creek Sno-Park, and there is no access between the two. Westbound traffic must drive all the way to the Hyak/Rocky Run Exit 54 to return to the eastbound sno-park.) A sno-park permit with Special Groomed Area sticker is required.

The Tour: The trail begins as an unsigned corridor through the trees from the northwest end of the parking lot. This trail heads west for 50 feet through the trees, then turns abruptly left (south) at an

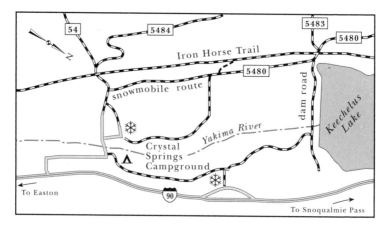

unmarked intersection. Note the narrow road on the right; it is the return leg of the loop.

Wander through the forest on a quiet, nearly level, groomed skier trail. After a mile in the forest, picnic tables announce your arrival at Crystal Springs Campground. Shortly beyond is Stampede Pass Road No. 54; you may need to remove your skis and walk. Go right, crossing the Yakima River on the car bridge. Continue along the road for 500 feet to an intersection with the road to the Crystal Springs Sno-Park. Walk right, into the sno-park, and head straight to a signpost, which marks the start of the groomed cross-country ski trail.

The trail takes you around a gravel pit, where there is usually a snowmobile rodeo of riders bombing here and there, then heads into the relatively peaceful forest. At the end of a mile, the groomed skiers' trail intersects Lost Lake Road 5480. Cross the road and contour up the steep hillside to the Iron Horse railroad grade to find a well-groomed trail at the top. Head right.

At the 3-mile point the railroad grade crosses Road 5480. Your third right turn for the day takes you off the railroad grade and onto the main road. Cross the road and continue straight, on Keechelus Lake Dam Road. Cross over (or around) a snow-covered gate, then ski along the top of Keechelus Lake Dam. In good weather, make this your picnic site, as it's the best viewpoint. Enjoy the snow-capped peaks rising above the lake and the ice-clogged Yakima River flowing from it.

On the far side of the dam, note the maintenance buildings in a clearing below. Descend a ramp and ski across the clearing on the left side of the buildings, then head straight into the forest on a wide trail paralleling a line of telephone poles. When you reach an open flood plain, find a trail, marked with blue diamonds, on your left. The marked trail leads to a bridge over a stream, followed by a short, steep climb. At the top, take a left turn to return to the sno-park.

Small stream crossed on That Dam Loop

61 KENDALL—KNOBS, LAKES, AND LOOPS

Open to: skis and snowshoes
Surface: forest road
Rating: more difficult
Round trip: 7 miles
Skiing time: 4 hours
Elevation gain: 1,700 feet
High point: 4,400 feet
Best: December–April
Avalanche potential: moderate
Map: *Green Trails* Snoqualmie Pass #207

Open slopes, grand views, and two small lakes nestled in the forest are just some of the features of this vast area below Kendall Peak. This is a unique sno-park in the Snoqualmie Pass area, where snowmobiles are not allowed and the cross-country trail groomer never ventures. A sno-park permit is required; however, the Special Groomed Area sticker is not. Arrive early to secure a parking spot, and be prepared for a lot of company.

One of the reasons this area has been left undeveloped is there is some uncertainty as to how long the sno-park will remain open. Developers intending to build vacation houses in Gold Creek valley wish to eliminate the sno-park and all recreation access to the area. We hope that skier outrage will convince the Forest Service and the State Parks Department to find a way to keep this area open. If you would

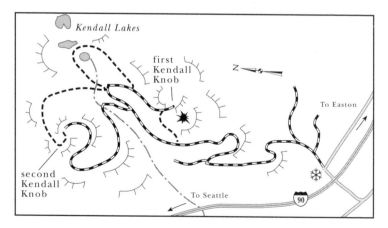

like to help save public parking at Snoqualmie Pass, please write a letter to: North Bend District Ranger, 42404 SE North Bend Way, North Bend, WA 98045. Also write to: Washington State Parks and Recreation Commission, 7150 Cleanwater Lane KY-11, P.O. Box 42650, Olympia, WA 98504-2650.

Access: Drive Interstate 90 east from Snoqualmie Pass 2 miles to Hyak/ Rocky Run Exit 54. Park in the Gold Creek Sno-Park on the north side of the freeway, along the plowed section of the old highway (2,640 feet).

The Tour: Ski up Gold Creek valley on level road. At 1/8 mile, the road turns uphill and climbs quite steeply. The road forks at the 1/2-mile point, stay left and switchback up through an old clearcut. Two major spur roads are passed, the first on the right and the second on the left, as your road heads into the first of two steep switchbacks, where the views start to get exciting. At 2 miles (3,600 feet), the road swings north through a band of trees, then crosses an old clearcut with excellent views of the skiers on the slopes at Summit Central. Pass a spur road on the left, then a road on the right, as you head up into a fold of the hill. At 3 1/4 miles the road divides at a switchback; go right and continue climbing until the road reaches a narrow saddle on a ridge. Go right and ski to the road's end on a flat landing atop the 4,400-foot summit of the first Kendall Knob.

If you are still looking for more adventure, consider a short side trip to Kendall Lakes. The lakes offer a peaceful backcountry escape as well as an outstanding run down through the trees. From the narrow saddle directly below the first Kendall Knob, go left and climb up over two short rises. At the top of the second rise, leave the road. Head left into the trees, then traverse north to a stream drainage. Turn uphill and follow the stream to the lowest lake (4,300 feet), a short 1/2 mile above the first Kendall Knob. The second lake lies another 1/4 mile up the valley. This is the turnaround point, as serious avalanche hazard lies beyond.

For the return trip, ski straight down the valley from the lakes to intersect the road leading to the first knob. Widely spaced trees provide telemarkers with fun obstacles to negotiate, and the snow remains powdery long after the exposed slopes turn to mush.

For some excellent telemarking and views galore, try out the slopes up the main road on the second Kendall Knob for 3 1/8 miles. At this point you will have passed the switchbacks, skied through the forest, crossed the old clearcut, and traversed a recent clearcut slope, to a point where a steep hill rises on the left. Shortly beyond, a road takes off on the right and then another road branches off to the left. Take the lefthand road and ski across the clearcut. You will descend slightly to cross Coal Creek and then climb again. The road ends in an open basin near the top. Continue on, breaking your own trail for the final 1/4 mile to the 4,720-foot summit of the second knob.

For the descent, the slopes heading due west down from the summit are the most open and stable. The slopes on the south side are steep and rocky and should only be skied in very stable conditions.

Evening view of Snoqualmie Pass

62 THE IRON HORSE TRAIL

Open to: nonmotorized
Surface: groomed
Rating: easiest
Round trip: up to 15 miles
Skiing time: up to 6 hours
Elevation gain: 70 feet
High point: 2,540 feet
Best: mid-December–February
Avalanche potential: high
Map: *Green Trails* Snoqualmie Pass #207

A nearly level tour? Perfect for beginners and young families? Ideal for skating or an aerobic diagonal-stride workout? Yes, yes, and yes!

For this rare gem of a tour we can thank the hard-working Rails-to-Trails program, whose energetic pursuit of the abandoned Milwaukee railroad grade has saved it from the hands of greedy land grabbers and preserved this national treasure for recreational use. At this time, the 7 1/2-mile section of the old railroad grade on the east side of Snoqualmie Pass, between Hyak and Stampede Pass Road, is groomed and reserved for skiers' use during the winter months.

This section of the railroad grade is particularly scenic, and skiers will find sections of quiet forest as well as views from the shores of Keechelus Lake of Kendall Knob, Gold Creek valley, Chikamin Ridge, and Mount Catherine.

The railroad grade provides an almost level tour, and the State Park provides a double set of groomed ski tracks, which are ideal for practicing the long, gliding, diagonal stride of the traditional skier, while the open area between the tracks allows for the high-speed, leg-stretching skate of the nouveau skier.

The railroad grade has many possible turnaround points for round-trip skiers, or, with a car shuttle, you can arrange an 8-mile, one-way tour to the Crystal Springs Sno-Park on Interstate 90. A sno-park pass with the Special Groomed Area sticker is required for parking.

Access: Drive Interstate 90 east from the Snoqualmie Pass summit to Hyak/Rocky Run Exit 54. Following the boat ramp signs, go left just before the Summit East Ski Area entrance and follow a narrow road that parallels Interstate 90 for 0.5 mile. Just before the Department of Transportation complex, go right. After 0.1 mile, go right again, following the State Park signs to the sno-park skiing and

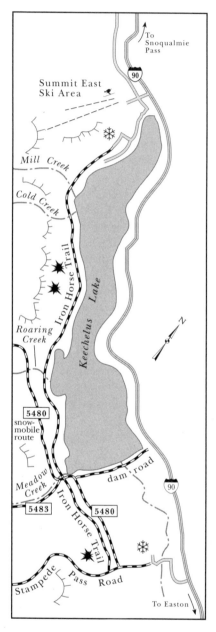

inner-tubing area (2,540 feet).

The Tour: The tour begins on the west side of the parking area and follows the well-maintained railroad grade south. This is a popular tour and you will be sharing the tracks with all types of skiers, from beginners to experts, ages two to ninety-five years old.

The railroad grade follows the access road for 1/8 mile, then passes a snow-covered parking area. Soon after, the trail bends and begins its swing around the west side of Keechelus Lake. The railroad grade stays in the trees as it rounds a cove to cross first Mill Creek, then Cold Creek, at 1 1/4 miles. The tour continues through the trees for another 1/2 mile then returns to the lakeshore.

At 2 1/2 miles the railroad grade passes under a cliff, a very dangerous area when the snow is unstable. When the trains used to travel this route, they were sheltered here by two snow sheds. Old woodwork from the sheds can still be seen on the hillside above. A large red sign warns you of the danger before you enter this area. Use considerable caution and do not linger when passing through this hazardous area. The avalanche area lasts for 1/4 mile, after which the tour is once again relatively avalanche-free.

The railroad grade parallels the lake for a time, then plows across a small peninsula before returning to the lakeshore. At 4 1/4 miles you will cross the Roaring Creek bridge. Continue south, dodging in and out of the trees with occasional views until, at 5 3/4 miles, you cross Meadow Creek and soon after arrive at an intersection. To the left lies the Keechelus Lake dam, a great place for a sunny-day picnic and the ideal turnaround point if you are heading back to the north end of the lake.

The railroad grade crosses Meadow Creek Road and continues south. The road and railroad grade are close together in this section, and there is a constant roar of snowmobiles on the road below, shredding the quiet peace of winter. A second avalanche chute is crossed at 7 miles. When the avalanche hazard is high, it is best to descend to the road to cross this section, then return to the railroad grade for the final 1/2 mile.

At 7 1/2 miles the railroad grade crosses Stampede Pass Road. Go left here to ski out to the Crystal Springs Sno-Park.

Iron Horse Trail near Crystal Springs Sno-Park

63 MOUNT CATHERINE LOOP

Open to: skis only
Surface: groomed
Rating: backcountry
Loop trip: 10 1/2 miles
Skiing time: 6 hours
Elevation gain: 1,520 feet
High point: 4,060 feet
Best: mid-December–April
Avalanche potential: low
Map: *Green Trails* Snoqualmie Pass #207

Not long ago, cross-country skiers were stereotyped as long-haired hippies. Their wooden skis smelled of pine tar. They wore scratchy woolen clothes and used bamboo ski poles that left peace-sign imprints in the snow. Those so-called "granola" skiers used to drive to Snoqualmie Pass, park with the downhill skiers, and then head out to the uncharted forest behind the ski areas.

Today the uncharted forests have been replaced by groomed ski trails, with two sets of machine-made tracks for classic skiers and a wide lane for skaters in the middle. This is a marvelous place to witness how modern technology has transformed the sport. The "granola" skiers have shed their natural skin for one of plastic: skis, poles, boots, and even clothing.

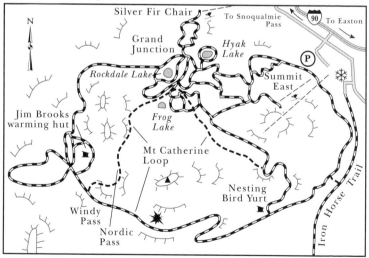

Thanks to The Mountaineers and the Sierra Club, as well as cheerful cooperation from the Summit Nordic Center, backcountry skiers can still access their traditional telemarking grounds and complete the ever-popular loop around Mount Catherine. This is a difficult route that is partially on groomed trails and partially on steep, forested hillsides.

Access: Drive Interstate 90 east from the Snoqualmie Pass summit to Hyak/Rocky Run Exit 54. Following the boat ramp signs, go left just before the Summit East Ski Area entrance and follow a narrow road that parallels Interstate 90 for 0.5 mile. Just before the Department of Transportation complex, go right. After 0.1 mile, go right again, following the Iron Horse State Park signs to the sno-park skiing and inner-tubing area (2,540 feet).

The Tour: Ski east from the parking area on the groomed railroad grade. After a level, and very easy, 3/4 mile, look to the right for a blue diamond on a tree just before the railroad grade crosses Mill Creek. Leave the groomed railroad grade and head uphill on a difficult trail that contours through the forest, heading steadily up the hillside.

After a couple of short switchbacks, the trail ends on the groomed cross-country trail, which originates at the Summit Nordic Center. Go left on what is called a "shared corridor" and follow the groomed road. After 1/4 mile, the road dips, crosses Mill Creek (2,660 feet), and then begins to climb. At 1 3/4 miles, reach a well-signed intersection. The best method for the loop is to continue straight ahead for the long, steady climb to Windy Pass.

At 3 miles is the first of two switchbacks and the beginning of great views. Use caution at the second switchback; it seems to be the literal downfall of many skiers, and those heading uphill should definitely be ready to jump out of the way. Reach aptly named Windy Pass at 5 miles (3,800 feet). The common corridor ends here, and skiers without passes must go off the groomed trail and head across the open slopes.

Ski to the right and climb the steep slope to the trees, then continue on up the hillside to the narrow, forested Nordic Pass (4,000 feet). Staying on the route as it heads down through the dense forest becomes a challenge. Keep on the left (north) side of the valley, following the occasional marker until you reach a logging road at 6 miles. Continue straight ahead to find a well-marked trail maintained by The Mountaineers and the Sierra Club.

The trail route takes you down the untracked slopes, paralleling but avoiding the groomed tracks. When there is sufficient snow to cover all the small trees and scrub brush, skiing can be excellent. The trail ends at the upper reaches of the Mill Creek valley. The common corridor comes back into effect, and groomed trails are followed for nearly a mile to an outstanding viewpoint over Keechelus Lake, Mount Margaret, and Keechelus Ridge (3,200 feet).

Beyond the viewpoint the road drops. Skiers afraid of the outstanding claims of gravity in this area may even walk the upper section. The loop portion ends at 9 miles. Go left and descend back to the Iron Horse Trail.

Skiing a groomed trail

64 SUMMIT NORDIC CENTER

Open to: skis and snowshoes
Surface: groomed
Rating: easy to most difficult
Round trip: up to 30 miles
Skiing time: 4 or more hours
Elevation gain: 500 feet
High point: 3,808 feet
Best: mid-December–March
Avalanche potential: moderate
Maps: *Green Trails* Snoqualmie Pass #207 and resort handout map

High above Snoqualmie Pass chairlifts, and a world apart from the rat race of alpine skiers and snowboarders, is an intricate web of outstandingly groomed cross-country ski trails. With twenty-eight trails to choose from, a main lodge with heated bathrooms and food service, two warming huts to relax in, a rental shop for gear you don't own or simply forgot to bring, lessons aimed at making your day on skis more enjoyable in this mountainous terrain (they teach you how to go down hills), and night skiing on Wednesdays, this resort rivals Sun Mountain in the Methow Valley.

A trail pass may seem expensive, but it comes with a ride on the chairlift, allowing skiers to be *whooshed* up from the valley floor to the ridge crests 500 vertical feet above.

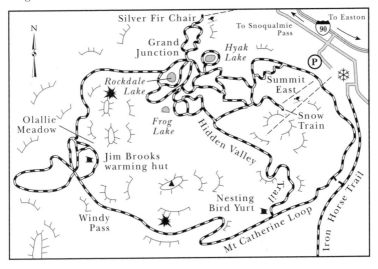

Access: Drive Interstate 90 to the Hyak/Rocky Run Exit 54, located on the east side of the Snoqualmie Pass summit. If coming from the west, drive straight ahead from the end of the exit ramp into the Summit East/Hyak area. If coming from the east, go left off the exit to find the entrance on the left. Go 0.1 mile into the Summit East/Hyak area, then take a left on Hyak R.E. Descend a short 1,000 feet, then turn right on Keechelus Drive. Follow this narrow road for 0.1 mile to the entrance of the main parking area. Overnight parking is allowed. The lodge is located directly up the hill, to the left. A sno-park permit is not needed to park here.

The Tour: Once you have purchased your trail pass, you are set to explore. True novices should consider trying out their skis on the lower loops, followed by a tour on the Mount Catherine Loop to a scenic vista over Keechelus Lake. Skiers with any kind of previously learned descending skills should head up to the Keechelus Chair and ride to the top. After you get off the chair, descend straight down the hill to find the start of the Nordic trail system. The first trail is called Snow Train, and it leads down to the main network of trails, which connects with the Grand Junction and Inner Loops area. Not all junctions are marked, and not all junctions make sense. Ski to enjoy and explore.

Descending from Keechelus Chair

If you choose to ski out to Grand Junction, you can take the Rockdale Trail over to Olallie Meadow and Jim Brooks warming hut in just 3.8 kilometers (2 1/4 miles). Use caution if you decide to head down to the Nesting Bird Yurt at the lower end of the Hidden Valley Trail. The trail drops over a cliff and is very tricky when icy.

Rockdale and parts of the Mount Catherine Loop cross avalanche zones. Gates are put up when the snow is unstable, and skiers are not allowed to pass. Ask about snow conditions before you buy your ticket if the closing of those trails will disrupt your day.

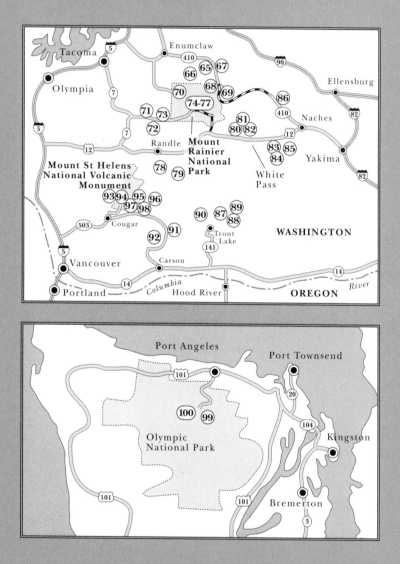

South Cascade and Olympic Regions

From the crater rims of Washington's loftiest volcanoes to gently rolling foothills, the South Cascades offers a plethora of skiing experiences. From groomed trails at White Pass to ice fields on Mount Rainier, skiers can spend years exploring the possibilities here.

The Olympic Mountains, on the other hand, offer very limited skiing opportunities. The mountains at the center of the range are extremely steep and avalanche prone, and skiing is too risky to be recommended. The variable weather and radically fluctuating snow line make it nearly impossible to rely on the foothill areas for ski touring. The only place where there is enough snow for an extended period throughout the winter is Hurricane Ridge. Both of the Olympic Mountain tours start there.

Both the South Cascade and Olympic Regions are subject to frequent variations in the weather. Skiers should always carry waterproof outwear, even for short trips. Road conditions can vary radically from day to day. Plowing is infrequent in some of the more isolated locations, and drivers should come prepared with a shovel and tire chains.

65 SUNTOP MOUNTAIN SNO-PARK

Huckleberry Creek
Open to: skis only
Surface: groomed
Rating: easiest
Round trip: 9½ miles
Skiing time: 4 hours
Elevation gain: 700 feet
High point: 2,900 feet
Best: mid-December–February
Avalanche potential: low
Map: *Green Trails* Greenwater #238

Suntop Lookout Road
Open to: skis only
Surface: groomed
Rating: most difficult
Round trip: 10–11 miles
Skiing time: 6 hours
Elevation gain: 2,180, or 3,030 feet to summit
High point: 4,420, or 5,279 at summit
Best: December–March
Avalanche potential: low to saddle, high to summit
Map: *Green Trails* Greenwater # 238

If we were rating sno-parks on a scale of one to ten, Suntop would receive a twenty. Not long ago, this entire area was overrun by snowmobiles. Skiers were harassed regularly, and backcountry campsites

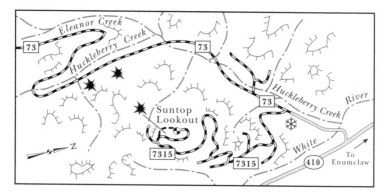

were blitzed by speeding machines. Thanks to the cooperation of the state-funded sno-park system and the Forest Service, this area has been turned into a true haven for skiers.

The Suntop Sno-Park is the starting point for two very different types of tours. One is an easy glide on a nearly level road up the Huckleberry Creek valley. The second is a steep climb to a spectacular viewpoint on Suntop Mountain.

Access: Drive Highway 410 east from Enumclaw 24.2 miles, then turn right on Huckleberry Creek Road No. 73. The road usually is plowed for the 1.4 miles to the sno-park (2,240 feet). A sno-park pass is required.

Huckleberry Creek: Ski around the gate to an intersection. Go straight on broad, nearly level Huckleberry Creek Road No. 73 to an intersection at 1/4 mile. Stay left, watching for elk and deer tracks in the snow as you ski. Spur roads abound, and with them are numerous opportunities for exploration and snow play. At 3/4 mile you will reach a major intersection; stay left on Road 73 and ski through beautiful old-growth forest. This congenial tour has numerous places that make excellent turnaround points, should small legs (or inexperienced ones) get tired.

Before long the road brushes near the creek. The tour continues through the forest of Huckleberry Creek valley, then returns to the creek again at about 1 1/2 miles. Look for spur roads on the right if you would like to take a closer look at the water. The road wanders away from the creek and returns to it several more times.

At 4 miles the road crosses a narrow avalanche chute. The chute slides early in the season and at regular intervals thereafter. Be cautious here at all times and particularly so during or just after heavy precipitation. The grooming ends at 4 3/4 miles, where Road 73 crosses Huckleberry Creek. The road continues on, climbing to the crest of Huckleberry Ridge (see Tour 66 for details).

Suntop Lookout Road: From the sno-park, ski around the gate to an intersection. Turn left and head uphill on Road 7315. The climb is steady and the road slips rapidly through a green-and-white patchwork of forest and clearcut, passing an occasional side road. By the end of the first mile you will reach the first of many viewpoints overlooking the White River valley and east to Dallas Ridge. Near the 2-mile point, Spur Road 301 branches to the right, offering views over Huckleberry Creek, and 1/2 mile farther, Spur Road 401 branches to the left, ending in a clearcut overlooking the White River valley.

At about 5 miles, the road makes a final switchback to the forested

Mount Rainier from Suntop Mountain

4,420-foot saddle below Suntop. This is the best place to end the tour. Between the saddle and the summit, the road crosses several extremely dangerous avalanche slopes. Most of the views seen from the summit can be found by continuing straight across the saddle for 1/2 mile to excellent vantage points of Mount Rainier.

For those choosing to continue to the summit of Suntop despite the very real hazard of avalanches, go right and follow the road up from the saddle to the edge of the trees. Ski (climbing skins are a must) or hike directly up the south rib to the lookout, following the summer trail. Do not ski the road beyond the edge of the trees, as both the east and west sides of the summit pyramid are extremely hazardous. After heavy snowfall, no route to the summit is safe, and skiers should turn back at the saddle.

66 GRAND PARK

Open to: skis and snowshoes
Surface: forest roads and trails
Rating: backcountry
Round trip: 21 miles
Skiing time: 2–3 days
Elevation gain: 3,540 feet
High point: 5,640 feet
Best: January–March
Avalanche potential: moderate
Maps: *Green Trails* Greenwater #238 and Mt. Rainier East #270

Any strong, competent skier with decent routefinding skills and a couple of days to spare can reach the wide meadows of Grand Park, just a stone's throw from the northeast base of what locals refer to as "The Mountain"—Mount Rainier. Camping on a clear night in Grand Park in full view of The Mountain is a once-in-a-lifetime experience, and skiing across the broad meadow under a full moon is truly memorable.

Access: Drive Highway 410 east from Enumclaw 24.2 miles, then turn right on Huckleberry Creek Road No. 73. The road usually is plowed for the 1.4 miles to the Suntop Sno-Park (2,240 feet), where a sno-park pass is required.

The Tour: From the sno-park, follow Road 73 (the Huckleberry Creek Trail; see Tour 65 for details). The road starts off as a nearly level cruise. Stay left at 1/4 mile. After a mile in the trees, the road enters clearcuts in Huckleberry Creek valley and parallels the creek. At 4 miles, cross a narrow avalanche chute. The chute slides early in the season and at regular intervals thereafter. Be cautious here at all times and particularly so during or just after heavy precipitation.

At 4 3/4 miles, Huckleberry Creek (2,960 feet) is crossed. From this point the road gains elevation for 1 1/2 miles, then, at the 3,680-foot

Grand Park and Mount Rainier

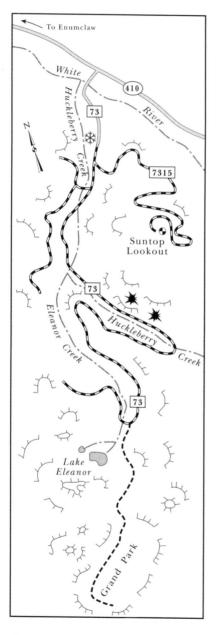

level, bends sharply into the Eleanor Creek drainage. The climb becomes less urgent, and after 2 more miles the road again turns abruptly to cross Eleanor Creek (4,480 feet). Leave the road and enter the forest left (east) of the Eleanor Creek crossing. Head straight ahead to the trees, and in a few yards you will cross the park boundary.

The next 3 miles is an unmarked backcountry route, through the trees to Grand Park, that requires a good map. From the National Park boundary, head straight through the forest, going south-southeast, keeping to the left of the small valley, between Scarface to the west and the ridge to the east. If you come to Lake Eleanor, you have gone too far to the west and need to head east for 1/2 mile, before skiing a southwest course up a rolling ridge. There is a short, steep descent, followed by a traverse across an open bench; stay to the right. You may spot blazes and other signs of a summer trail from Lake Eleanor on. When the bench ends, the trail continues to follow the ridge, climbing steeply along the left side of a forested hump to reach the edge of the meadows 2 miles from the road. Continue forward, staying generally to the right of the ridge crest, to reach the vast expanse and awesome views of 5,600-foot Grand Park.

67 CORRAL PASS

Open to: all users
Surface: forest road
Rating: most difficult
Round trip: 9 miles to the pass
Skiing time: 6 hours
Elevation gain: 3,000 feet
High point: 5,700 feet
Best: December–mid-May
Avalanche potential: low
Maps: *Green Trails* Mt. Rainier East #270, Greenwater #238, and
   Lester #239

Here's a tour for the entire snow season—be it late fall, midwinter, or early spring. And don't limit your explorations of the Corral Pass environs to day-use only; the tent sites here are notably scenic.

Corral Pass Road starts at 2,700 feet and climbs, and climbs, and then climbs some more, gaining 3,000 feet in just 4 1/2 miles. No matter how fast you start at the bottom, your momentum will slow before you reach the top. Carry a lot of water and energy food, and pace yourself; the goal is worth the effort.

Access: Drive Highway 410 from Enumclaw east through Greenwater and on. Note the mileage as you pass the Four Season Mountain Resort, and continue east for 0.5 mile to Corral Pass Road No. 7174, located on the lefthand side of the highway. Corral Pass

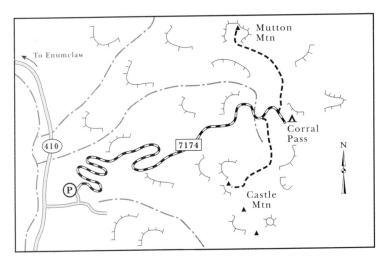

Skiers' camp above Corral Pass, Mount Rainier in distance

Road starts by winding past a power station and vacation cabins for 1/2 mile to an intersection (2,850 feet). Ideally you should park at the intersection; if you must park lower on the road, take care not to block anyone's cabin access. In midwinter, parking is difficult, especially if the snow level has been below 3,000 feet for a week or so. If you cannot find a place to park along Road 7174, you will need to rethink your plans and go elsewhere. Suntop Mountain Lookout (Tour 65) and Grand Park (Tour 66) are good alternatives.

The Tour: From the intersection, go right, up Road 7174, and climb. Steep switchback follows steep switchback until you arrive at an open meadow below Castle Mountain (5,300 feet) after 3 3/4 miles. If time allows, ski the delightful slopes at the south and southwest end of the meadow, on an offshoot ridge of Castle Mountain.

Corral Pass is reached at 4 1/2 miles (5,700 feet). Ski right at the pass to find a large open area, parking lot, summertime picnic area, and winter campsite. For an alternative campsite, continue along the road to Corral Pass Campground, located on a small, frozen stream running through the trees.

For the best views, ski north to Mutton Mountain. From Corral Pass, ski straight east, up the hillside and through a band of trees. At the first open area, turn north and climb up to the ridge top. Continue north over several small rolls until the ridge drops off in front of your skis. Descend west to a saddle, then climb to rounded Mutton Mountain (5,900 feet). If you got this far without noticing the view, now is the time to feast your eyes. Mount Rainier fills the horizon to the southwest, while Mount Stuart and the Snoqualmie-area peaks rise to the east. Finally, Noble Knob to the north and Castle Mountain to the south scratch the sky as well.

192

68 SILVER CREEK SKI ROUTE

Open to: all users
Surface: forest road
Rating: easiest
Round trip: up to 23 miles
Skiing time: 1–2 days
Elevation gain: up to 1,742 feet
High point: up to 4,232 feet
Best: mid-December–March
Avalanche potential: low
Map: *Green Trails* Mt. Rainier East #270

The Silver Creek Ski Route offers winter access to the White River area of Mount Rainier National Park. The route follows Highway 410 from the Crystal Mountain turnoff to Mather Junction, then heads deeper into the park to end in old-growth forest at White River Campground. The tour passes through an amazing winter wonderland of snow-laced trees, ice-covered creeks, and unexpected vistas. Elk inhabit this area throughout the winter, and ski tracks are often potholed with their hoofprints.

Access: Drive east on Highway 410 to the end of the plowing at the Mount Rainier National Park boundary. Turn left on the Crystal Mountain access road for 100 feet, then go right to enter the Silver Springs Sno-Park (2,740 feet). (The fate of this sno-park is uncertain; check with the National Park office or Enumclaw Forest Service office before you go.)

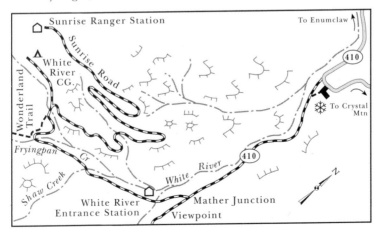

The Tour: Starting at the information board at the northwest end of the sno-park, ski into the trees. Traverse southwest 100 feet to meet Highway 410 at the entrance arch to Mount Rainier National Park. Ski under the arch, then up the road under a dense forest cover. The highway heads up the White River valley; however, you will ski a mile before actually seeing the river.

The road climbs gradually through old-growth timber. Elk tracks are everywhere. If you should happen to be on this route at sundown or in the dark, use caution to avoid running into these large animals.

Near the 2-mile point, the road carves its way across a steep bank with an excellent view of the White River. The climb steepens, not drastically, but just enough to offer an enjoyable glide on the way back. At 4 miles pass the Crystal Lakes Trail on the left. Continue up the road, passing the gravel pile before reaching 3,686-foot Mather Junction at 4 1/2 miles from the sno-park.

When, and only when, the snowpack is stable, skiers may continue on up Highway 410 for another 1/2 mile to a viewpoint over the White River valley to The Mountain. The viewpoint is a broad turnout located on the righthand side of the road (3,840 feet). Turn around here; beyond, the road crosses one avalanche slope after another.

From Mather Junction, skiers heading into the park should go right on Sunrise Road and descend for the next mile. At 5 1/2 miles, the road crosses Klickitat Creek (3,460 feet) and resumes a very gradual climb. The White River Ranger Station and entrance booths are passed at 5 3/4 miles.

The next 2 miles are spent cruising west. At 7 miles the road crosses Shaw Creek. The Owyhigh Lakes trailhead is passed at 7 3/4 miles. Near the 8 1/2-mile point the road crosses Fryingpan Creek and soon after passes the Wonderland Trail. Burrowing through the old-growth forest, the road heads around the base of Goat Island Mountain, then crosses the White River at 10 miles. Beyond the bridge the road divides; go left and continue up the White River valley on a narrow road that reaches the campground at 11 1/2 miles.

Pick your campsite carefully. Avoid camping under large trees that might dump snow or drop old branches on your tent in the middle of the night. (No drinking water or services are available at the campground.)

Giant icicles adorn the hillside along the Silver Creek Ski Route

69 CHINOOK PASS AND NACHES PEAK

Chinook Pass
Open to: skis and snowshoes
Surface: open slopes
Rating: most difficult
Round trip: 4 miles
Skiing time: 2 hours
Elevation gain: 832 feet
High point: 5,432 feet
Best: November–December
Avalanche potential: low
Map: *Green Trails* Mt. Rainier East #270

Naches Peak (false summit)
Open to: skis and snowshoes
Surface: open slopes
Rating: backcountry
Round trip: 7 miles
Skiing time: 4 hours
Elevation gain: 1,760 feet
High point: 6,360 feet
Best: November–December
Avalanche potential: moderate
Maps: *Green Trails* Mt. Rainier East #270 and Bumping Lake #271

Skiing in the Chinook Pass–Naches Peak area starts when the first major snowstorm hits the Cascades. There is great fun to be had challenging the open bowls leading to Dewey Lakes or simply enjoying the incomparable views of Mount Rainier.

The skiing season around Chinook Pass starts and ends early. Beginning as soon as Chinook Pass is closed for the winter, it ends when

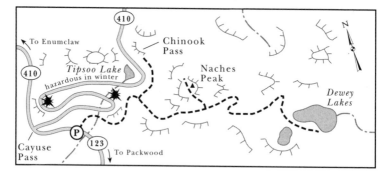

4,694-foot Cayuse Pass is snowed in, usually by mid- to late-December. In late spring there is often another week or two of skiing before the snowplows come to end the fun.

Note: Do not even consider skiing up Highway 410 to Cayuse Pass or Chinook Pass during the midwinter months. The road crosses several steep avalanche slide areas, making travel extremely hazardous. Just getting from Cayuse Pass to Chinook Pass requires a careful following of the directions below.

Access: From Enumclaw, drive Highway 410 for 41 miles to the summit of Cayuse Pass. Cross the pass and park in one of the turnouts just beyond. A sno-park pass is not required for this tour.

Chinook Pass: On skis, contour through the trees below Chinook Pass Highway, heading southeast for 1/4 to 1/2 mile, before heading uphill. Be sure to stay well away from the highway and in the protection of the trees. After 1/2 mile of steep ascent, the route bisects the highway where it makes a switchback north. Follow Highway 410 to reach 5,294-foot Tipsoo Lake and excellent views of Mount Rainier from the snowbound bowl. The road can be followed for the final 1/2 mile to Chinook Pass. Skiing beyond the pass is not recommended, as the steep slopes are avalanche prone.

Naches Peak (false summit): From Tipsoo Lake, follow the road another 500 feet and climb to the smaller, upper Tipsoo Lake. Ski south up a lightly timbered ridge to an open slope below a ridge. Traverse west to gain that ridge, avoiding the cornices above. Once on the ridge crest, follow its south side to the false summit of Naches Peak, the 6,360-foot chief viewpoint of the trip. From the false summit, ski out to Dewey Lakes, or just be satisfied with a great run back to the car. Sections of the descent are steep, so be sure your turns and stopping ability are in good form.

Mount Rainier from the shoulder of Naches Peak

70 MOWICH LAKE

Open to: skis and snowshoes
Surface: forest road
Rating: more difficult
Round trip: 11 miles
Skiing time: 6 hours
Elevation gain: 1,410 feet
High point: 4,960 feet
Best: March–April
Avalanche potential: low
Map: *Green Trails* Mt. Rainier West #269

Nestled in the forest at the base of glacier-wrapped Mount Rainier, Mowich Lake is an excellent tour for a day or a weekend outing. While the area has prime skiing throughout the winter, access problems make it best to leave this tour for the spring, when the roads are snowfree to the park boundary.

Access: Drive Highway 410 to Buckley. At the west end of town, turn south on Highway 165 for 10.5 miles, passing through Wilkeson and crossing the Fairfax Bridge over the Carbon River. At the junction beyond the bridge, take the right fork to Mowich Lake. A "Road Closed" sign here indicates that there is no winter plowing or maintenance. The first 1.3 miles of pavement is followed by 10 miles on dirt. The boundary of Mount Rainier National Park and the start of the tour are reached at 11.3 miles (3,550 feet).

The Tour: Ski the road through dense forest, passing the Paul Peak Picnic Area 3/4 mile from the park boundary. The climb is gentle but steady to the end of the valley. At 3 miles (4,280 feet), the road makes a long curve to the south. The lake and road end are reached at 5 1/2 miles (4,960 feet).

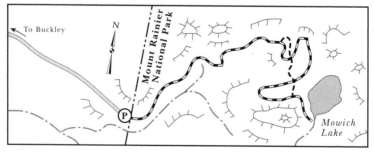

Campsites are found at the road's end on the south side of the lake, and viewpoints are on the west side. For vistas, ski left from the high point of the road and head up a forested ridge until Mount Rainier comes into sight over the lake. Watch the thundering spring avalanches cascade down the sheer rock face of Willis Wall.

Mount Rainier from Mowich Lake

71 DNR ROAD 92 SNO-PARK (COPPER CREEK HUT)

Open to: skis and snowshoes
Surface: mostly groomed road
Rating: more difficult
Round trip: 6 miles
Skiing time: 3 hours
Elevation gain: 900 feet
High point: 4,200 feet
Best: mid-December–mid-March
Avalanche potential: low
Map: *USGS* Ashford

Copper Creek Hut is the easiest of the Mt. Tahoma Trails Association system huts to access. Even if your skiing skills are not the greatest, you may still sample the joys of skiing into an isolated but comfortable mountain hut. The tour is not only easy, it is a lot of fun, with gradual climbs and excellent views over the Nisqually River valley, the Sawtooth Ridge, and Mount Rainier. This is also a delightful tour for day skiers, who can ski to the hut or to the open ridge tops beyond.

Access: From the town of Elbe, drive east on Highway 706 for 6.5 miles, then go left on a narrow road signed for the "92 Road Access," the "Central District Access," and the "Elbe Hills ATV" area. The road passes several houses, then heads out for a long climb up DNR forest lands. The intersections are well signed, and turns at all forks, after the first, are to the right. After 6.3 steep and rough miles, the road arrives at the ridge-top sno-park (3,300 feet). **Note:** Do not head up these steep and difficult roads without chains and a shovel in your car. On heavy snow years, the sno-park may be moved a mile or two down the road. Skiers staying at the hut must be prepared for this contingency.

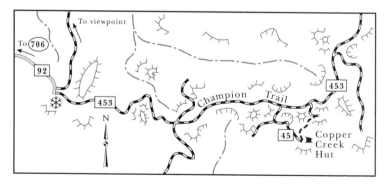

Copper Creek Hut

The Tour: Two routes take off from the parking area. On the left, a mainline forest road heads northeast for 1 1/4 miles to a rarely visited viewpoint. The Champion Trail to Copper Creek Hut is the narrow path on the right. This initial steep climb is the most difficult section of the tour. Once on the crest of the hill, the trail begins an easy contouring ascent to the east.

At the end of the first 1/2 mile, the Champion Trail joins a wide forest road and descends to the right (east). Two short descents take you to the base of a gradual but steady climb along the ridge. Routefinding is easy and intersections are well marked. You will pass several minor spur roads, as well as one major service road that branches right at 1 1/2 miles. Shortly after, the road divides. Stay right on Road 453 and continue to climb.

The Champion Trail heads up and along a broad ridge crest to views of Mount St. Helens and Sawtooth Ridge, then steepens for a climb to a forested saddle and the first views of Mount Rainier. The road continues its gradual ascent around the north side of the knoll to reach a second saddle and intersection at 2 1/2 miles. If the hut is your goal, descend to the right on Road 45 for 500 feet, then take the first left. This road starts by going down, but soon begins a steep climb up an exposed hillside that ends at the hut (4,200 feet).

If the hut is not the goal of your tour, continue straight at the Road 45 intersection on the Champion Trail. After 1/4 mile, the trail begins a steep and exposed climb to the excellent touring on the open ridges above the hut.

201

72 ROAD 1 SNO-PARK (SNOW BOWL AND HIGH HUTS)

Snow Bowl Hut
Open to: skis and snowshoes
Surface: groomed
Rating: most difficult
Round trip: 9 miles
Skiing time: 6 hours
Elevation gain: 2,130 feet
High point: 4,350 feet
Best: mid-December–March
Avalanche potential: low
Maps: *USGS* Sawtooth Ridge and Anderson Lake

High Hut
Open to: skis and snowshoes
Surface: groomed
Rating: most difficult
Round trip: 10 miles
Skiing time: 6 hours
Elevation gain: 2,503 feet
High point: 4,743 feet
Best: mid-December–March
Avalanche potential: low
Maps: *USGS* Sawtooth Ridge and Anderson Lake

On a long, cold winter night, it is hard to imagine anything more appealing than sitting in a warm hut and sharing dinner with friends while the snow falls outside. Thanks to the hard work and dedication of the Mt. Tahoma Trails Association volunteers, cross-country skiers have three public huts to choose from. Copper Creek Hut is located off the DNR Road 92 Sno-Park and is discussed in Tour 71. This section features Snow Bowl Hut and the very scenic High Hut.

Reaching these two huts is never an easy task. The access roads are steep, demanding considerable effort to ascend and, when icy, even more effort to descend. Skiers who have never toured with an overnight pack should factor that challenge into the equation as well. Arrive at the trailhead early and allow plenty of time for the trip. Inexperienced skiers may wish to add a pair of snowshoes to their load, just to be on the safe side. (Snowshoers should stay to the side of the groomed road and never leave dangerous holes or lumps for skiers.)

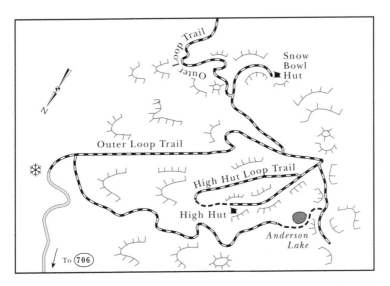

Reservations are available on a first-come basis, from December 15 to the end of March. For a hut reservation form, send a self-addressed, stamped envelope to Mt. Tahoma Trails Association, Attn: Hut Reservation Program, P.O. Box 206, Ashford, WA 98304.

Access: From the town of Elbe, drive Highway 706 east 7 miles toward the Nisqually Entrance of Mount Rainier National Park. Turn right on a road signed to the South District Trails. After 1.2 miles, this rough, narrow road divides; stay right, and cross the Nisqually River. At 3.1 miles you will reach a T intersection; go left. A gate is passed at 5 miles, and at 6.6 miles the plowing ends at the Road 1 Sno-Park (2,240 feet).

The Tour: The trip begins with a very steep ascent from the sno-park. If snow is absent from the road, be prepared to hike until you find it. After 1/4 mile the road divides (2,620 feet). To the right is the 2 1/2-mile non-groomed trail to Anderson Lake. For the huts, continue straight, climbing steeply up the forested valley on the regularly groomed Outer Loop Trail. The climb seems relentless, with only two much too short, level sections where you can stand without slipping backward. Catt Creek is crossed at 2 miles (3,420 feet), and soon after the road switchbacks, reaching the ridge crest and an intersection at 2 3/4 miles (3,880 feet).

For Snow Bowl Hut, go left, still on Outer Loop Trail, and follow it along the crest of the ridge. The road climbs, then descends, then climbs again in typical ridge crest fashion. The grooming ends around the 3-mile point. However, this does not mean you must make your way through the unyielding wilderness. This well-used route continues on a road that climbs along the south side of the ridge. Pass a spur road on the right and one to the left before reaching the tour's 4,350-foot high point and a view of Snow Bowl Hut.

From the high point, the road descends to an intersection and excellent views of Mount Rainier. Go right, leaving the Outer Loop Trail, and follow the often windblown ridge crest for the final 1/2 mile to the hut (4,300 feet). Snow Bowl Hut lives up to its name. The hut is located at the top of a beautiful, open, north-facing slope, where the snow is sheltered from the wind and sun. Few visitors can resist taking at least a couple of runs down the bowl, carving a squiggly track on the soft snow.

If High Hut is your destination, stay right when you first reach the ridge crest at 2 3/4 miles. Continue the steep climb for another 3/4 mile to a major intersection near a copse of trees at 4,030 feet. Go right for the final mile-long trudge to find the hut on the crest of a windblown ridge. About halfway up you will pass the High Hut Loop Trail; at this point stay left, and leave the longer Loop Trail as an option for your return. Of the three huts in the Mt. Tahoma trails system, High Hut has the largest view. Mount Rainier dominates, grandly towering over the hut and filling the northeastern horizon. To the northwest you can see all the way to the Olympics, and at night there is a brilliant glow from the Puget Sound cities. To the east and south, the Goat Rocks, Mount Adams, and Mount St. Helens can be seen over a sea of lesser summits.

Snow Bowl Hut

73 COPPER PASS

Open to: all users
Surface: ungroomed forest road
Rating: more difficult
Round trip: 8 miles
Skiing time: 4 hours
Elevation gain: 1,100 feet
High point: 4,500 feet
Best: mid-December–March
Avalanche potential: low
Maps: *USGS* Mt. Wow and Ashford; *Green Trails* Mt. Rainier West #269

Beyond a doubt, this is the most scenic ski area outside Mount Rainier National Park. This tour has something for everyone: scenery, views, open slopes for telemarking, and miles of roads for exploring.

Access: From the town of Ashford, drive 3.4 miles toward the Nisqually Entrance to Mount Rainier National Park. Turn left on Copper Creek Road No. 59 and follow it as far up as you can go. In previous years, this road was plowed for 4.4 miles by the sno-park system. The old sno-park was an ideal starting place. However, at the time of this writing, no plans had been made to continue this expensive plowing, so skiing must start at the snow line. A side road at the 2.8-mile point offers an alternate starting point when conditions are bad. No permit is required for parking (3,700 feet).

The Tour: From your parking site, ski up Road 59. Once the road reaches the ridge crest it turns north and contours, climbing gradually. Ski past the Lake Christine Trail access road, which in years past has been the winter haunt of snow-busting four-wheel-drives. Avoid the motorized jamboree and continue straight on Road 59, skiing

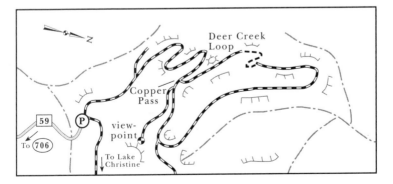

Mount Rainier from the forest road near Copper Pass

past a gate. The climb is steady but not steep as the road contours around the hillside into the Copper Creek drainage. On clear days you will have a magnificent view that includes Mount St. Helens, High Rock, Sawtooth Ridge, and Mount Adams.

One mile beyond the Lake Christine intersection, the road divides (3,900 feet). Stay right, and soon after begin a couple of gradual switchbacks. At 2¾ miles, reach the 4,500-foot Copper Pass at the crest of the ridge and a glorious view of Mount Rainier.

Once you have absorbed the initial impact of this view, it is time to check out your options. The road divides at the pass. Road 59, the one you have been following, crosses the ridge. It heads east, descending and then climbing to the next ridge before traversing north 4 miles along the border of the Glacier View Wilderness, with few views.

Your most scenic option from the pass is to take the road to the right. This road follows the ridge crest south for a mile to the base of Mount Beljica, offering spectacular views for little effort. Near the base of Mount Beljica, the road divides; go left for a steep climb to the ultimate viewpoint at 4,860 feet.

74 REFLECTION LAKES

Open to: nonmotorized
Surface: forest roads and trails
Rating: more difficult
Round trip: 3 miles
Skiing time: 2 hours
Elevation gain: 538 feet
High point: 5,100 feet
Best: January–mid-April
Avalanche potential: low
Map: *Green Trails* Mt. Rainier East #270

During the summer, Reflection Lakes live up to their name, reflecting a regal image of Mount Rainier, framed beautifully by delicate wildflowers. Summer visitors pause briefly to click cameras and then drive on, heading to Paradise and the numerous park amenities found there. However, once the lakes are covered with snow, reflecting nothing but the sun, they are transformed into a popular destination for day trips and overnight outings.

Access: From the Nisqually Entrance to Mount Rainier National Park, follow Paradise Road to Narada Falls Viewpoint (4,572 feet). The large parking area is plowed for winter users, and the warming hut and restroom facility is kept open.

The Tour: From the parking lot, the aim is to gain Stevens Canyon Road on the top of the steep hill straight ahead. Don't attempt to climb

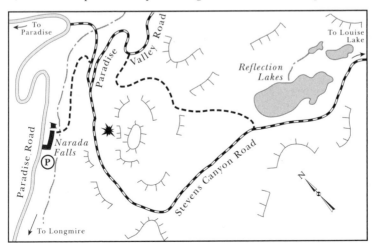

Nisqually River valley

directly up the open slope behind the warming hut; the avalanche hazard makes this approach dangerous. Look near the warming hut for a marked trail that heads into the forest, ascending the forested valley, located between the open slopes and the road to Paradise.

Once you reach the snow-covered Stevens Canyon Road, go to the right. Before long the road divides; if the snow is stable, stay right and follow the road across the windswept hillside above the warming hut. The traverse is followed by 1 mile of easy skiing to the lakes.

When the snowpack is unstable, and there is a possibility of avalanches, go left at the intersection and ski up old Paradise Valley Road. After 1/4 mile, go right on a well-signed but very steep and very narrow winter trail that climbs over Mazama Ridge (5,100 feet), then descends back to Stevens Canyon Road. Once down, ski left along the road 1/8 mile to the largest Reflection Lake (4,854 feet). If in doubt about which way to go, ask a ranger before starting.

At the lake, an obvious option is to wander the snowy meadows. Another is to visit Louise Lake. To do so, continue on the road, passing the two main Reflection Lakes. At the head of Stevens Canyon, the road makes a broad bend and descends to a lower bench and Louise Lake. You may also leave the road at the head of the bend and descend the open slope to the lake (4,597 feet).

Other popular tours in the lakes area are the Tatoosh Range (Tour 75) and Paradise Valley Road (Tour 76).

75 TATOOSH RANGE

Open to: nonmotorized
Surface: open slopes
Rating: backcountry
Round trip: 5 miles
Skiing time: 4 hours
Elevation gain: 1,432 feet
High point: 6,000 feet
Best: January–April
Avalanche potential: moderate
Map: *Green Trails* Mt. Rainier East #270

As viewed from a small saddle on the side of Castle Peak in the Tatoosh Range, the enormous bulk of Mount Rainier fills the entire northern horizon. Below lies a basin whose deep snow generally is much drier than that across the valley at Paradise, and the steep slopes are ideal for telemarking.

Access: From the Nisqually Entrance to Mount Rainier National Park, drive to the Narada Falls Viewpoint parking area (4,572 feet).

The Tour: Ski the winter trail to Reflection Lakes (4,854 feet) (see Tour 74). Skiers who have hiked this area in the summer will be familiar with the two trails from the Reflection Lakes vicinity that head into the Tatoosh Range—the Bench and Snow Lakes Trail and the Pinnacle Saddle Trail. Both are highly avalanche-prone in winter. There is, however, a relatively avalanche-free entry to the Tatoosh Range via Castle Saddle.

Ski Stevens Canyon Road halfway around the first Reflection Lake. At a convenient point, leave the road and start uphill into a big basin with a steep headwall. The avalanche-free route follows the Pinnacle

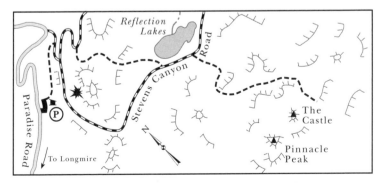

Saddle Trail up the right side of the basin to the fringe of trees atop a rib. Once on the rib, leave the trail and head up through the open forest at the rib's crest. When the rib steepens and becomes impassable, cross the top of the headwall and climb into another big basin between Pinnacle Peak on the right and The Castle on the left. Follow the tree line on the left of the basin. Where the trees end, climb the last 200 feet of steep open slopes on the east side of Castle to the crest of the Tatoosh Range (6,000 feet).

Mount Rainier from Tatoosh Range

76 MAZAMA RIDGE

Open to: skis and snowshoes
Surface: open slopes
Rating: backcountry
Round trip: 6 miles
Skiing time: 4 hours
Elevation gain: 900 feet in, 900 feet out
High point: 5,700 feet
Best: January–mid-May
Avalanche potential: moderate
Map: *Green Trails* Mt. Rainier East #270

The snowy meadows of Mazama Ridge lie at the edge of some of the best midwinter telemarking slopes in the Paradise area. The ridge is easy to access, has excellent campsites, and the scenery is unbelievably photogenic.

Mazama Ridge is a fun objective in most weather and snow conditions and, with careful navigation, can even be skied in a whiteout. If choosing to ski the loop, be advised that sections of the return leg of the tour on Stevens Canyon and Paradise Valley Roads are prone to avalanches and should be skied with caution. Talk with the ranger at Paradise before starting out.

Access: Drive to the Nisqually Entrance of Mount Rainier National Park, then on to the end of the plowed road at Paradise. The tour starts at the southeast corner of the upper parking lot (5,450 feet).

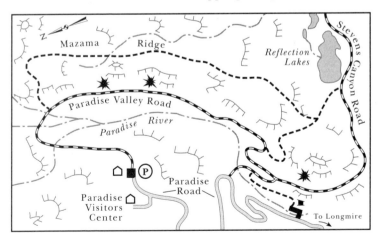

The Tour: Follow snow-covered Paradise Valley Road on a traversing descent below the Paradise Inn. Directly after crossing the third bridge (5,200 feet), turn left and head uphill. If you have climbing skins, this is the time to put them on.

The initially steep climb abates when you reach a sloping bench. Stay to the right of the creek and ski to the base of the next steep slope at the upper end of the bench. Make a right turn at the base of the hill and switchback up to the summit of Mazama Ridge (5,700 feet).

Once on the ridge crest, take time to explore the rolling meadowlands, uninhibited by summer signs that tell you to "Stay on the Trail" and "Keep off the Meadows." Ski over a cushion of snow, north toward Panorama Point or to the open basin below Paradise Glacier a little to the east, to find the telemarking slopes. Excellent campsites abound.

To ski the loop, head down Mazama Ridge, staying to the right of center as you traverse the crest of the ridge. Near the southern end of the ridge, the broad plateau falls away. Ski just east of the ridge crest, angling across several steep, open, south-facing slopes and through several thick bands of trees until you reach the winter trail to Reflection Lakes. Go left and descend with your best telemark through the heavy timber to Stevens Canyon Road. On the road, ski to the left for 100 feet to reach the first lake at 2 1/2 miles (4,854 feet).

To return, ski west from Reflection Lakes on Stevens Canyon Road. Back at the Reflection Lakes Ski Trail you must make a choice. To continue on the road means crossing a steep avalanche slope above Narada Falls, which is only safe when the snowpack is stable. If following the road, ski about halfway across the avalanche slope, then head uphill on Paradise Valley Road. If the snowpack is unstable or you simply love the excitement of skiing steep, tree-studded hillsides, then follow the orange stakes marking the trail, up over Mazama Ridge and down to Paradise Valley Road.

The final leg of the loop is the steady ascent of Paradise Valley Road. Views, weather permitting, can be excellent here. The road traverses below Mazama Ridge, passing under an avalanche chute halfway up the valley. When the snow is unstable, you must drop down to the valley floor and ski around the avalanche slope before returning to the road.

Skiing the open slopes on Mazama Ridge

77 GLACIER VISTA AND CAMP MUIR

Glacier Vista
Open to: nonmotorized
Surface: open slopes
Rating: backcountry
Round trip: 3 miles
Skiing time: 2 hours
Elevation gain: 1,022 feet
High point: 6,336 feet
Best: December–April
Avalanche potential: low
Map: *Green Trails* Mt. Rainier East #270

Camp Muir
Open to: nonmotorized
Surface: open slopes
Rating: mountaineer
Round trip: 9 miles
Skiing time: 8 hours
Elevation gain: 4,500 feet
High point: 10,000 feet
Best: mid-October–mid-July
Avalanche potential: moderate
Map: *Green Trails* Mt. Rainier East # 270

Although the snow is best on the meadows and snowfields here from November to mid-June, diehard skiers come here year-round for a few turns. Winter skiers generally are satisfied with the steep slopes at Glacier Vista below Panorama Point. Those continuing to Camp Muir should be proficient mountaineers ready to deal with sudden whiteouts

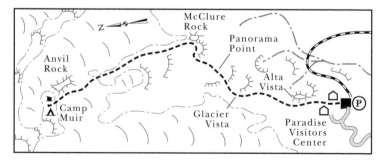

Gigantic view from Camp Muir

and blasting winds. In summer, skiers must hike to the base of the permanent ice field above Pebble Creek (7,500 feet), and even in these milder months should always be prepared for sudden changes in weather.

Note: When snow conditions are unstable or an east wind is blowing, Panorama Point has high potential for slab avalanches. Do not climb Panorama Point after a heavy snowfall, when the wind blows from the east, or during winter rains.

Access: Drive to the Nisqually Entrance of Mount Rainier National Park, then on to the end of the plowed road at Paradise. The tour starts at the upper Paradise parking lot (5,450 feet). At the start and finish of the trip, register in the logbook at the ranger's office.

The Tour: Ski up from the parking lot, working your way around the inner-tubing area and then climbing along the left side of Alta Vista to a saddle. Follow the flat-topped ridge crest past forlorn clumps of wind-blown trees to Glacier Vista at 1½ miles (6,336 feet). This overlook of Nisqually Glacier is an ideal picnic spot and turnaround for winter skiers.

To proceed to Camp Muir, climb the southwest rib of Panorama Point through a broken line of dwarf trees. Skis generally should be removed in favor of postholing.

Once on top, put the skis back on and head north across the summit of Panorama Point, angling to the right until you reach the base of a prominent rock outcrop named McClure Rock. Stay to the left of these rocks and the next rocks, Sugar Loaf, and aim for the knob, Anvil Rock, and stay to the left of it. The final, long snowfield to Camp Muir (10,000 feet) is not really the longest—it just seems that way.

Take special care on the descent. If visibility is poor, stick close to the tracks you made going up. Mistakes on the descent route may take you way out of your way—like all the way down to Nisqually Glacier, or farther out of your way over a cliff.

78 BURLEY MOUNTAIN LOOKOUT

Open to: nonmotorized
Surface: forest road
Rating: most difficult
Round trip: up to 18 miles
Skiing time: 2 days
Elevation gain: 3,931 feet
High point: 5,304 feet
Best: November–December and March–April
Avalanche potential: moderate
Map: *Green Trails* McCoy Peak #333

Like a tiny island in the middle of the vast ocean, Burley Mountain is a narrow rib of rocks jutting out of a vast green sea of trees. On a rare clear day, the view is wondrous, encompassing snow-covered meadows and Washington's southern volcanoes.

The trek from the valley floor to the lookout is extremely arduous. The route follows a steep and narrow forest road. Near the top, snowdrifts make routefinding difficult and even dangerous. However, if you reach the top, you can spend one or more nights in the old Burley Mountain Lookout and spend the days skiing over the ridge crest. (Advance reservations are required to stay at the lookout. Contact the Cowlitz Valley Ranger Station at 10024 U.S. Highway 12, Randle, WA 98377; or call 360-479-1100.)

Access: Drive to Randle. Turn south off Highway 12 at the grocery store and follow the combined Forest Roads 23 and 25. At 0.9 mile, the road splits. Stay left on Cispus Road No. 23 for the next 8.1 miles.

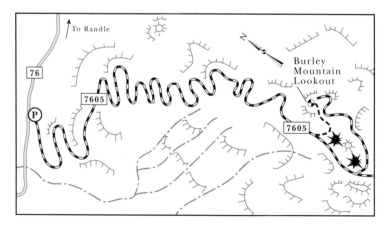

Turn right at Road 28, heading toward Cispus Center, for 1.4 miles, then take another right on Road 76. Continue on for 3.3 miles, passing through Cispus Center and the small community of Tower Rock, before making a left turn on Road 7605. Drive to the snow line. Be sure to have traction devices in the car, and leave it pointing downhill, in case conditions change while you are at the lookout. This road is not plowed.

The Tour: Burley Mountain Road starts off by climbing and never stops until it reaches the top. The first 6 miles are nondescript switchbacks through dense second-growth forest. Several unmarked spur roads are passed. If in doubt, always pick the road that is going up and you won't go wrong.

After 6 long miles, the road reaches a broad bench at 4,260 feet and levels off to traverse the open meadows below the summit cliffs. This is a good location for a campsite. Beyond the meadows the road heads south to the ridge crest. Stay with the road until it begins to traverse an open hillside, then follow the arrow that points up to a low saddle (4,800 feet). (If the snow is unstable, you must leave the road before it begins the exposed traverse. Once you see the open hillside, retreat back around the corner and head up the sparsely timbered hillside. Keep climbing until you reach the top. Do not stray too far to the left; that is where the cliffs are.)

If you stayed on the main route, go left from the saddle and begin a traversing climb along the west side of the ridge crest. In 1/8 mile, reach a second saddle. Continue to climb the last 1/4 mile toward the relay station and lookout, now visible on the hillcrest above.

Before heading into the lookout's dark interior, let the eye wander southwest toward the steaming remains of the once-mighty Mount St. Helens, then farther east to the still-mighty Mount Adams, and finally to the mightiest of all, Mount Rainier.

The lookout is a very primitive facility. During the winter, the shutters must remain closed and propane lights provide the only light. The lookout was originally designed to be staffed during the summer only, and on stormy nights the wind finds all the chinks and holes. For heat, the lookout has a woodstove, but, to date, the wood supply has been limited. Price per night is very reasonable, and there is space for up to four people.

Burley Mountain Lookout

79 HORSESHOE LAKE

Open to: multiple use
Surface: trail, and groomed for snowmobiles
Rating: backcountry
Round trip: 11³/₄ miles
Skiing time: 6 hours
Elevation gain: 1,200 feet
High point: 4,100 feet
Best: mid-December–mid-March
Avalanche potential: low
Map: *Green Trails* Blue Lake #334

Despite the rough setting in the center of snowmobile country, this tour is a definite gem. The trip begins with a 3-mile ski up a groomed snowmobile road. The constant rip and roar of the machines demands nerves of steel; however, the second half of the tour is on a skier-only trail that tunnels through snow-laden trees to Horseshoe Lake.

Overall, this tour is not difficult and, if skiing ability were the only factor, it could be rated as *more difficult.* However, the trail is not well marked and routefinding is challenging. At least one person in the party should be competent with map and compass.

Access: Drive Highway 12 to Randle, then head south on Highway 131. After 0.9 mile, the road divides; stay left on Road 23. After 18.7 miles, go left again on Road 21 for the next 4.8 miles to an intersection with Road 56. Go right on Road 56, passing Adams Fork Campground, which may have one loop open. Cross the Cispus River and continue on Road 56 for another 3.1 miles before turning right on Road 5603 for a final 0.3 mile to the Orr Creek Sno-Park (2,900 feet). **Note:** This is a

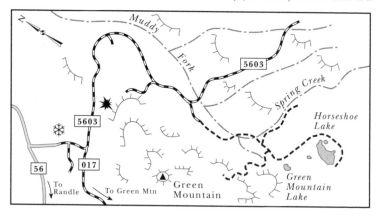

low-priority road that may not be plowed for several days during major winter storms. Always carry a shovel and be prepared to chain up.

The Tour: From the sno-park, ski south on Road 5603. At 1/4 mile pass Spur Road (5603)017 to Green Mountain (a great tour when Road 5603 is annoyingly busy). For now, stay with the snowmobiles and continue up the well-groomed Road 5603.

After passing the 3-mile mark, continue on to the next corner, then go right on a narrow, ungroomed spur road signed to the Spring Creek Trail. Leave the snowmobiles (hopefully) as you follow the road around the edge of a large clearcut. The road parallels a line of uncut trees for 1/4 mile and then bends right, heading across a plantation of young trees that extends all the way to the base of Green Mountain. As you head out into the plantation, the road disappears in the nearly level field of snow. Look left to the line of trees along the southeast side of the giant plantation, then head for a point about a third of the way to the base of Green Mountain. If there are no other ski tracks to follow, you may have to scout around a bit to find the narrow trail cut, marked with a blue diamond, which heads through the dense grove of trees.

This first section of trail is well marked with blue diamonds. The trail passes through a dense line of trees, then skirts a marsh and an old burn. At 4 miles from the sno-park, the trail crosses Spring Creek, and your reassuring line of blue diamonds comes to an end. Cross the creek, then continue straight ahead with just a single line of trees between you and the marsh, and you should be on the trail.

This skier-only trail is very peaceful as it climbs gradually through the forest. The main noises are the swish of your skis and the thump of your poles. At 4 1/2 miles, pass a signed trail to Keenes Horse Camp. Continue straight, and at 5 1/4 miles, pass to the right of small, forested Green Mountain Lake (4,050 feet).

Continuing through the forest, the rate of ascent increases for the final 1/2 mile. An intersection with the Chain of Lakes Trail marks your arrival at Horseshoe Lake. Follow the trail as it traverses along the left side of the lake to reach the campground at 5 3/4 miles (4,100 feet). You may find a few snowmobiles around the campground; however, you can avoid them by skiing into the trees.

Horseshoe Lake Campground

80 WHITE ROAD SNO-PARK

Open to: skis and snowshoes
Surface: ungroomed forest road
Rating: easiest
Round trip: 7 miles
Skiing time: 4 hours
Elevation gain: 480 feet
High point: 4,800 feet
Best: January–March
Avalanche potential: low
Map: *Green Trails* White Pass #303

This short tour is full of surprises and a sure crowd pleaser. White Road (formerly called Yellowjacket Road) is nearly level and easy to ascend and descend, which pleases the beginners. The clearcuts please telemarkers and telemarker wanna-bes. And everyone is sure to be pleased by the views, especially skiers seeking the best in mountain scenery but not really wanting to tackle lofty summits. This area has been designated for nonmotorized winter sports. Only a moderate number of snowmobiles get "lost" here, which is also pleasing.

Access: From the summit of White Pass, drive Highway 12 west 0.7 mile, then turn north on White Road No. 1284. Park well off to the side, allowing road-maintenance equipment free access to the work center (4,320 feet).

The Tour: Ski up the road, gaining elevation gradually along the tree-lined route. The first clearcut is passed at the ½ mile point. The broad, open basin is the best area for beginner telemarkers to practice

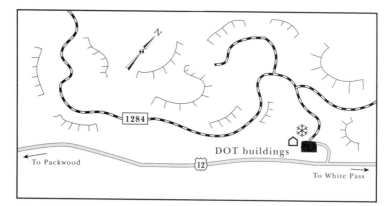

their skills. The road then turns south, and the upper lifts of the White Pass Ski Area come into view. Across the valley, massive Hogback Ridge dominates the horizon. The road soon bends west and gradually the entire Cowlitz River Valley unfolds before your eyes, another segment of the giant panorama being added with each clearcut traversed. At first only Chimney Rock is visible, but, ultimately, views extend deep into the Goat Rocks, all the way to 7,930-foot Old Snowy Mountain. To the north, the Tatoosh Range dominates the skyline.

The visual climax of the trip, and the trip's end, is reached at 3 1/2 miles (4,800 feet). The road rounds a corner and Mount Rainier springs into full view, high and mighty above other peaks. Take a long lunch break before heading back to enjoy the miles of vistas from the opposite perspective.

Skiers on White Road

81 WHITE PASS—PACIFIC CREST TRAIL

Open to: skis and snowshoes
Surface: trail
Rating: backcountry
Round trip: 7–16 miles
Skiing time: 1–3 days
Elevation gain: up to 1,200 feet
High point: 5,600 feet
Best: January–April
Avalanche potential: low
Map: *Green Trails* White Pass #303

Ski to one subalpine lake or to ten. Climb to the top of one of the rounded hills for the sheer pleasure of coming down, or climb to the summit of several. Tour a single snow-covered meadow, or explore twenty of them.

Skiers making one-day trips along the Pacific Crest Trail will find an easy destination in Deer and Sand Lakes. Those with two or more days can ski deep into Cowlitz Pass, a wonderful base camp for explorations in the center of the William O. Douglas Wilderness.

Access: Drive Highway 12 to the White Pass summit and park in the overnight parking lot (4,400 feet) near the motel.

The Tour: This tour begins 1/2 mile below the summit of White Pass. Ski through a narrow band of trees to a prepared cross-country track around Leech Lake (renamed White Pass Lake by the ski resort). Turn right, paralleling the track to the northeast end of the lake and the Pacific Crest Trail.

The Pacific Crest Trail starts off in forest, switchbacking up a small knoll; the way is usually well tracked and easy to follow as far as Deer

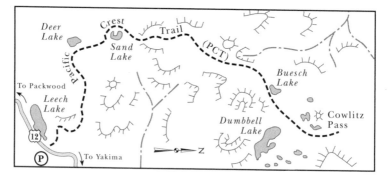

Lake. After a new snowfall, however, someone has to be first, and it may be you, so be sure to carry a map and compass to navigate over the forested ridges. A brief description to Deer Lake: After leaving Leech Lake, when nearing the top of the first hill, head left over a shallow saddle, then contour left around the backside of the open hill above Leech Lake. At 2 miles pass a large meadow on the right. Continue climbing to the left (west) up a steep ridge. A short descent down the opposite side leads to 5,206-foot Deer Lake.

Beyond Deer Lake the trail turns north (right). Head along a broad, lightly forested ridge crest interspersed with pocket-size meadows. Sand Lake (5,295 feet) lies 1/2 mile beyond Deer Lake and is much more difficult to spot; its odd shape makes it look more like a meadow than a body of frozen water. Day skiers will find Sand Lake, 3 1/2 miles from the start, to be an ideal turnaround point.

The route beyond is a steady climb along the east side of the ridge, in view of Spiral Butte (an infant volcano), with occasional looks south to the Goat Rocks and Mount Adams. At 5 miles (5,600 feet), the trail bends right to contour the east side of a partially forested hill and starts a descent that ends 1 mile later, at Buesch Lake (5,080 feet). The trail skirts the right side of the lake, then climbs northeast to Cowlitz Pass (5,200 feet) and camping.

Numerous tours can be made from a base camp here. Skilled backcountry skiers may enjoy the ascent of 6,340-foot Tumac Mountain (another potential Mount St. Helens) to excellent views. Other skiers find plenty of room for exploration among the lakes or in Blankenship Meadows on the north side of Tumac.

Continuing north on the Pacific Crest Trail from the lakes looks inviting on the map, but avalanche potential increases dramatically.

Skier at Sand Lake

82 WHITE PASS CROSS-COUNTRY TOURING CENTER

Open to: skis only
Surface: groomed
Rating: easiest to most difficult
Round trip: up to 10 miles
Skiing time: 3 or more hours
Elevation gain: 300 feet
High point: 4,700 feet
Best: mid-December–March
Avalanche potential: none
Map: *Green Trails* White Pass #303

Skimming the edges of the William O. Douglas Wilderness and the Goat Rocks Wilderness, the trails of the White Pass Cross-Country Touring Center seem to whisk you straight away from the busy resort area into the depths of the forest primeval. Views from this high mountain location are amazingly enticing, though somewhat hard to come by.

The excellently groomed tracks are laid out in a series of well-designed loops ideal for beginners to experts, with grooves for diagonal striding and a wide platform in the center for skating.

The trails are open and freshly groomed Thursdays through Sundays, and on holidays from 9:00 A.M. to 4:00 P.M. Lessons on diagonal striding, skating, and telemarking are offered. The resort has rentals, day care services, overnight accommodations, and food service. A per-person trail fee is charged. The rate is the same for adults as for children.

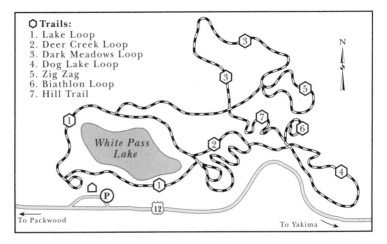

○ Trails:
1. Lake Loop
2. Deer Creek Loop
3. Dark Meadows Loop
4. Dog Lake Loop
5. Zig Zag
6. Biathlon Loop
7. Hill Trail

Access: Drive Highway 12 for 20 miles east of Packwood (or 54 miles west of Yakima) to the summit of White Pass (4,400 feet). The touring center is located on the north side of the highway and is accessed from the central parking lot.

The Tour: The touring center buildings are located on a low hill overlooking a lake. In the summer, this lake goes by its official name of Leech; however, during the snowy months of winter, the name is changed to the more appealing appellation of White Pass Lake. A loop around the lake, whichever its name, is a must. Here you are treated to the area's best scenery. From White Pass Lake you will alternately see Spiral Butte, Hogback Mountain, and densely forested hillsides. On the north side of the lake you will find a trail to take you up to the Dark Meadows Loop, where you can glide through the forest. It is in the Dark Meadows area that you will find the most challenging trail—the Zig Zag. When icy, this trail can be a real ski breaker.

On the east side of White Pass Lake is the start of the Deer Creek Loop. This trail descends through the forest to an intersection with the Dog Lake Loop, the Hill Trail, and the Biathlon Loop. The Dog Lake Loop does not reach the lake, nor does it have a view of the lake. Skiers who wish to visit the lake should follow the ungroomed Beaver Cutoff Trail. The Hill Trail climbs with breathtaking steepness for 0.7 kilometer (½ mile) to the Dark Meadows Loop. Views along this trail are quite good.

The Hill Trail

83 ROUND MOUNTAIN ROAD

Open to: skis and snowshoes
Surface: ungroomed
Rating: more difficult
Round trip: 9 miles
Skiing time: 5 hours
Elevation gain: 1,280 feet
High point: 4,320 feet
Best: January–March
Avalanche potential: low
Map: *Green Trails* White Pass #303

Although primarily on a road that tunnels through dense forest, the Round Mountain Tour occasionally yields beautiful, head-on views of the Goat Rocks, with Old Snowy, Ives Peak, and Gilbert Peak, cloaked in their winter whites, dominating the skyline. From road's end, backcountry skiers, capable of reading a map for direction and the slopes for avalanche hazard, will find access to a north-facing bowl just below the summit of Round Mountain. It's a great slope for cranking turns and a superb location for burning film.

Access: Turn south off Highway 12 at 26.2 miles west of the Highway 410 junction or 7.6 miles east of White Pass. Follow Tieton River Road No. 12 for 3.3 miles to the North Fork Tieton River Sno-Park (3,040 feet). Walk or ski 1/4 mile back to Round Mountain Road No. 830.

The Tour: The road climbs steadily for 1/2 mile, passing Road 831, making a switchback, and then leveling off at a viewpoint of the Goat Rocks. Continue on; more views of the Goat Rocks, Clear Lake,

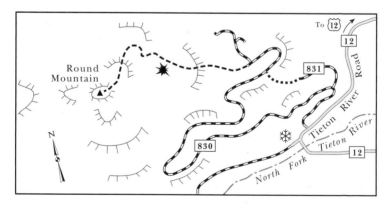

North Fork Tieton River valley from Round Mountain Road

Pinegrass Ridge, and Russell Ridge await you. For the next 3 1/2 miles, the road alternates between lackadaisical climbing and level traversing. At 4 1/2 miles the road ends at the Round Mountain trailhead (4,320 feet).

Skiers with mountaineering abilities making the summit push, or backcountry skiers looking for some excitement, may shortcut Road 830 by skiing up Road 831, which provides a breathtakingly straightforward ascent to the trailhead. Ski to the end of Road 831, then don climbing skins and head to the right, through the trees, to a logging clearing. Ski up the steep clearing to rejoin Road 830. A right turn will lead you to road's end.

The summit of Round Mountain is a steep climb from the end of the road. Head up the mountain, sticking to the ridge crest until reaching the edge of the trees at about 5,100 feet. This is a potentially unstable area. When the stability of the snowpack is questionable, turn around here and enjoy the run down through the trees. If stable conditions allow, traverse left and climb to the summit ridge. Follow this ridge southwest to the old lookout site (5,971 feet). Before returning, ski off the north side of the ridge and scribble a signature or two in the tantalizing powder bowl.

84 NORTH FORK TIETON RIVER

Open to: skis and snowshoes
Surface: some trails machine groomed
Rating: easiest to more difficult
Round trip: 2–9½ miles
Skiing time: up to 5 hours
Elevation gain: up to 140 feet
High point: 3,300 feet
Best: January–mid-March
Avalanche potential: low
Map: *Green Trails* White Pass #303

Five tours start from this small sno-park, presenting skiers with an unusual number of choices when they first arrive. With the exception of the mountaineers' route to the summit of Round Mountain, these tours are all scenic and nonstrenuous, making this an ideal touring area for your entire, extended family. In 2001, the Ski-n-Yurt was built on a spur road off the North Fork Tieton River Road. This is an independent commercial venture, and skiers are welcome to rent the facility for overnight stays. When unoccupied, the yurt is open to all and is a great picnic site. If interested in renting the yurt, contact the Little Red School House in Naches at (509) 653-2041.

For details of the Round Mountain trip, see Tour 83. The remaining four tours are described below.

Access: Turn south off Highway 12 at 26.2 miles west of the Highway 410 junction or 7.6 miles east of White Pass. Follow Tieton River Road No.12 for 3.3 miles to the North Fork Tieton River Sno-Park (3,040 feet).

West Loop: This is a 2-mile tour with a *more difficult* rating. The tour starts at the upper end of the sno-park with an ascending traverse

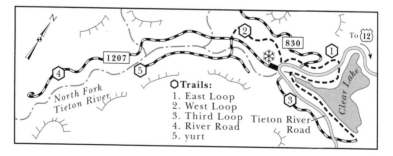

Trails:
1. East Loop
2. West Loop
3. Third Loop
4. River Road
5. yurt

of the forested hillside. Before long the trail crosses the first of several clearcuts, with views of the towering walls of the North Fork Tieton valley. The most challenging portion of the loop is a run through the trees on a narrow trail. At the end of the first mile, the loop route descends to intersect Forest Road 1207. Go left and complete your loop with an easy 1-mile road ski back to the sno-park.

East Loop: Varied scenery is the attraction of this easy 2-mile loop. From the sno-park, walk a few feet back down Tieton River Road to find a blue diamond on the left, where the loop begins. The trail meanders through forest and clearcuts at the base of Round Mountain, paralleling the road north for a mile. You then must walk or ski across the road to find the return loop along the shores of Clear Lake.

Third Loop: This 2-mile loop has one short, steep descent, which accounts for its *more difficult* rating. From the sno-park, walk across the North Fork Tieton River Bridge and then on up the road for 200 feet, until you find a forest road on the right. Ski uphill to a three-way intersection and go left for a gradual ascent. At the time of this writing, many of the blue diamonds that used to mark this route were missing, including the one that should mark the next intersection. At 3/4 mile, go left on a narrow spur road that descends through a clearcut. At the base of the clearcut, make a short traverse and then descend down to the road.

On the pavement, walk a few feet to the right to find a snow-covered road and follow it down into a camping area. Stay with the road until you find a blue diamond on the left, then ski the marked trail back along Clear Lake to the North Fork Tieton River Bridge.

North Fork Tieton River Road: This is the easiest of the five tours that originate from the sno-park. Best of all, this tour can be skied after the snow has melted from the other three loops.

The directions for this tour are delightfully simple. From the upper end of the sno-park, follow groomed Road 1207 southeast along the valley floor through forest and clearcuts. Near the 1-mile point, pass the West Loop intersection on the right and the yurt access road on the left. (To reach the yurt, cross the river, then go right at the intersection. Ski upvalley for 2 1/2 miles.) At 1 1/4 miles, North Fork Tieton River Road descends to cross Hell Creek, then climbs in a gradual fashion to cross Miriam Creek at 2 1/2 miles. Do not turn around until you have seen the view of Bear Creek Mountain, Devils Horns, Tieton Peak, and the Goat Rocks from a bend in the road at 2 3/4 miles.

The road ends at 4 3/4 miles, at the boundary of the Goat Rocks Wilderness. A small campground and a trailhead mark the turnaround point.

End of road loop on North Fork Tieton River Road

85 LOST LAKE

Open to: all uses
Surface: forest road
Rating: more difficult
Round trip: 10 miles
Skiing time: 6 hours–2 days
Elevation gain: 1,250 feet
High point: 3,800 feet
Best: January–March
Avalanche potential: none
Map: *Green Trails* Rimrock #304

Have no fear, Lost Lake is lost no more. In summer, a paved road winds up from the valley floor to a small lakeside campground nestled below the fortresslike summits of Divide Ridge. In winter, the road becomes a snow-covered avenue through parklike forests of ponderosa pine. A camp at Lost Lake is ideally situated for exploring the many roads and trails that criss-cross the area's meadows and lakes.

Access: Drive Highway 12 east from White Pass 16.4 miles (or 0.6 mile west of Hause Creek Campground). Turn south on Tieton Road and drive 0.2 mile to a large sno-park on the right (2,550 feet). A Forest Service information sign marks the start of the Goose Egg Trail, a fun 4-mile ski through the forest for novices. If there is ample snow, park here. If not, turn left on Lost Lake Road No. 1201 and continue driving to the snow line.

The Tour: Elevation is gained gradually on the first mile of Lost Lake Road. Several spur roads are passed—three on the right and two on the left—then the uphill grade increases slightly. Few views enhance

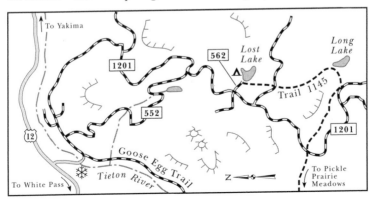

your enjoyment as you climb, but the white snow, green pine needles, orange-red bark of the ponderosa, and blue sky more than compensate. After 2½ miles, snow-plastered Bethel Ridge highlights the northern horizon. At 4¾ miles, go left on Spur Road 562 for the final ¼-mile push to Lost Lake and the campground (3,800 feet).

Lost Lake Road

86 PLEASANT VALLEY LOOP

Open to: skis and snowshoes
Surface: forest roads and trails
Rating: easiest to most difficult
Round trip: up to 14 miles
Skiing time: up to 8 hours
Elevation gain: 10–400 feet
High point: 3,600 feet
Best: January–mid-March
Avalanche potential: none
Map: *Green Trails* Bumping Lake #271

Shadowed by the steep walls of Fifes and American Ridges, the snow lingers in Pleasant Valley long after it has melted on the surrounding hillsides, leaving skiers free to enjoy the 14 miles of looping trails until early springtime.

The Pleasant Valley Loop divides into three sub-loops, two of which are challenging, and a third loop that was created to accommodate the needs of beginning skiers. The Pleasant Valley area is forested and best skied after a fresh snowfall. Icy trails, difficult creek crossings, and deep tree wells are persistent hazards when skiing on old snow.

Access: From the intersection of Highways 410 and 12, follow 410 for 33.3 miles toward Chinook Pass to Hells Crossing Campground (3,280 feet). Alternate starting points are located at the Crow Lake Way trailhead, Pleasant Valley Campground, and the Union Creek trailhead. Limited parking may also be found at Lodgepole Campground. Be sure to carry tire chains and a shovel; Highway 410 is plowed on a low-priority basis.

The Beginners Loop: This loop begins at Hells Crossing Campground on the north side of Highway 410. It is approximately 2 miles long and is rated *easiest*. The loop is on an old road and is definitely pleasant.

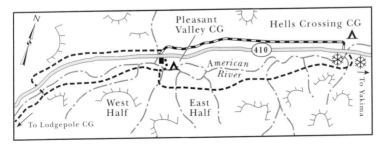

Log bridge over the American River

Pleasant Valley Loop—East Half: This 8-mile section of trail runs from Hells Crossing Campground to Pleasant Valley Campground and back. The two legs of the loop, on opposite sides of the American River, differ radically. The southeast leg follows a narrow trail along a rolling hillside and is rated *most difficult.* The northwest side follows a skid road that is wide, open, and nearly level the whole distance—good skiing for everyone. The only point of possible confusion on this loop is the unsigned three-way intersection located across the American River from Pleasant Valley Campground. This intersection should not cause problems if you keep on the lookout for it, ski straight through it, and do not wander off following the wrong line of blue diamonds.

Pleasant Valley Loop—West Half: The west half of this loop is a challenging 6 miles of trail skiing, from Pleasant Valley Campground to the American River Bridge and back. Both legs on this portion of the loop are rated as *most difficult* due to the short, steep climbs and descents through the trees. At the upper end of the loop you must walk the road across the American River and then climb a steep snowbank along the left edge of the road to find the trail on the opposite side.

On the southwest side of the American River, the trail divides. The loop route goes left, heading northeast, back down the river to Pleasant Valley Campground, while the trail on the right makes a challenging roller-coaster run along Highway 410 to Lodgepole Campground. At Pleasant Valley Campground, be alert for an unsigned intersection. Here one trail heads north toward the campground, while the second trail continues downvalley to Hells Crossing.

87 BIG TREE LOOP

Open to: skis and snowshoes
Surface: groomed
Rating: easiest
Loop trip: 4 3/4 miles
Skiing time: 3 hours
Elevation gain: 400 feet
High point: 2,850 feet
Best: January–February
Avalanche potential: none
Map: *Green Trails* Mt. Adams West #366

Loop through a majestic pine and fir forest to the base of one of the largest known ponderosa pine trees, the Trout Lake Big Tree. Roads are narrow but smoothly groomed, and, weather permitting, you will be treated to a stunning view of Mount Adams.

Access: Follow Highway 14 along the Columbia Gorge to Bingen, then head north on Highway 141 for 23 miles to Trout Lake. Where the road divides at the Trout Lake Service Station (a Chevron Station in 2000), stay to the right, and to the right at all subsequent major intersections. At 4.8 miles from Trout Lake, shortly after the county road becomes Forest Road 82, you will find the entrance to Pine Side Sno-Park on your right (2,750 feet).

The Tour: The trailhead is located across Road 82 from the

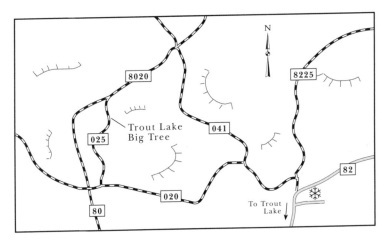

entrance of the sno-park. Take the lower of the two trails and begin with a gradual descent on Spur Road 041. The road is lined with tall pines that create an impressive corridor under a cover of fresh snow.

After a 3/4-mile descent, you will arrive at the start of the loop portion of the tour (2,650 feet). Stay to the left and continue your journey beneath towering trees. Wildlife abounds in this area; watch for snowshoe hares or squirrels prancing over the snow, and the tracks of larger animals such as deer and elk.

A second junction is reached at 1 3/4 miles (2,580 feet). Here an alternate, unsigned, but well-marked route heads right, following Spur Road 025 in a meandering backdoor approach to Trout Lake Big Tree. This ungroomed trail is narrow and has a real wilderness feel.

If you prefer the easier—and certainly quicker—approach on groomed trails, continue straight ahead for 1/8 mile to intersect Road 80. This broad and very open mainline road sweeps you uphill for the next 1/2 mile of steady climbing.

The next intersection is nearly undetectable, as the well-groomed trail seamlessly switches you off the mainline road onto narrower Road 8020 at the 2 1/2-mile point. A nearly level 1/4 mile beyond, the trail reaches the Big Tree entrance. A picnic table is located at the far side of this 200-foot-tall megalith and is an excellent location for lunch, if you can clear the snow off of the benches.

From the Trout Lake Big Tree, the loop continues on Road 8020, climbing gradually northeast for the next 3/4 mile to a clearcut with a

dominating view of Mount Adams. Beyond the view-point the road descends steadily, winding down a narrow canyon above Hole-in-the-Ground Creek. The descent continues until the road reaches an inter-section with Spur Road 041, which closes the loop portion of the tour.

The final 3/4 mile is spent following your own tracks back to the sno-park.

Sign at Trout Lake Big Tree

88 PINE SIDE LOOPS

Open to: some multiple use
Surface: machine groomed
Rating: more difficult
Loop trip: 6 1/3 miles
Skiing time: 3 hours
Elevation gain: 930 feet
High point: 3,680 feet
Best: January–February
Avalanche potential: none
Map: *USFS* Mt. Adams Ranger District

This is the perfect sylvan scene, where snow-covered trees line the route as you pass from one forest glade to the next. The only sounds heard are other high-spirited skiers swooshing down the rolling hills. Okay, the glades are actually clearcuts, your route is a logging road, and the high-pitched whine of snowmobiles occasionally drowns out the voices of the skiers; however, the Pine Side Loops are still a delightful place for a half-day tour by yourself or with a large group.

The loops originating from Pine Side Sno-Park are groomed and tracked for skiers, perfect for the classic kick-and-glide style of skiing.

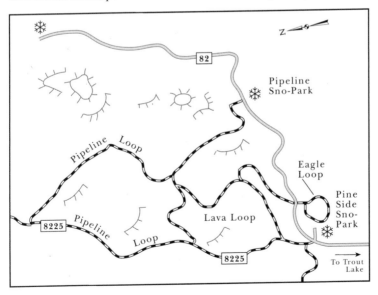

Skaters may use the untracked lane, although it is a bit narrow if you have a wide stride.

Access: Follow Highway 14 along the Columbia Gorge to Bingen, then head north on Highway 141 for 23 miles to Trout Lake. Where the road divides at the Trout Lake Service Station (a Chevron Station in 2000), stay to the right, and to the right at all subsequent major intersections. At 4.8 miles from Trout Lake, shortly after the county road becomes Forest Road 82, you will find the entrance to Pine Side Sno-Park on your right (2,750 feet).

The Pine Side Sno-Park is the first of two accesses to the loops. The second access, known as Pipeline Sno-Park, is located 2.4 miles

Ski trail through meadow on Lava Loop

farther up Road 82, at the Spur Road 101 intersection, and, as of 2001, had parking for up to eight vehicles. If you choose to start your tour here, add an extra 2 1/2 miles to the overall mileage.

Note: Forest Road 82 is only plowed once a week. Always carry a shovel and tire chains for your car.

The Tour: This tour description starts from the Pine Side Sno-Park. Trail maps are available at the trailhead outhouse and the Mount Adams Ranger Station in Trout Lake. All access points are well marked and all trails and intersections are signed.

From the Pine Side Sno-Park, cross the access road and begin your tour by skiing up Road 8225, following signs for the Lava and Pipeline Loop. The road climbs steeply for 1/3 mile to an intersection. Go right on Lava Loop and ski beneath a band of trees before beginning to climb through a series of logging clearings. After a short 1/2 mile of steady ascent, you will arrive at an intersection with Eagle Loop. Stay left and continue the climb. An intersection marks the top of Lava Loop, at 1 1/2 miles. At this point you may either go left and return to the sno-park, or take a right and continue on to Pipeline Loop.

Pipeline Loop begins 500 feet south of the top of the Lava Loop. From the intersection, head left and continue the steady up-hill grind. (If you go right here, you will reach Pipeline Sno-Park in 1 1/3 miles). After a moderately steep, mile-long ascent, the trail bends sharply to the left and narrows. Grooming may be less immaculate here as the terrain rolls and the trail winds between the narrowly spaced trees. A wide clearcut at 3,680 feet marks the start of the descent.

After a hectic few minutes of dodging trees, the Pipeline Loop reaches Road 8225. This is a shared road, so watch for snowmobiles and don't let inexperienced skiers get too spread out from the group. (If you are interested in a little bit of exploring, a right turn on Road 8225 will lead to miles of ungroomed roads, including several that will take you down to intersect Tour 87, Big Tree Loop). The descent of Road 8225 is rapid and may even require a bit of the old snowplow action to keep the speed in check. After 1 1/2 miles, pass an access to the top of Lava Loop. When the snowmobiles are thick, you may prefer to return to skier-only trails. Watch for elk as you descend. Even if you do not see the animals, you may find their deep tracks crossing the road near the clearcuts.

At the 6-mile point you will pass the lower Lava Loop entrance. Keep straight, but slow down here; the final plunge to the parking lot is a steep one.

89 GOTCHEN CREEK

Open to: all uses
Surface: forest roads and trails
Rating: more difficult
Round trip: 6½ miles
Skiing time: 3 hours
Elevation gain: 668 feet
High point: 4,520 feet
Best: mid-December–March
Avalanche potential: low
Map: *USFS* Mt. Adams Ranger District

A high plateau at the base of Mount Adams is an ideal location for skiing, exploring, and close-up views of the mountain. The plateau is criss-crossed with a maze of logging roads for skiers to sample, while the huge, wide clearcuts are an invitation for family fun. Towering over all, the ice-covered mass of Mount Adams creates a stunning background.

Two main roads branch off from the parking area. The tour described here traverses a series of logging roads to Gotchen Creek. Qualified backcountry skiers can continue on from the end of the road and head up to the ridge crests for some telemarking descents. (When the snowmobiles are attacking the area in force, the self-propelled may want to look at Spur Road 200 as an alternative.)

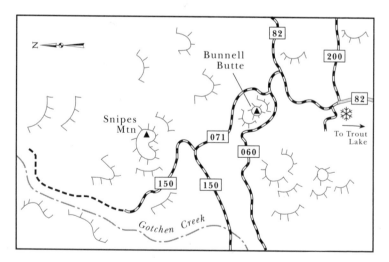

Access: From Highway 14 in the Columbia Gorge, turn north at Bingen and follow Highway 141 for 23 miles to the town of Trout Lake. Where the road divides at the Trout Lake Service Station, stay right, following signs to the Mount Adams Recreation Area. After heading north for 1.4 miles, the road divides again; stay right. At 2.4 miles, the road divides again; stay right, on a road signed to the sno-parks. Pass the Pine Side Sno-Park at 4.8 miles and continue up the rather rough Forest Road 82 for another 4.4 miles to the end of the plowing at the Smith Butte Sno-Park (3,852 feet). **Note:** The access road to the sno-park is plowed once a week only. Driving can be nasty on a snowy weekend. Always carry tire chains and a shovel.

The Tour: The sno-park is located at the intersection of Road 82 and Spur Road 200, which branches off to the right. The Gotchen Creek route heads north from the sno-park, following Road 82 over gently rolling terrain. This area is not usually groomed, so early arrivals must be ready to break trail.

After skiing past clearcuts and second growth for 3/4 mile, the road divides; go left on Spur Road 060. A short descent is followed by a level traverse along the edge of a broad clearcut. At 1 mile, reach the north end of the clearcut and Spur Road 071. Go right and ski along the base of Bunnell Butte, skirting the northern edge of the broad clearcut before ducking into the forest.

Reach a wide intersection at 2 miles (4,040 feet) and ski to the right on Spur Road 150. A steady ascent will bring you to road's end along the edge of Gotchen Creek at 3 1/4 miles (4,520 feet).

When the snow conditions are right, there is excellent skiing on the sparsely forested hillsides above. To continue, head uphill, keeping Gotchen Creek to your left, and climb until you are tired; then turn back for an enjoyable run through the trees.

Mount Adams from meadow near Smith Butte

90 ATKISSON SNO-PARK: ICE CAVE/NATURAL BRIDGES/ PETERSON RIDGE

Ice Cave/Natural Bridges
Open to: skis and snowshoes
Surface: ungroomed roads and trails
Rating: easiest
Loop trip: 4 miles
Skiing time: 2 hours
Elevation gain: 200 feet
High point: 2,900 feet
Best: January–February
Avalanche potential: none
Map: *Green Trails* Willard #398

Peterson Ridge
Open to: skis and snowshoes
Surface: forest roads and trails
Rating: more difficult
Round trip: 9 miles
Skiing time: 4 hours
Elevation gain: 940 feet
High point: 3,640 feet
Best: January–mid-March
Avalanche potential: low
Maps: *Green Trails* Willard #398 and Mt. Adams West #366

The roar, the snarl, and the belching exhaust of the snowmobiles at the popular Atkisson Sno-Park is enough to scare away any skier. However, if you can get past the noise-shock of the parking area, you will find miles of snowmobile-free trails reserved for skiers. In fact, the only things skiers and snowmobilers share are the parking area, an outhouse, a shelter with picnic tables and a woodstove (bring some wood), and a few feet of trail.

Three skier-only tours begin at the sno-park. Two of the tours are easy loops; the Natural Bridges loop explores an old, collapsed lava tube in the Big Trench area, while the Ice Cave loop circles the entrance of another lava tube on old forest roads. The third tour takes you to views of Mount Adams from the crest of Peterson Ridge.

One of the most exciting features of this area is the availability of

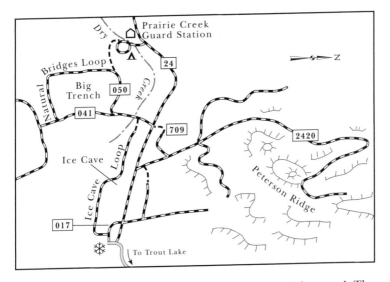

the old Prairie Creek Guard Station cabin for overnight rental. The facility sleeps up to six people and can be accessed by self-propelled trails or by a 2 1/4-mile dash on the groomed snowmobile highway. For information or reservations, write: Mount Adams Ranger District, 2455 Highway 141, Trout Lake, WA 98650. Or call: (509) 395-3400.

Access: From Highway 14 in the Columbia Gorge, head north on Highway 141 for 23 miles to Trout Lake. (If you are coming from the west, you may use Alternate Highway 141 and shorten your drive by a couple of miles.) At Trout Lake, the road divides; stay to the left, on Highway 141, and start watching your mileage. You will pass the Mount Adams Ranger Station before reaching an intersection at 1.7 miles. Go left, still on the narrow, sporadically plowed Highway 141, and drive until you reach another intersection, at 5.7 miles. Turn left and go the final 0.2 mile to the Atkisson Sno-Park (2,700 feet).

Ice Cave Loop: From the sno-park, follow the snowmobiles into the woods for 30 feet, to Spur Road 017. Go left. After 100 feet, the snowmobiles will head off to the right. The nonmotorized route follows a narrow old road through a second-growth forest.

After winding across the nearly level edges of Peterson Prairie for a mile, you will arrive at an intersection with the short spur trail to the Ice Cave. The Ice Cave is located 150 feet to the right. Snow-covered stairs and icy footing in the cave make it a very treacherous place to visit, but the icicles streaming off the ceiling are amazingly beautiful.

It is fun to grab a couple of flashlights (never explore a cave with just one) and explore from the stairs. Unfortunately, when the icicles are at their best, the floor of the cave is impossible to walk on. If you would really like to look around in the cave, come back in the summer.

To return to the loop, head back to the main trail and go right, skiing west for another mile to intersect Spur Road 041. The Natural Bridges loop is to the left, and the Ice Caves loop heads right, soon crossing the snowmobile-groomed Road 24. Once safely across the road-cum-snowmobile racetrack, follow the blue diamond markers on a cross-country trip through the forest for a short distance before turning right on Spur Road 709. At 2½ miles, this road ends and the loop route heads right, on Peterson Ridge Trail No. 2420. After paralleling a clearcut for ¼ mile, the route heads left across the snow covered countryside. The loop ends with a right turn that leads to Road 24. Cross the road and continue straight. You will rejoin the snowmobiles for the final ¼ mile of the loop back to the sno-park.

Natural Bridges Loop: Natural Bridges is a 3-mile extension of Ice Cave loop, with the added benefit of views as well as a couple of climbs and swooshing descents. Starting at the sno-park, follow the Ice Caves loop for the 2 miles to intersect Spur Road 041. Go left and climb for the next ½ mile to a clearcut at the crest of a low hill. Turn right and head west on Spur Road 050, paralleling the Big Trench. Little of this area can be seen or explored in the winter, as the covering of snow makes it hard to find the features and dangerous to look for them.

After heading west for ½ mile, the trail divides. Straight ahead a trail leads on ½ mile to Peterson Prairie Campground and the rental cabin. The Natural Bridges loop makes a 90-degree turn and heads left, along an exposed section of the trench, for a short ½ mile before making another left turn. When you reach Spur Road 041, go left once again to close the loop.

Peterson Ridge: This trip can be skied either as an extension of the Ice Cave Loop or independently. If you ski the entire Ice Cave Loop in addition to the Peterson Ridge Trail, your total will be 10¼ miles. However, if you head out from the sno-park and go right with the snowmobiles, as described below, you can reduce the trip to 9 miles.

From the sno-park, follow the snowmobiles into the woods for 30 feet. Where the trail divides, stay to the right and ski up the ¼-mile-long shared corridor to Road 24. Cross the groomed road and follow the blue diamond marked "Ice Cave Loop" for the next ¾ mile. (As a speedier alternative, you may follow the groomed snowmobile road.)

After crossing a broad clearcut, the trail intersects Road 2420; go right. The route to the ridge is well marked and easy to follow. Descend briefly to cross Dry Creek, then climb gradually, passing clearcuts and the eastern edge of Lost Meadow. At 4 miles from the sno-park, Road 2420 makes a radical turn to the right (3,450 feet), and the final 1/2 mile is spent in a climbing traverse to the crest of Peterson Ridge (3,650 feet).

Long spears of ice near the entrance to the Ice Cave

91 McCLELLAN MEADOWS LOOP

Open to: skis only
Surface: groomed and forest roads and trails
Rating: more difficult
Loop trip: 4¹/₄ miles
Skiing time: 3 hours
Elevation gain: 420 feet
High point: 3,050 feet
Best: mid-December–February
Avalanche potential: none
Maps: *Green Trails* Lone Butte #365 and Wind River #397; *USFS* Wind
  River Ranger District

The Wind River Winter Sports Area is one of the most intriguing sno-parks in the state. Skiers have a myriad of forest roads to tour, starting at seven different sno-parks. Of these seven sno-parks, four are reserved for nonmotorized winter sports.

In the nonmotorized area, skiers will find 15 miles of forest roads groomed and set with tracks, as well as another 15 miles of non-groomed roads and trails. Tour lengths vary from an easy 1¹/₄-mile romp on the groomed Old Man Loop to the challenging 12¹/₂-mile Road 65 Loop, which follows ungroomed roads and hiking trails.

The McClellan Meadows Loop is a combination loop, with both groomed roads and ungroomed trails. Plenty of opportunities exist for stride-and-glide–type touring, as well as for telemarkers to weave their magic over open hillsides. Except for one very tricky descent and one challenging climb, the skiing on this loop is not difficult.

Access: From Highway 14 in the Columbia River Gorge, drive

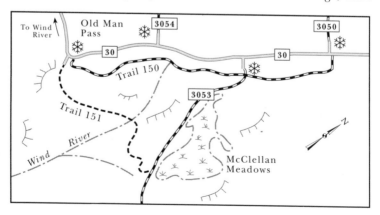

north to Carson, then continue into the mountains on Wind River Road. After 7 miles, Wind River Road becomes Forest Road 30. Proceed for another 14 miles, to Old Man Pass (3,050 feet), then descend 1.6 miles to the Road 3053 Sno-Park, located on the right (2,900 feet). **Note:** Road 30 is plowed on a low-priority basis. Driving can be difficult, and all cars, even those equipped with four-wheel-drive, should carry tire chains and a shovel. A sno-park permit is required.

The Tour: Start your tour at the restroom. Head into the forest, then go right on groomed Trail 150. The next 1 1/2 miles are spent climbing steadily through the forest, paralleling the main road, to the 3,050-foot crest of Old Man Pass. Where the trail ends, it dumps you onto Road 30. The easiest course is to remove your skis and descend to the road, then head left about 20 feet to the start of Trail 151.

Trail 151 is a true trail, narrow and ungroomed, leading you directly to adventure by swooping down through a clearcut to cross Wind River, a rather small creek (2,780 feet). The trail then climbs. The upward journey begins with a moderate traverse that turns into a steep scramble up a narrow cut to the top of a 3,000-foot ridge. At 3 miles, Trail 151 intersects the McClellan Meadows Trail (Road 3053) and ends. The meadows lie straight ahead through a narrow band of trees, but may be difficult to access due to a small creek. When there is sufficient snow, it is fun to explore the meadowlands looking for tracks of its native inhabitants.

The loop route turns left here, and heads northeast on the well-groomed Road 3053 for 1 1/4 miles, to the Road 3053 Sno-Park. There is an intersection just before the sno-park; go left, then take an almost immediate right, to return to the start at 4 1/4 miles.

Trail 151

92 HARDTIME LOOP

Open to: skis only
Surface: groomed
Rating: more difficult
Loop trip: 10½ miles
Skiing time: 5 hours
Elevation gain: 580 feet
High point: 3,280 feet
Best: mid-December–mid-March
Avalanche potential: none
Maps: *Green Trails* Wind River #397 and Lone Butte #365; *USFS* Wind River Ranger District

Hardtime—well, maybe if it was really icy. Otherwise the loop is smooth skiing all the way.

Access: From Highway 14 in the Columbia River Gorge, drive north to Carson, then continue into the mountains on Wind River Road. After 7 miles, Wind River Road becomes Forest Road 30. Proceed for another 14 miles, to Old Man Pass (3,050 feet), then descend 1.6 miles to the Road 3053 Sno-Park, located on the right (2,900 feet). *Note:* Road 30 is plowed on a low-priority basis. Driving can be difficult, and all cars, even those equipped with four-wheel-drive, should carry tire chains and a shovel. A sno-park permit is required.

The Tour: From the Road 3053 Sno-Park, walk past the information

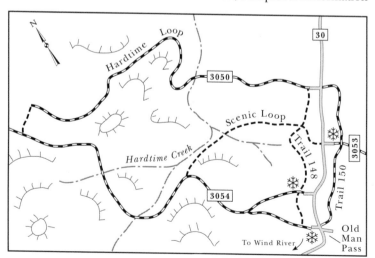

board, then ski into the woods for 20 feet to intersect the Hardtime Loop; take the trail on the right. You will return to this point on the trail to your left. The trail tunnels through the forest while gradually climbing for 1½ miles to the 3,050-foot summit of Old Man Pass. Cross to the west side of Road 30 and follow the well-marked trail back into the woods.

As you head through the trees, you will pass several intersections; stay left. The Hardtime Loop is joined by the Scenic Loop, and together the two loops head up the hillside on groomed Road 3054. The Indian Heaven Wilderness comes into view as you reach the first large clearcut, at 2¼ miles. At 3¼ miles, the Scenic Loop branches off to the right. (You can cut the trip in half by following this well-marked but ungroomed trail back.) The Hardtime Loop continues straight ahead. A short descent leads to a crossing of Hardtime Creek, and is followed by more gradual climbing.

At 6¼ miles, the loop route leaves Road 3054 and heads into the trees, following a line of blue diamond markers. Depending on conditions, this section of the loop may or may not be groomed, but

markers and nearly level terrain ensure an easy crossing to the next road. This pleasant interlude ends at 6½ miles, where the trail meets Road 3050 (3,200 feet).

Go right and ski down groomed tracks. In the next mile you will find several exhilarating descents through the forest and clearcuts, with views of Mount St. Helens, Mount Rainier, and Mount Adams. At 8½ miles, recross Hardtime Creek (2,700 feet), then begin a gradual climb to Road 30 (2,898 feet). At 10 miles, recross Road 30 and follow the rolling Hardtime Loop Trail for a final ¾ mile back to the Road 3053 Sno-Park.

Road 3054

93 COUGAR SNO-PARK

Kalama Ski Trail
Open to: skis and snowshoes
Surface: trails and forest roads
Rating: easiest to most difficult
Round trip: up to 26 miles
Skiing time: 1 hour to 3 days
Elevation gain: 2,302 feet
High point: 3,360 feet
Best: January–February
Avalanche potential: none
Maps: *Green Trails* Mount St. Helens #364 and *USGS* Goat Mtn.

Climbers Bivouac
Open to: all uses
Surface: roads groomed for snowmobiles
Rating: more difficult
Round trip: 9 1/2 miles
Skiing time: 4–5 hours
Elevation gain: 1,515 feet
High point: 3,765 feet
Best: January–March
Avalanche potential: low
Map: *Green Trails* Mount St. Helens #364

A casual glance at the Cougar Sno-Park is often enough to cause normally careful drivers to put pedal to the metal and depart at great

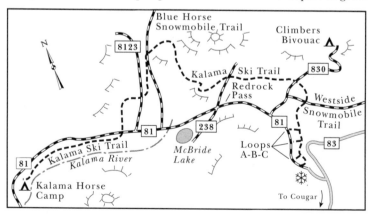

speed. The noise of the snowmobiles, the massive trailer and truck combinations, and the exhaust are enough to frighten anyone. If this has been your impression of Cougar Sno-Park, it is time to look again.

Starting just inside the gate is a nonmotorized trail system that runs for 13 miles along the south side of Mount St. Helens. The lower section of trail has several access options and numerous excellent views of the mountain. Skiers do not need to cover the entire distance for a rewarding day's outing; a few miles will do.

Climbers Bivouac is an alternative destination. Located on the flanks of the mountain, this primitive camping and summer staging area for climbers makes an incredibly scenic destination and ideal campsite.

Access: Exit Interstate 5 at Woodland and drive east on State Route 503 for 28.8 miles to Cougar. Go straight through town for another 6.8 miles, then turn left on Forest Road 83. After 3 miles the road divides (2,250 feet). Go left on Road 81, and immediately look for a place to park; on weekends you should arrive early. Snowmobiles rarely visit on weekdays. A sno-park permit is required.

Kalama Ski Trail: The ski trail begins about 30 feet up the snowmobile raceway. The first section is one of the hardest. The narrow trail climbs steadily through dense second growth, with an occasional view. The pathway, rated *most difficult,* is at its best when there has been a recent snowfall to soften the tread. When it is icy, consider skipping the lower portion altogether. The Kalama Ski Trail has three alternate access points. The Loop A access is located a short 1/2 mile up Road 81, the Loop B access can be found 1 mile up Road 81, and the Loop C access is found 1 1/2 miles up the road. When conditions are less than optimal, ski up the road to the Loop B trail access. From that point, the trail is nearly as easy to ski as the road.

The Kalama Ski Trail crosses the Westside Snowmobile Trail, and soon after, at about the 3-mile point, crosses Spur Road 830. At 5 miles, ski across Trail 238. A left turn here will take you across the snow-covered lava field to intercept Road 81 at Redrock Pass. The Kalama Ski Trail spends the next 2 miles climbing to its 3,360-foot high point, then begins descending, crossing the Blue Horse Snowmobile Trail and then, 3/4 mile beyond, crossing Road 8123. Near the 11-mile point, the trail crosses Road 81 and spends the final 2 miles sandwiched between the road and the Kalama River.

Climbers Bivouac: This fun tour can be skied entirely on roads or in conjunction with the Kalama Ski Trail. Snowmobiles are allowed on the road for the entire distance, but are rarely seen on the upper 3 miles.

From the Cougar Sno-Park, follow Road 81 for 1³/₄ miles to a wide, groomed, and well-signed intersection. Following signs to the Climbers Bivouac, go right and head uphill for ¹/₂ mile to a second well-signed intersection. Head to the left and begin the long uphill climb on Spur Road 830. To reach the spectacular views, you have to ski the entire distance. From the bivouac, Mount Adams stands tall to the east, while Mount St. Helens stands as tall as she is still able, domineering the northern skyline. Don't be surprised to find you are sharing the tour with numerous climbers. The Climbers Bivouac is the starting point for climbs up the Ptarmigan Trail to the Monitor Ridge Route. All ski tours to the summit require a permit.

Mount St. Helens viewed from Climbers Bivouac

94 MARBLE MOUNTAIN

Open to: all uses
Surface: groomed for snowmobiles
Rating: more difficult
Round trip: 11 miles
Skiing time: 6 hours
Elevation gain: 1,488 feet
High point: 4,128 feet
Best: January–mid-March
Avalanche potential: low
Map: *Green Trails* Mount St. Helens #364

A full day of views and a fantastic, uninterrupted 2 1/4-mile descent ensure that this tour will never lose its spot as one of the best ski trips in the state.

Access: Exit Interstate 5 at Woodland and drive east on State Route 503 for 28.8 miles to Cougar. Go straight through town and continue east for 6.8 miles, then turn left on Forest Road 83. After 3 miles, pass the Cougar Sno-Park. Stay right on Road 83 for another 2.7 miles, to the huge Marble Mountain Sno-Park at the end of the plowing (2,640 feet). When the main parking area is full of trailers and big rigs, use the single vehicle parking area at the head of Road 8312. When both lots are full, you must descend a mile back to the Over Flow lot, and that is no fun at all! Be sure to display your sno-park permit, no matter which lot you choose.

The Tour: Either follow the skier signs out of the lower side of the main parking area, or head right out from the single vehicle parking lot. From the main lot, follow the snowmobile route across Road 83, through the woods, and then down to the Road 8312 gate. The tour begins with

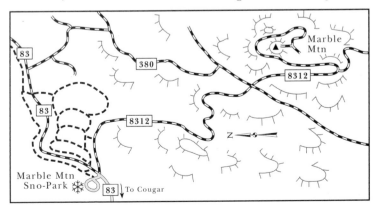

an easy downhill glide on the snowmobile-groomed Road 8312. The gradual descent takes you past the lower entrance to Marble Loop. Cross June Lake Creek and pass Trail 245B to Beaver Loop. After crossing East Fork Swift Creek at 3/4 mile, it is time to switch gears and climb.

The climb is steady, traversing into a small side valley and then abruptly turning east to open slopes. Starting at 2 miles are tremendous views of the south side of Mount St. Helens, from the crater rim down the gleaming white slopes, through the Worm Flows formations to the forest below.

At 2 3/4 miles, the road heads up to a narrow fold in the hills and arrives at the Four Corners junction in another 1/4 mile (3,360 feet). Go right on an easy glide over broad, rolling clear-cut slopes. Here the road levels, and it's time to practice skating on the snowmobile-packed (but not machine-groomed) surface.

The road starts to climb again near 4 1/4 miles, spiraling its way to the 4,128-foot summit of Marble Mountain and views of Mount St. Helens, Mount Adams, Mount Rainier, Mount Hood and Mount Jefferson, Swift Reservoir, endless clearcuts, roads, and forests. (On a clear day you may prefer to cut a mile from the total by leaving Road 8312 at the summit and descending west to rejoin the road below.)

Snowmobiles are in evidence on this road nearly every day. Although the road is too short for the machines to get in a full day's exercise, the open meadows above the 3-mile point draw them in. Start your trip early, but not so early that you are ready to leave the summit before the first snowmobilers arrive. Watching them try to

turn their snowmobiles in the limited space at the top is as good as a trip to the circus. If you feel that snowmobiles do not belong on this road, please send a letter to: District Ranger, Mount St. Helens National Volcanic Monument, Amboy, WA 98601.

If you enjoy loops, you can return to the start by following Spur Road 380 from Four Corners. The road heads over a hill, then divides. Go left for a 3-mile trip down to intercept Road 83, just 2 1/2 miles from the sno-park.

Skier near Four Corners Junction

95 JUNE LAKE LOOP

Open to: skis and snowshoes
Surface: forest roads and trails
Rating: more difficult
Loop trip: 5 miles
Skiing time: 3 hours
Elevation gain: 560 feet
High point: 3,200 feet
Best: January–February
Avalanche potential: low
Map: *Green Trails* Mount St. Helens NW #364S

June Lake is a five-star destination. It gets stars for having a lake, a waterfall, unlimited views of snow-covered Mount St. Helens, sheltered campsites, and a loop for those so inclined.

Access: Exit Interstate 5 at Woodland and drive east on State Route 503 for 28.8 miles to Cougar. Go straight through town and continue east for 6.8 miles, then turn left on Forest Road 83. After 3 miles, pass the Cougar Sno-Park. Stay right on Road 83 for another 2.7 miles, to the huge Marble Mountain Sno-Park at the end of the plowing (2,640 feet). When the main parking area is full of trailers and big rigs, use the single vehicle parking area at the head of Road 8312. When both lots are full, you must descend a mile back to the Over Flow lot. Be sure to display your sno-park permit.

The Tour: From the sno-park, there are three ways to cover the

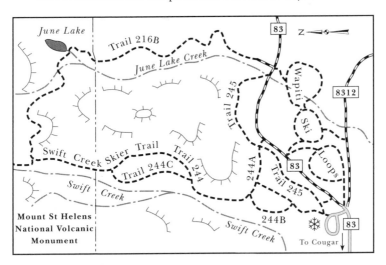

³/₄ mile to the June Lake trailhead. The easiest is to join the snowmobiles and ski-groomed Road 83 for ³/₄ mile. The road is accessed from the lower side of the northern end of the parking area. If you prefer skier-only trails, try Pine Martin Trail No. 245. This delightful trail starts from the upper north end of the parking loop and parallels Road 83 for 1 mile. Where the trail ends, go left and ski the road over the Lake Creek road bridge to find a large sign marking the June Lake trailhead on your left (2,700 feet). Your third option is to follow the Wapiti Ski Loops, located on the south side of Road 83, to the June Lake trailhead. If you choose this option, be sure to pick up a map at the warming hut before you head out.

Once you reach the June Lake Trail (216B), follow the well-marked route up an old clearcut, first on road, then on a broad trail. Ahead, Mount St. Helens is in full view. At 2 ¹/₈ miles from the sno-park, the trail officially enters Mount St. Helens National Volcanic Monument. A short, steep drop is followed by a short climb to a bridged creek crossing. Ski out onto an open bench. June Lake and the waterfall are to your right, bounded by steep cliffs (3,100 feet). The level area near the lake offers excellent campsites. Stay back from the edge of the lake; it is difficult to determine where the lakeshore starts in this broad, flat field of snow.

Skiers opting to make the loop should climb the open slope beyond the lake, heading toward the mountain. (This route is marked.) Near the top of the slope, go left and ski down to a small wooded bench (good campsites). Cross the bench and climb up and over a steep rib, angling toward the mountain.

At ¹/₂ mile from June Lake is the Swift Creek Skier Trail, a narrow corridor through the forest well marked by blue diamonds. If you followed the Swift Creek Skier Trail to the right, you would be on the climbers' route up the mountain. The loop route turns left and descends Trail 244 down the Swift Creek valley. The trail divides twice, giving you options for more challenging descents on Trails 244C and 244B. The ski trail joins a snowmobile road shortly before the parking area.

Descending Swift Creek Skier Trail

96 SASQUATCH LOOPS

Open to: skis and snowshoes
Surface: forest roads and trails
Rating: most difficult
Round trip: 8 miles
Skiing time: 4 hours
Elevation gain: 740 feet
High point: 3,440 feet
Best: January–February
Avalanche potential: low
Map: *Green Trails* Mount St. Helens NW #364S

For the views, for the challenge, and for the pure joy of skiing—the Sasquatch Loops take you away from the noise, hustle, and smell of the snowmachines, away from the crowds of fellow skiers, and out into the quiet forest plantations at the base of Mount St. Helens.

If the loops are skied in a clockwise direction, you will climb the steepest sections of the trail and find all descents to be gradual. For a challenge, reverse the loop. If you want out early, you can shortcut 3 miles by taking the Middle Loop Trail. Routefinding is the main challenge for skiers doing the entire loop. The blue diamonds that mark the route of the upper sections of the loop are often snow-covered or completely missing, demanding some luck and considerable common sense to make your way around the entire route.

Access: Exit Interstate 5 at Woodland and drive east on State Route 503 for 28.8 miles to Cougar. Go straight through town and continue east for 6.8 miles, then turn left on Forest Road 83. After 3 miles, pass

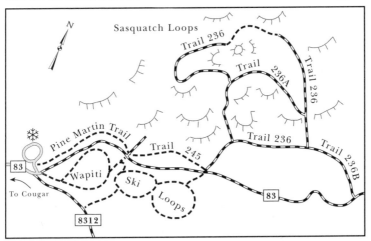

the Cougar Sno-Park. Stay right on Road 83 for another 2.7 miles, to the huge Marble Mountain Sno-Park at the end of the plowing (2,640 feet). When the main parking area is full of trailers and big rigs, use the single vehicle parking area at the head of Road 8312. When both lots are full, you must descend a mile back to the Over Flow lot. Be sure to display your sno-park permit.

The Tour: From the upper end of the parking area, ski Pine Martin Trail No. 245 for 1 3/4 miles to its end at the base of the Sasquatch Loops. The trail cuts through the thick forest and can be slow going, so if you are short on time or low on energy, you may join the snowmobiles and race along Road 83 for 1 1/2 miles from the sno-park to the start of the Sasquatch Loops (2,763 feet).

The Sasquatch Loops start on the left side of Road 83, a few feet from the end of the Pine Martin Trail. Ski to the large map board that marks the trailhead, then head uphill for 1/4 mile to an intersection and the start of the loop portion of the tour (2,870 feet). Take the left fork and head through a band of trees to an open basin. The trail contours around the basin, climbing rapidly along an old road. At 2 3/4 miles, the trail reaches the crest of a ridge and intersects a wide logging road (3,280 feet). To the right is the shorter Middle Loop Trail No. 236A. The Long Loop heads left, contouring around the ridge to views of Marble Mountain and Mount Adams. After passing a weather station, the road swings west around the ridge to a view of the Worm Flows on the side of Mount St. Helens.

Your routefinding difficulties begin where the road ends (3,430 feet). Continue straight ahead on a trail, marked with blue diamonds, that traverses around the hillside and then descends to a broad, flat ridge top. Head straight across the open ridge. About halfway across, the trail disappears. At this point you should angle off to your left. You will find the trail again about 200 feet from the wall of trees along the northwest side of a clearcut. Parallel the trees until you find a narrow road. The road soon divides; stay right and follow it on to a second intersection, at 4 1/4 miles, and again go right.

Descend at a steady rate down a road that serves as a riverbed during spring runoff. At 5 1/4 miles, the Middle Loop Trail No. 236A is passed on the right. Continue down for 1/4 mile to reach the Trail 236B intersection. Go right on Trail 236 to reach the end of the loop portion of your tour, at 6 miles. Retrace your tracks back to Road 83. To return to the sno-park, you may ski the road (quickest), return via Pine Martin Trail No. 245, or, if you are looking for fun, cross Road 83 and wander through the Wapiti Ski Loops.

Skiers crossing narrow bridge on Wapiti Ski Loops

97 LAHAR VIEWPOINT

Open to: all uses
Surface: trails and road groomed for snowmobiles
Rating: easiest
Loop trip: 8 miles
Skiing time: 5 hours
Elevation gain: 410 feet
High point: 2,930 feet
Best: mid-December–March
Avalanche potential: none
Map: *Green Trails* Mount St. Helens #364

An early start will help you avoid the rush along this popular multiple-use road. The destination is the massive mudflow area that turns into a beautiful, open, snow-covered plain in the winter. This vast, sparkling plain rises to the gleaming slopes of Mount St. Helens, and the overall result is an ice sculpture that would win first prize in any contest.

On the weekends, snowshoers, hikers, and an endless stream of snowmobilers share this tour with the skiers. The snowmobilers use the road as an access to the mudflow, where they are free to head across the open slopes, climbing to the Plains of Abraham and on to a view over Spirit Lake from Windy Ridge.

Skiers may avoid much of the noise and smell by spending the first and last portion of the tour on skier-only trails. Skiing these trails is neither as quick nor as easy as following the groomed road used by the snowmobiles, but it is a whole lot more peaceful.

Access: Exit Interstate 5 at Woodland and drive east on State Route 503 for 28.8 miles to Cougar. Go straight through town and continue east for 6.8 miles, then turn left on Forest Road 83. After 3 miles, pass the Cougar Sno-Park. Stay right on Road 83 for another 2.7 miles, to the huge Marble Mountain Sno-Park at the end of the plowing (2,640

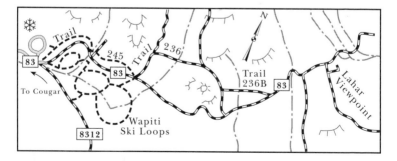

feet). When the main parking area is full of trailers and big rigs, use the single vehicle parking area at the head of Road 8312. When both lots are full, you must descend a mile back to the Over Flow lot. Be sure to display your sno-park permit.

The Tour: If you have beginners in your party or are getting the suggested early start, then start your tour by skiing up Road 83. You may access this road by the snowmobile ramp located at the lower side of the parking loop. Road 83 is then followed for 4 1/4 miles to the Lahar area, where you leave the forest and enter the open plain (2,930 feet). When you are done staring at Mount St. Helens, swing around for a view of Mount Adams to the east and Mount Hood to the south.

If you choose to avoid the road, walk the upper end of the parking loop and scramble up the bank to find the start of Pine Martin Trail No. 245. This trail parallels Road 83 for 1 3/4 miles, passing the start of the Swift Creek Trail and the June Lake Trail before it ends at the Sasquatch trailhead. You can continue to avoid the road by following Sasquatch Trail No. 236. You will add an extra mile to your trip length and an extra 1/2 hour of skiing time. Ski up Sasquatch Trail No. 236 for 1/4 mile to the first intersection, then go right, heading up a low hill for 1/2 mile to a second intersection. Continue straight on rarely used Trail 236B, which heads east to end at Road 83, at the 3 1/4-mile point. Go left for the final 2 miles to the Lahar area.

Once you reach the open plains of the mudflow, descend to the intersection and head left, still following Road 83. The groomer does not go here, and neither do the majority of the snowmobilers. You can angle down and across the plains for 3/4 mile to reach road's end at Lava Canyon. Do not venture out on the trails in this area; they are steep, slippery, and very hazardous.

If you armed yourself with a map before starting out, try the Wapiti Ski Loops on the way back. These trails may be accessed from Road 83, opposite the start of the Sasquatch Trails. The Wapiti Ski Loops will bring you back to the Marble Mountain Sno-Park after some pleasant meandering through the forest and meadows.

Skier on the open Lahar plains below Mount St. Helens

98 MOUNT ST. HELENS

Open to: skis and snowshoes
Surface: trail and open slopes
Rating: mountaineer
Round trip: 8 miles
Skiing time: 8 hours
Elevation gain: 5,725 feet via Worm Flows
High point: 8,365 feet
Best: January–May
Avalanche potential: moderate
Map: *Green Trails* Mount St. Helens #364

Mount St. Helens, or what remains of it, is a telemarkers' haven. The slopes are uniform, and when the sun softens the snow, they are ski-able by anyone who can do a kick-turn.

But skiing Mount St. Helens is not a cakewalk. When the snow refuses to soften, the icy slopes are a horror to three-pinners, and nasty, even fatal slips are possible. In addition, there are dangers to skiing any major peak that demand the skill and judgment of experienced mountaineers.

Skiing above 4,800 feet on Mount St. Helens requires a permit. An unlimited number of these permits are self-issued daily between November 1 and May 15. From May 16 through October, however, only a hundred permits are issued per day; fifty of these permits may be reserved in advance by writing to: Mount St. Helens National Volcanic Monument Headquarters, Route 1, Box 269, Amboy, WA 98601. The remaining fifty permits are available at Jacks Restaurant

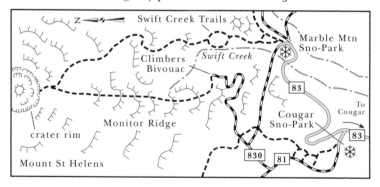

in Yale, on a first-come basis on the day of the tour. When eruption hazard is high, all permits are invalidated.

Access: For the Worm Flows route, drive to the Marble Mountain Sno-Park, as described in Tour 94. For the Monitor Ridge Route, park at the Cougar Sno-Park, as described in Tour 93.

The Worm Flows: During the winter months, this is the easiest route to access. The trip begins at the upper side of the parking loop, just above the warming hut. Climb the snowmobile ramp and head into the trees for 20 feet, to the first intersection. Go straight and follow the blue diamonds through the forest to Swift Creek Ski Trail No. 244. At 1/4 mile, Trail 244B branches off to the left. Either Trail 244 or 244B may be used; Trail 244 is the easiest. Follow the trail of your choice to its intersection with Trail 244A, an old logging road, then go left, climbing steadily up the Swift Creek valley.

Near the 1-mile point, the trail divides again. Both trails go to the same place, so either take the steeper Trail 244C on the left or stick with Trail 244 and continue the ascent. Shortly after the two trails rejoin you will reach the June Lake Trail intersection, at 2 1/4 miles (3,500 feet). Continue straight along the snow-covered ridge. The climb abates as you leave the trees, then increases as you cross Swift Creek and head toward the base of the mountain.

At 2 3/4 miles (3,800 feet), pass the last campsites and begin the long haul up the mountain. Pick an elevated area for your ascent, following the twisty turns of one of the Worm Flows to the crest of Monitor Ridge, which you reach at around the 7,200-foot level. Once on the ridge, angle a bit to the west for your final push to the 8,300-foot crater rim. The actual 8,365-foot high point is located 3/4 mile to the west. Use extreme caution as you approach the crater rim. A huge, 50-foot cornice usually extends off the rim over the crater. Posts have been placed to let you know where the rim is. If the posts are covered with snow, stay far back from the edge.

The Monitor Ridge Route: From the Cougar Sno-Park, ski up to the Climbers Bivouac, as described in Tour 93. Follow Ptarmigan Trail No. 216A to timberline. Once out of the trees, turn right and follow a gully up to a small bench (4,800 feet), where the real climb begins. Ski west, climbing a steepish slope to the ridge top, then head north toward the crater rim, skiing up a series of narrow gullies and ribs on the west side of Monitor Ridge. At 6,200 feet, the last gully peters out and a steep (often icy) slope must be cautiously traversed or avoided by dropping below it. When the snow is unstable, the slope should be completely avoided by climbing to the ridge above and following the exposed rocks to the main snow slopes.

Once the steep slope is traversed, climb to the right (east), following the natural roll of the terrain up Monitor Ridge to the crest at 7,200 feet. On the left, skirt a large bowl, which is prone to avalanche when the snow is unstable. Once on the ridge, turn north and ski the open slopes toward the crater.

Skier descending from the Worm Flows

99 OBSTRUCTION POINT

Open to: nonmotorized
Surface: forest road
Rating: most difficult
Round trip: 16 miles
Skiing time: 2 days
Elevation gain: 1,300 feet
High point: 6,200 feet
Best: January–April
Avalanche potential: moderate
Map: *Custom Correct* Hurricane Ridge

The Obstruction Point Trail follows a primitive, single lane road along the steep flanks of Hurricane Ridge to high alpine meadows on snow-covered ridge tops, with panoramic vistas over Olympic National Park. Ambitious and energetic skiers can reach the meadows and return in a single day; however, the ideal way to enjoy the tour is to spend the night. Skiers with two days have plenty of time to leave their neatest telemark signatures on all the slopes.

Although an overnight trip is undoubtedly the best way to enjoy the area, it is not a trip to be undertaken lightly. Cars cannot be left overnight anywhere near the trailhead, and skiers are faced with a hitchhike up the road. Weather can be vicious, making a campsite in the meadows risky in uncertain weather.

Access: From Port Angeles, drive 17 miles up the Hurricane Ridge road to Hurricane Ridge. Before setting out, pay the usage fee and register your tour at the Hurricane Ridge Visitor Center. Once checked in, drive back to the trail sign at the parking lot entrance, drop packs, skis, and extra skiers, then drive back down the road several miles to the well-signed but frequently moved overnight parking area.

The Tour: Following narrow Obstruction Point Road, the tour

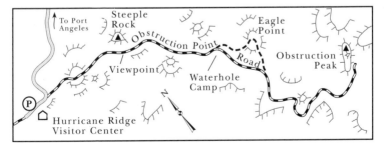

Steeple Rock and Eagle Point from Hurricane Ridge

begins with a steeply descending traverse along a very exposed hillside. Don't be afraid to take off your skis and walk. Just keep your shoe holes away from the ski tracks. The rapid descent continues until the road reaches the forested crest of the ridge. The descent then moderates but continues as you follow the ridge east. Near the 1-mile point, the road begins to climb, breaking into the open 1/2 mile later on the south side of Steeple Rock. Views extend over the Bailey Range and the Alaskan-looking, 7,965-foot lord of the area, Mount Olympus. If the snow is icy or the weather is bad, make the edge of the clearing the turnaround.

Beyond the clearing the road reenters forest, traverses around two more small hills, and at 3 1/2 miles reaches forested Waterhole Camp (5,000 feet), a good enough destination if you are running late; keep in mind that the road back to Port Angeles is gated at dusk.

Waterhole Camp is the last protected and level site on this tour. Ski to your right to find the outhouse, and left or right of the road for campsites. If the weather is stable and you trust the local weather report, you may want to continue on and find a camp on the open slopes above.

The road now climbs, gaining 750 feet in the next 1 1/2 miles while traversing the south side of 6,247-foot Eagle Point. The last 3 miles to Obstruction Point cross open meadows above tree line, exposing skiers to grand views, sometimes dangerously icy hills, and perhaps bad weather. The final mile climbs to the end of Obstruction Point Road (6,150 feet), with excellent views and scenic good-weather campsites. Travel beyond the point is not recommended due to high avalanche potential.

At the end of your tour, be sure to return to the visitor center to sign out on the register.

100 HURRICANE HILL

Ridge Road
Open to: nonmotorized
Surface: forest roads
Rating: more difficult
Round trip: 3 miles
Skiing time: 2 hours
Elevation gain: 200 feet
High point: 5,200 feet
Best: January–mid-April
Avalanche potential: none
Map: *Custom Correct* Hurricane Ridge

Hilltop
Open to: nonmotorized
Surface: trails
Rating: backcountry
Round trip: 6 miles
Skiing time: 4 hours
Elevation gain: 760 feet
High point: 5,757 feet
Best: January–mid-April
Avalanche potential: moderate
Map: *Custom Correct* Hurricane Ridge

Don't expect to be alone amid the scenery that led the United Na-
tions to designate Olympic National Park a World Heritage Park. In

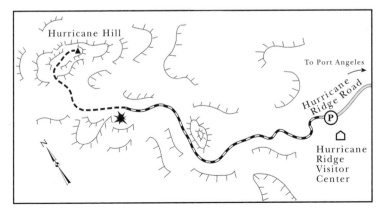

good weather, throngs of Nordic skiers swarm the unplowed road from Hurricane Ridge Visitor Center. Once the road ends, backcountry skiers continue cross-country to the summit of Hurricane Hill for more views and glorious telemark descents of the steep bowls.

Access: From Port Angeles, drive 17 miles up the Hurricane Ridge road to Hurricane Ridge. Register your trip destination at the visitor center (5,200 feet).

The Tour: Ski west from the lodge, skirting the downhill ski area, following the route of the snow-covered road. The road is easy to follow once it enters the trees and begins its descent along the ridge crest. At 1 mile the road levels, passes the picnic area, then climbs a bit to end at 1 1/2 miles.

An information board at the end of the road marks the turn-around point for skiers. Beyond here it is a difficult 1 1/2-mile climb to the crest of Hurricane Hill, and competence in telemarking and backcountry travel is essential. Also, skiers need to keep an eye on the weather, which can change from balmy sunshine to a blinding blizzard in a very short time. Be prepared for a quick retreat.

Part of the way is on a very narrow ridge with a knife-edge crest. Stay atop the ridge and climb over a small knoll rather than trying to traverse its very steep and dangerous sides. Ski down the far side of the knoll, wary of cornices on the north (right), then go around a second knoll to the foot of Hurricane Hill.

A rock outcrop amid stunted, wind-blasted trees marks the 5,757-foot summit. Gaze over Port Angeles, the Strait of Juan de Fuca, Victoria, Vancouver Island Mountains, the British Columbia Coast Range, and, of course, Mount Baker. Reach for another sandwich and turn to gaze over the Elwha Valley and Bailey Range to Olympus.

Windswept crest of Hurricane Ridge

APPENDIX A

HANDY LIST OF ADDRESSES AND SUGGESTED READING

Avalanche Conditions
North and Central Cascades: (206) 526-6677
Southern Cascades: (503) 808-2400

Groomed Area Snow Conditions
Lake Easton State Park: (509) 656-2586
Lake Wenatchee State Park: (509) 763-3103
Leavenworth Winter Sports Club: (509) 548-5115
Methow Valley Sport Trails Association: (800) 682-5787
Mt. Tahoma Ski Trails Association: (360) 569-2451
Rendezvous Outfitters, Inc.: (800) 422-3048
Spokane Parks and Recreation: (509) 625-6200

Forest Service and Park Service Phone Numbers
Chelan Ranger Station: (509) 682-2576
Cle Elum Ranger Station: (509) 674-4411
Cowlitz Valley Ranger Station: (360) 479-1100
Glacier Public Service Center: (360) 599-2714
Lake Wenatchee Ranger Station: (509) 763-3103
Leavenworth Ranger Station: (509) 548-5817 or (509) 548-6977
Mount Adams Ranger District: (509) 395-3400
Mount Baker Ranger District: (360) 856-5700
Mount Rainier National Park: (360) 569-2211
Mount St. Helens National Volcanic Monument: (360) 274-5473
Naches Ranger District: (509) 653-2205
North Cascades National Park: (360) 856-5700
Olympic National Park: (360) 452-4501
Republic Ranger District: (509) 775-3305
Skykomish Ranger Station: (360) 677-2414
Verlot Public Service Center: (360) 691-7791
White River Ranger Station: (206) 825-2571
Wind River Ranger Station: (509) 427-5645
Winthrop Ranger Station: (509) 996-22

Addresses

Mount Adams Ranger District
2455 Highway 141
Trout Lake, WA 98650

Mount St. Helens National Volcanic Monument
Route 1, Box 269
Amboy, WA 98601

Mt. Tahoma Trails Association
P.O. Box 206
Ashford, WA 98304

Republic Ranger District
P.O. Box 468
Republic, WA 99166

Websites

Forest Service National Avalanche Center: *www.nwac.noaa.gov/*
Mountain pass road and weather information: *www.traffic.wsdot.wa.gov
    /gov/sno-info/*
Sno-park information: *www.parks.wa.gov/winter/*
White Pass information and maps: *www.skiwhitepass.com*

SUGGESTED READING

Avalanche Safety

Daffern, Tony. *Avalanche Safety for Skiers, Climbers, & Snowboarders,* 2d
    ed. Seattle: The Mountaineers Books.
Tremper, Bruce. *Staying Alive in Avalanche Terrain.* Seattle: The
    Mountaineers Books.

Enjoying the Outdoors (Proper Clothing, Ski Equipment, Winter Camping)

Graydon, Don, and Kurt Hanson ed. *Mountaineering: The Freedom of
    the Hills,* 6th ed. Seattle: The Mountaineers Books.

First Aid

Carline, Jan, Martha Lentz, & Steven MacDonald. *Mountaineering
    First Aid: A Guide to Accident Response and First-Aid Care,* 4th ed.
    Seattle: The Mountaineers Books.

Wilkerson, James. *Medicine For Mountaineering & Other Wilderness Activities*, 5th ed. Seattle: The Mountaineers Books.

Wilkerson, James, ed. *Hypothermia, Frostbite, and Other Cold Injuries: Prevention, Recognition, Prehospital Treatment.* Seattle: The Mountaineers Books.

How-To

Gillette, Ned and John Dostal. *Cross-Country Skiing,* 3rd ed. Seattle: The Mountaineers Books.

Parker, Paul. *Free-Heel Skiing: Telemark & Parallel Techniques for All Conditions,* 3rd ed. Seattle: The Mountaineers Books.

APPENDIX B

TOURS ORGANIZED BY SKI AREA

Ski Area	Sno-Park Pass Required	Special Groomed Area Sticker Required	Commercial Area	Groomed	Not Groomed	Reference
Atkisson	X				X	Tour 90
Blewett Pass	X				X	Tours 23, 24, and 25
Boulder Deer Creek	X			X	X	Tour 49
Boundary	X				X	None
Cabin Creek	X	X		X		Tours 57 and 58
Chiwawa Road	X	X		X		Tour 18
Cougar	X				X	Tours 93 and 98
Crow Lake Way	X				X	Tour 86
Crystal Springs	X			X		Tours 59 and 60
Cub Creek			X	X		Tour 40
Deer Creek					X	Tours 9 and 10
DNR Road 1	X			X		Tour 72
DNR Road 92	X			X		Tour 71

	1	2	3	4	5	
Downriver Golf Course	X			X		Tour 53
Echo Ridge	X			X		Tours 32 and 33
Echo Valley Nordic			X	X		Tour 31
Field's Spring State Park	X			X		Tour 54
Geophysical	X			X		Tour 51
Goose Egg	X				X	Tour 85
Hells Crossing	X				X	Tour 86
Highlands	X			X		Tour 47
Hurricane Ridge					X	Tours 99 and 100
Icicle	X				X	Tour 21
Kahler Glen Golf Course		X		X		Tour 17
Keechelus	X			X		Tours 59 and 60
Lake Easton State Park		X		X		Tour 56
Lake Wenatchee State Park North	X	X		X		Tour 17
Lake Wenatchee State Park South	X	X		X		Tour 17
Leavenworth, Golf Course			X	X		Tour 20
Leavenworth, Icicle River			X	X		Tour 20
Leavenworth, Ski Hill			X	X		Tour 20
Loup Loup (Bear Mountain)			X	X		Tour 35

Ski Area	Sno-Park Pass Required	Special Groomed Area Sticker Required	Commercial Area	Groomed	Not Groomed	Reference
Marble Mountain	X			X		Tours 94, 95, 96, 97 and 98
Mazama			X	X		Tours 36 and 45
Methow Valley Trails			X	X		Tours 36–46
Mount Baker					X	Tours 1, 2, 4, 5, and 6
Mount Rainier National Park					X	Tours 66, 68, 74, 75, 76, and 77
Mount Spokane	X	X		X		Tour 52
North Fork Tieton	X	May be coming soon		X		Tours 83 and 84
Orr Creek	X				X	Tour 79
Pineside	X			X		Tours 87 and 88
Pipe Creek	X				X	Tour 26
Pipeline	X			X		Tour 88
Pleasant Valley	X				X	Tour 86
Rendezvous			X	X		Tours 40, 41, and 43
Riverside State Park	X			X		Tour 53
Salmon Ridge	X			X		Tour 3
Satus Pass	X				X	None

Location				Tour
Sherman Pass	X		X	Tour 48
Smith Butte	X		X	Tour 89
Snoqualmie Pass Nordic Center		X	X	Tour 64
South Summit (Loup Loup)	X	X		Tour 34
Stehekin		X		Tours 29 and 30
Stevens Pass Cross-Country		X	X	Tours 14 and 15
Sun Mountain		X	X	Tour 37
Suntop	X	X		Tour 65
Swauk Creek Campground	X		X	Tour 27
Tronson Meadow	X		X	Tour 23
Twenty-five–Mile Creek	X		X	None
Union Creek	X		X	Tour 86
Upper Wolf		X		Tour 50
White Pass Touring Center		X	X	Tour 82
White Road	X		X	Tour 80
Wind River	X	X		Tours 91 and 92

APPENDIX C

TRAIL COMPARISON CHART

Chart Key

Distance. One-way mileages for each tour are listed by type. Groomed Ski Trails, Groomed Snowmobile Trails, Forest Road, Trail, and Open Slope. See Introduction, page 19, for definitions of these surfaces.

Rating. Only the least skill required to ski the area is listed. The ratings are E (easiest), D (more difficult), MD (most difficult), BC (backcountry), M (Mountaineer). See Introduction, page 21 for explanations of these terms. Some areas that are rated Easiest may also have trails that are More Difficult or Most Difficult.

Please note that the rating given may not always be in agreement with those given at the areas. More Difficult trails at some areas may actually be harder then Most Difficult at others. We have tried to remain consistent throughout the book in the ratings of the areas.

Elevation gain. The listed elevation is the amount of climbing needed to complete the trip. All elevations are given in feet.

Avalanche potential.
N = no avalanche potential
low = low avalanche potential
M = moderate potential for avalanches
H = high potential for avalanches at some point of the trip. Read tour directions before heading out.

For more information on Avalanche Potential and how it pertains to the daily avalanche hazard, please read the Introduction, pages 23 and 24.

Fees.
Yes = a fee will be collected at the trailhead.

Sno-Park permit.
Yes = you will need a sno-park permit to park at the trailhead.
Yes* = a sno-park permit with a Special Groomed Area sticker is required for parking.

Tour	Miles Groomed	Miles Groomed for Snowmobiles	Miles of Forest Road	Miles of Trail	Miles of Open Slopes	Rating	Elevation Gain	Avalanche Potential	Fees	Sno-Park permits
1. Heliotrope Ridge			5	6	2	BC	3,700	low		
2. North Fork Nooksack			3			E	400	low		
3. Salmon Ridge Sno-Park		6	2			E	1,200	low		Yes
4. Artist Point					5	BC	1,100	low		
Coleman Pinnacle					11	M	2,080	H		
5. Herman Saddle					3	BC	1,060	M		
6. Park Butte			5		4	BC	3,100	M		Yes
7. Kennedy Hot Springs				5		BC	2,300	H		
8. Schweizer Creek Loop			6	1		MD	1,800	low		
9. Deer Creek Road			3 +	1		D	1,500	low		
10. Big Four and Coal Lake			9			E	2,160	M		
11. Miller River			5	2		E	2,100	low		
12. Skyline Ridge					2	BC	1,200	low		
13. Smith Brook			2			D	800	H		
Lake Valhalla						BC	1,900	H		
14. Stevens Pass Cross-Country	8					E	1,220	low	Yes	
15. Lanham Lake				2	2	BC	1,283	N	Yes	
Jim Hill						M	3,805	M	Yes	

Tour	Miles Groomed	Miles Groomed for Snowmobiles	Miles of Forest Road	Miles of Trail	Miles of Open Slopes	Rating	Elevation Gain	Avalanche Potential	Fees	Sno-Park permits
16. Coulter Ski Trail / Scottish Lakes			7	10		MD / BC	2,800 / 2,000	low / M	Yes / Yes	
17. Lake Wenatchee State Park	14					E	430	N		Yes*
18. Chiwawa Sno-Park	5		6	4		E	680	N		Yes*
19. Little Wenatchee River Road			4 +			E	0	N		
20. Leavenworth	9					E	200	N	Yes	
21. Icicle Creek Road			4 +			E	780	low		Yes
22. Van Creek Loop		3	4			D	1,135	low		
23. Tronson Meadow Loops			10			D	500	low		Yes
24. Wenatchee Ridge		1	2			D	458	low		Yes
25. Haney Meadow				5		BC	1,860	M		Yes
26. Pipe Creek Sno-Park			4	1		MD	550	low		Yes
27. Old Blewett Pass Highway Skiers' Trails		4	2			D / D	1,030 / 250	low / N		
28. Iron Creek			3			E	700	low		
29. Stehekin Valley Trails	5					E	40	N		
30. Stehekin River Road	4		4			E	780	M		
31. Echo Valley	5					E	400	N	Yes	
32. The Outback	2		1 +	1		MD	1,524	N		

No.	Name										
33.	Echo Ridge	13					D	625	N		Yes
34.	Loup Loup—South Summit Sno-Park	13			1		E	700	N		Yes
35.	Loup Loup Ski Area—Bear Mountain	10					E	1,230	low	Yes	
36.	Methow Valley Community Trail	17 +					E	400	N	Yes	
37.	Sun Mountain	25					E	1,387	low	Yes	
38.	Pipestone Canyon			5			MD	750	low		
39.	Blue Buck Mountain			5			D	3,400	low	Yes	
40.	Rendezvous Pass Hut	5					D	1,345	N	Yes	
41.	Heifer Hut	5 ·	1				D	1,365	N	Yes	
42.	Buck Lake			2			MD	1,080	low	Yes	Yes
43.	Fawn Hut and Beyond	7+					MD	1,380	M	Yes	Yes
44.	Goat Mountain Road		2	5			D	2,640	low	Yes	Yes
45.	Mazama and Wilson Ranch	10					E	200	N	Yes	
46.	Early Winters—Base Camp	10 +					E	600	N	Yes	
47.	Highlands Sno-Park	5	7				E	1,000	low		Yes
48.	Sherman Pass Sno-Park				3		BC	1,000	H		Yes
49.	Boulder Deer Creek Summit Sno-Park	5		10		3	E	1,730	M		Yes
50.	Upper Wolf Trail System	2					E	30	N		

Tour	Miles Groomed	Miles Groomed for Snowmobiles	Miles of Forest Road	Miles of Trail	Miles of Open Slopes	Rating	Elevation Gain	Avalanche Potential	Fees	Sno-Park permits
51. Geophysical Sno-Park	8			3		E	100	N		Yes
52. Mount Spokane State Park	17					E	400	N		Yes*
53. Spokane's Sno-Parks	4+					E	200	N		Yes
54. Field's Spring State Park	5					E	430	N		Yes
55. Salmon La Sac Sno-Park	2+		5	2		E	4,083	M		Yes
56. Lake Easton Sno-Park	5					E	50	low		Yes*
57. Cabin Creek Nordic Ski Area	10					E	200	N		Yes*
58. Amabilis Mountain			8			MD	2,154	low		Yes*
59. Stampede Pass		8		2		D	1,300	low		Yes
60. That Dam Loop	4		1			D	80	low		Yes*
61. Kendall—Knobs, Lakes, and Loops			3+		2	D	1,700	M		Yes
62. The Iron Horse Trail	7					E	70	H		Yes*
63. Mount Catherine Loop	10 +			-1		BC	1,520	low		Yes
64. Summit Nordic Center	30					E	500	M	Yes	
65. Huckleberry Crk Suntop Lookout Rd	10					E	700	low		Yes
						MD	3,030	H		Yes
66. Grand Park	5		3 +	2		BC	3,540	M		Yes

No.									
67. Corral Pass		4+		1	MD	3,000	low		
68. Silver Creek Ski Route		12+			E	1,742	low	Yes	
69. Chinook Pass / Naches Peak				5+	MD / BC	832 / 1,760	low / M		
70. Mowich Lake	3	5+			D	1,410	low	Yes	
71. DNR Road 92 Sno-Park (Copper Creek Hut)	3				D	900	low	Yes	
72. Snow Bowl / High Hut	4+ / 5				MD / MD	2,130 / 2,503	low / low	Yes / Yes	
73. Copper Pass		4			D	1,100	low		
74. Reflection Lakes		1	-1		D	538	low		Yes
75. Tatoosh Range		1	-1	1	BC	1,432	M		Yes
76. Mazama Ridge		1		2	BC	900	M		Yes
77. Glacier Vista / Camp Muir				4+	BC / M	1,022 / 4,500	low / M		Yes / Yes
78. Burley Mountain Lookout		8		1	MD	3,931	M		
79. Horseshoe Lake	3		3		BC	1,200	low	Yes	
80. White Road Sno-Park		3+			E	480	low	Yes	
81. White Pass—Pacific Crest Trail			8		BC	1,200	low		
82. White Pass Cross-Country Touring Center	5				E	300	N	Yes	
83. Round Mountain Road		4+			D	1,280	low	Yes	
84. North Fork Tieton River	3		6		E	140	low	Yes	

Tour	Miles Groomed	Miles Groomed for Snowmobiles	Miles of Forest Road	Miles of Trail	Miles of Open Slopes	Rating	Elevation Gain	Avalanche Potential	Fees	Sno-Park permits
85. Lost Lake			5			D	1,250	N		Yes
86. Pleasant Valley Loop			8	6		E	400	N		
87. Big Tree Loop	4+					E	400	N		Yes
88. Pine Side Loops	6+					D	930	N		Yes
89. Gotchen Creek			3+			D	668	low		Yes
90. Ice Cave/Nat. Bridge			11	2		E	200	N		Yes
Peterson Ridge						D	940	low		Yes
91. McClellan Meadows Loop	4		-1	1+		D	420	N		Yes
92. Hardtime Loop	10			-1		D	580	N		Yes
93. Kalama Ski Trail		3	4+	13		E	2,302	N		Yes
93. Climbers Bivouac		3	4+			D	1,515	low		Yes
94. Marble Mountain		3	2+			D	1,488	low		Yes
95. June Lake Loop				5		D	560	low		Yes
96. Sasquatch Loops			4			MD	740	low		Yes
97. Lahar Viewpoint		4+				E	410	N		Yes
98. Mount St. Helens					4	M	5,725	M	Yes	Yes
99. Obstruction Point			8			MD	1,300	M	Yes	
100. Hilltop			1+		1+	BC	760	M	Yes	
Ridge Road						D	200	N	Yes	

INDEX

ABOUT THE AUTHORS

TOM KIRKENDALL and VICKY SPRING are experienced outdoor adventurers and enthusiastic skiers. This husband and wife team can be found outdoors in almost every season combining their love for hiking, backpacking, climbing, and cycling with careers in photography. Their two children tag along as models and tend to show up in a lot of pictures. No matter how busy they are, they make time to spend at least one week every summer on a volunteer trail crew helping to maintain the trails they enjoy. They hope to see you on one of those trips.

Tom and Vicky are co-authors of *Bicycling the Pacific Coast, Mountain Bike Adventures in Washington, An Outdoor Family Guide to Washington's National Parks and Monuments, 100 Hikes in*™ *the Alps, 100 Hikes in*™ *California's Central Sierra and Coast Range,* and a recreation guide to *Glacier National Park and Waterton Lakes National Park,* all published by The Mountaineers Books. Vicky also helps her father, Ira Spring, with the 100 Hikes series.